Sex Scandals in Amer

SEX SCANDALS IN AMERICAN POLITICS

A Multidisciplinary Approach to the Construction and Aftermath of Contemporary Political Sex Scandals

Edited by
Alison Dagnes

2011

Continuum International Publishing Group
80 Maiden Lane, New York, NY 10038
The Tower Building, 11 York Road, London SE1 7NX

www.continuumbooks.com

Library of Congress Cataloging-in-Publication Data
A catalog record for this book is available from the Library of Congress.

ISBN: 978-1-4411-8690-4 (PB)
          978-1-4411-8477-1 (HB)

Typeset by Newgen Imaging Systems Pvt Ltd, Chennai, India
Printed and bound in the United States of America

Contents

Contributors

Cynthia Botteron is Associate Professor of Political Science at Shippensburg University in Pennsylvania. With Charles H. Kennedy, she co-edited and contributed to *Pakistan 2005* (2006) and contributed to *New Perspectives on Pakistan: Contexts, Realities, and Visions for the Future*, edited by SaeedShafqat (2007). Her work focused on the motivations and impact of constitutional changes undertaken by President Musharraf. Her current research, *Constitutional Qualifications for Public Office: A Global Comparative Studył*, captured the full range of requirements for national office of all countries of the world to uncover new representation-types. She received her doctorate from the University of Texas–Austin.

Alison Dagnes is Associate Professor of Political Science at Shippensburg University in Pennsylvania. She is the author of *Politics on Demand: The Effects of 24-Hour News on American Politics* (2010), and she frequently speaks on the topic of the modern media. Her current research examines ideology and political satire. Prior to receiving her doctorate in Political Science from the University of Massachusetts at Amherst, Dr. Dagnes was a producer for C-SPAN in Washington, DC.

Cynthia Drenovsky is a Professor of Sociology at Shippensburg University, where she has taught courses on research design, family sociology, and gerontology for the past 20 years. She is a former president of the Mid-Atlantic Council on Family Relations. Her current research includes studies on family change and community attitudes toward hospice care. She has most recently published in the *American Journal of Hospice and Palliative Medicine*.

James D. Griffith's training was in applied experimental psychology, where he did work in advanced quantitative methodologies and program evaluation. He currently has three primary research interests that include risk-taking behaviors, general program evaluation, and jury decision-making. His teaching interests include: General Psychology, Legal Psychology, Industrial-Organizational Psychology, and Statistics.

Stephanie Jirard, a former trial attorney, has been a lieutenant in the U.S. Navy JAG Corps, a Trial Attorney at the Department of Justice, Civil Division, an Assistant U.S. Attorney, an Assistant Federal Public Defender, and an Assistant Public Defender in one of Missouri's capital litigation units. She is an Associate Professor of Criminal Justice at Shippensburg University and her research interests include federalism, advocacy skills, and evidence law. Her book, *Criminal Law, Criminal Procedure and the Constitution,* was published by Pearson Prentice Hall in 2008.

Richard A. Knight began his career in higher education by serving as Director of Forensics and instructor of communication at West Texas A&M University. He then earned his doctorate in Speech Communication with an emphasis in Political Rhetoric at the University of Southern Mississippi, and turned to a full-time career in the class-room. He currently teaches in the Department of Human Communication Studies at Shippensburg University, offering courses in rhetoric, nonverbal communication, and persuasion. Dr. Knight's published research includes studies in political apologia, post-presidential rhetoric, and the role of humor in professional organizations.

Mark Sachleben is Assistant Professor of Political Science at Shippensburg University in Shippensburg, PA. He teaches classes in international relations, comparative politics, global governance, and human rights. He is the author of *International Human Rights: Considering Patterns of Participation, 1948–2000*(2004), the co-author of *Seeing the Bigger Picture: American and International Politics in Film and Popular Culture*, Second Edition (2011), and has written articles and chapters on pedagogy and international politics. Dr. Sachleben received his PhD from Miami University (Ohio) in 2003.

Carrie Sipes is an Assistant Professor at Shippensburg University and teaches public relations in the Communications Journalism Department. Her research interests focus on persuasive communication messages and she conducts research on political advertising and the behavioral aspects of public health campaigns. Additional research interests include the psychological and cultural aspects of mediated messages.

Jan Smith, Associate Professor of Geography/Earth Sciences at Shippensburg University, teaches courses in Geographic Information Systems (GIS), cartography, and regional geography. Recently, she has been interested in using GIS to understand the development of a sense of place and to delineate perceptual regions. Dr. Smith served as President of the National Council for Geographic Education (2008) and is currently the Coordinator of the Pennsylvania Alliance for Geographic Education.

CHAPTER 1

Introduction

Alison Dagnes

Comedian Chris Rock once said: "A man is only as faithful as his options," which may go a long way toward explaining the adulterous behavior of certain prominent men. While not all (or even most) famous men are lascivious adulterers, the scores of men famous for their vast sexual conquests alongside their varying talents have proven that, for some women, celebrity is one powerful aphrodisiac. The categories of prominent men with raging libidos are fairly obvious, and each category exemplifies a different reason that famous men may stray: athletes are preternaturally competitive; actors are exceptionally self-involved; and rock stars are engrossed in a lifestyle that not only permits such behavior but actually encourages it.

To elaborate, there are athletes who have been caught in affairs off the course, court, or ball field: Tiger Woods made international news for his sexual behavior; Wilt Chamberlain wrote a book about his conquests, which numbered in the tens of thousands; and Magic Johnson contracted HIV, and then admitted to extensive sexual liaisons outside of his marriage(Cole 1994). For athletes, the source of their sexual cravings may come with the territory of intense competition. According to University of Pennsylvania sociologist Elijah Anderson, an athlete's sexual conquest is tantamount to his athletic prowess: "The physical emphasis, the independence, the doing of battle with other men all underscore the male identity and dominance" (Wahl and Wertheim 1998). In addition to athletes, there are actors who garner as many headlines for their off-screen romances as they do for their box office draw. Warren Beatty, Jack Nicholson, Colin Farrell, and Bradley Cooper are well known Lotharios, and the fame they garner for their sex lives is fodder for the 24/7 news cycle that constantly puts famous faces into the public realm. A study in the *Journal of Research in Personality* showed that entertainment celebrities are "significantly more narcissistic" than is the general population, which means that women who feed into this narcissism are likely to attract the attention of those desiring it (Young 2006). The actors who gain attention from their love lives also gain the fame (or infamy) from such behavior, which can be constructive for their careers; the sexual behavior complements the narcissism, which complements the profession. Finally, there are musicians with infamous sexual appetites such as Steven Tyler, Mick Jagger, Lenny Kravitz, and many of the performers at The Monsters of Rock Tour. For rock stars, the groupie phenomenon is not only prevalent, it is infamous enough to be fodder for a plethora of songs about the colossal availability of promiscuous women.[1] Bad behavior on the part of rock stars is so rampant and established that when a rock star settles down and stops bedding multiple partners at once, then *that* action alone garners attention. In short, famous and accomplished men have many opportunities when it comes to sexual relationships, and many of these famous men stray, for a variety of reasons.

Thus, if Washington, DC, is considered Hollywood for ugly people and if former Secretary of State Henry Kissinger is correct in his assertion that "power is the ultimate aphrodisiac" (*The New York Times,* October 28, 1973), it is important to add a fourth category of prominent men to any examination of sex scandals: politicians. Political sex scandals are different from other types of celebrity scandals because, although they can garner the same level of extreme media attention, the nature of a politician's celebrity is different from that of an athlete, actor, or rock star. A politician may be famous, but he is famous for the leadership role he plays in government and for the promises he makes to the public in terms of good character and model behavior. An athlete only promises he can hit a golf ball or make a basket, an actor only agrees to be good looking and entertaining, and a rock star only pledges that he will act the part of a rock star. Contrary to this, a political figure swears that he will act as a representative of the greater public, and with this pledge he brings his constituents with him into any situation. Tiger Woods was publicly convicted of more than a dozen affairs outside his marriage, and he may have embarrassed his wife, but he certainly did not embarrass the people of South Carolina, as did former governor Mark Sanford when it became public knowledge that he had cheated on his spouse with his Argentinean mistress. Thus, while politicians may be as competitive as athletes, as narcissistic as actors, and as imbued in a particular lifestyle as rock stars, none of these explanations alone suffices to explain a politician's philandering. This book tackles the difficult questions of how and why politicians cheat on their wives—and what happens when they do.

There have been scholarly examinations of political sex scandals, especially in the wake of President Bill Clinton's impeachment for lying about his conduct with White House aide Monica Lewinsky, but those assessments took a narrower view of the topic, focusing solely on idiosyncratic aspects of the events that unfolded. Here, we examine political sex scandals from a wide variety of disciplinary viewpoints to examine the social, rhetorical, political, legal and psychological ramifications of political infidelities. We propose that political sex scandals are a special breed of humiliation, involving more than just politics: They necessitate studies into human communications theory, sociological perspectives on sex, analysis of constituent and media reactions to bad behavior, and a layered examination of the psychology of one who would reveal a carefully constructed version of himself on the campaign trail and then risk his success with illicit behavior. This book approaches this single topic from a number of angles in the hopes of demonstrating the distinctiveness of political sex scandals, even in an age where scandal is so ubiquitous.

Sex Scandals Today

We note at the outset of this endeavor that political sex scandals are not new, nor are they necessarily a growing problem in America today. Certainly, sex scandals have occurred from the very founding of our government, with consistency and regularity. While he was Treasury Secretary, Alexander Hamilton had an affair with Maria Reynolds, a woman described by Hamilton biographer Richard Brookhiser as a "whore" and a "blackmailer" (Brookheiser 1999). Our twenty-second president, Grover Cleveland, was named as the father of an illegitimate child during his 1884 presidential campaign, inspiring the chant: "Ma, ma, where's my pa? Gone to the White House, ha haha!" President Warren G. Harding was rumored to have had several mistresses, including one who took $20,000 in hush money and another who bore his child. President Franklin Delano Roosevelt's affair with Lucy Mercer was ongoing throughout his life and, according to historian Doris Kearns Goodwin, Roosevelt died in Warm Springs, Georgia, with Lucy Mercer at his side(Goodwin 1994). President John F. Kennedy was legendary in his extramarital behavior, to the point that his affairs are used today as a differentiating mark to distinguish the old press corps (which restrained from reporting on such stories) from the modern media circus (which feeds on them). Wilbur Mills was a congressman who was caught with a stripper, Gary Hart was a senator who was caught with a spokes model, and Bill Clinton was a president who was caught with an intern. We understand: political sex scandals are nothing new.

One thing that is new, however, is the media system, which has expanded exponentially in the past 250 years of our nation, thanks to technological innovation and financial reward. We went from a nation that used poorly circulated pamphlets to disseminate opinion to one with a 24-hour news cycle, complete with instant updates and immediate information available to everyone, on television and through the internet. This expansive media that includes an immeasurable number of electronic and print outlets brings with it constant coverage of anything that will make money for the media agent. The media are able to report on every politician's apology, every nuance of his explanation, the reactions from every interest group, and every political development. Thus, not only are political sex scandals an important specific type of scandal, they are ripe for study, since there is so much more information on these scandals available to scholars today.

Although a study by the Pew Research Center in 2007 suggested that an overwhelming majority of the American public was tired of celebrity scandal stories, the public continues today to tune in and watch any new scandal as it comes to light (Rivas 2007). This is most likely because sex scandal stories are interesting, easy to understand, and universally attention-grabbing. Yet, despite their fascinating content, few academics have broached the subject of political sex scandals. Historian John Thompson (2000) and scholars Paul Apostolidis and Juliet Williams (2004) have written two of the most comprehensive and scholarly examinations of the subject. Thompson takes an historical view of political scandals and argues that although media developments are important, so too are what he calls the "broad changes in the social context of politics" (Thompson 2000). According to Thompson, the increasing emphasis in American politics on personal traits and character strength over policy and ideological stands has led to an environment that pays attention to personal failings more than to other political dynamics (Thompson 2000, 8). Apostolidis and Williams examine the history and context of sex political scandals and root their analysis within the framework of the Clinton sex scandal. They focus on the private/public divide as the center point of an examination:

> The myriad and continuing historical adjustments through judicial decisions and public policy changes, of what is commonly thought of as "the state's power to intervene in religious affairs," reflect the fact that neither the public nor the private realm is an entity that exists with an enduring, stable self-identity; rather, both are continually being reproduced and refashioned as the relations of power linking them together in a disciplinary matrix are altered. (Apostolidis 2004, 8)

Other scholarly work examines political sex scandals, presidential ones in particular (Markovitz 1989; Hagood 1998; Keeler 1985; Meyrowitz 1986; Callery 1992), and several books were published following the Clinton/Lewinsky scandal that chronicled the personal, political, and sociological implications of that particular scandal (Sharma 1998; Rozell 2000; Baker 2001; Busby 2001; Kalb 2007; Miller et al. 2009). Historian John H. Summers published a piece in the *Journal of American History* in 2000 about the politics of gossip and sex scandals in politics, examining the transformation of private discourse into public discussion. Summers comes to the very optimistic conclusion that the more public exposure of private matters suggests an expanded freedom of expression that is a positive influence in American society (Summers 2000). Taking a dimmer view of the same general topic, several political scientists have examined the suffering public trust as a result of this public coverage of private matters (Chanley et al. 2000; Nilson and Nilson 1980; Warren 2006). While each of these examinations explores the topic in depth, all address it from a singular perspective. We propose an interdisciplinary examination to take a more comprehensive view of political sex scandals.

What Is a Sex Scandal?

At *C-SPAN*, the public affairs network in Washington, DC, that broadcasts political events and persons, there are several words that network producers and writers are never allowed to use. One of these words is "scandal," because it is a word that is loaded with meaning and prejudice. Once the term "scandal" is used, a writer has stacked an event with salacious and sensational meaning, which goes against *C-SPAN*'s mission of impartial reporting. *C-SPAN*, always the calm and balanced observer, is a public service network and does not have to worry about ratings, so the word "scandal" is unnecessary. Yet for news organizations that have the financial imperatives to garner high ratings, "scandal" is a word that is often used because it specifically adds drama. A scandal attracts attention, bringing viewers and readers to a media outlet, thus begetting good ratings, which then leads to making money. Consequently, the American public often sees the word "scandal" in the mainstream press, to the point that one might speculate that the word is overused: It is generous applied, whether warranted or not.

The word "scandal" is often used in politics to impeach the character of a politician. Politics can be an unattractive sport, with participants flinging names at one another like "crook," and "liar," and "liberal." In the political world, if you are able focus on a scandal involving your opponent, you could make some serious points with your supporters. In 1998, Congress impeached President Clinton because he lied about a sex scandal, and he, thus, became only the second president in American history to face such a face impeachment proceedings. Despite the labyrnthian explanations and rationalizations for his impeachment, Clinton's political foes pointed to his "scandalous" behavior as reason for his political destruction. Political scandal results in political consequences.

Thus, despite C-SPAN's rejection of the word, we hear or see it often in other media, and actual scandal does occur in American politics with some frequency. The question can be legitimately asked, however, what *is* a scandal? What makes something truly scandalous, rather than simply interesting or dirty? Definitions are necessary. In his book on sex scandals, John Thompson lays out a thorough and first-rate definition for what constitutes a scandal. According to Thompson, a scandal must have the following five characteristics: First, it must involve some sort of "transgression of certain values, norms or moral codes." Second, it must contain an element of secrecy. Third, there must be some sort of disapproval of the action surrounding it. Fourth, accompanying the disapproval must be a public denouncement of the actions. Finally, the actions must damage the reputation of the individual. (Thompson 2000, 13–14) These definitions work because they illustrate the seriousness of the transgression and show that not only are internal factors involved but external ones, as well. Because our examination focuses specifically on sex scandals, we add to this comprehensive definition the corollary that there must also be some sort of sexual misbehavior involved, as well as some political fallout from the transgression. These are the elements of a political sex scandal, and these are the definitions with which we shall examine our case studies.

Chapter Summaries

Political Sex Scandals As They Shape Our Notions of Fidelity

Anne Houde writes in the *Proceedings of the National Academy of Sciences in the United States* that: "One of the triumphs of modern sociobiology is that evolutionary theory can explain why the sexes differ in their behavior along these lines in so many cases" (Houde 2001). While true, one of the triumphs of modern sociology is the ability to help explain how our national perceptions of sexuality and sexual behavior have evolved over time. What modernity has brought, in the form of technological development and a ubiquitous media system, is a constantly shifting understanding of what constitutes "sex." Is "sexting" the same thing as cheating? Does online sexual role-play count as infidelity? Is fellatio the same thing as intercourse? This last question was brought to light when President Clinton was impeached for perjury during the Paula Jones scandal. And thus, in Chapter 2, Cynthia Drenovsky examines the issue of our own national sexuality and how our cultural impressions of sex affect our understanding of political sex scandals.

The notion of fidelity is something that is viewed as crucial in American society, and yet because of the internet and the resulting increase in pornography many people today engage in behavior that can indeed count as infidelity without the act of genital penetration, thanks to the internet and the enormous increase in pornography. President Clinton helped usher in a new notion of sex in his defense of the Monica Lewinski affair. What is clear from this examination is that, in conjunction with the national media coverage of such scandals, when a politician gets caught *in flagrante*, this events helps us to shape our own perceptions of sex, sexuality, and sexual behavior beyond the political realm. Chapter 2 first explores American attitudes toward sex, and uses historical and sociological research to put our own identities into context. Drenovsky then examines the impact of the Clinton scandal on American family life, and also on our views about sexuality.

Reasons for Cheating

There are many reasons that people cheat on their spouses, and each case varies individually. We do not argue that political sex scandals occur more often than do everyday affairs, but we do maintain that they garner a significant increase of attention. Additionally, we contend that most of these political scandals occur when men cheat on their wives, but the reasons for cheating remain gender neutral. Ruth Houston, a self-proclaimed infidelity expert, has written about politicians who have cheated on their wives, listing a set of pop-psychological explanations for this behavior. Among the list are ego-embellishment, entitlement, the availability of opportunistic sex, the view of a mistress as a status symbol, and the perception that someone can get away with cheating. Yet, while all of these pop-psych explanations are amusing to contemplate, they lack scientific evidence to fully elucidate the reasons for infidelity among politicians. In Chapter 3, Jim Griffith, a psychology professor, examines the scientific reasons more completely, offering two explanations to account for these high-profile bad behaviors among politicians. The first is rooted within evolutionary psychology, which provides predictions as to who would be more likely to engage in various kinds of sexual behaviors and why. This integrative approach examines the ways human have adapted and evolved throughout time to see if a specific type of person might be more likely to stray. The second explanation is a combination of theories that have overlap but are cognitive in nature. Within this approach, cognitive biases exist under normal circumstances but are exacerbated develop when false-positive and false-negative biases over evolutionary history. Chapter 3 presents a thorough review of each perspective applied to political sex scandals.

Responses to Political Sex Scandals:
International, Constituencies, Media& Apologies

This book takes the stand that political sex scandals are not identical, and neither are the constituencies or political cultures within which they occur. Thus, in Chapter 4, Mark Sachleben establishes a framework that sets the parameters of sex scandal analysis. First, he identifies the different types of sex scandals, and then he determines the different political cultures in which sex scandals occur. Sachleben establishes a typology to help isolate factors to assess the impact of such scandals with the following categories: Sex scandal as personal failure; as professional failure; as hypocrisy; and as dalliances that are not scandalous. At that point, he examines the unique consequences of such events. What he finds is that sex and sex scandal are viewed quite differently in diverse societies with varied political cultures. While major political sex scandals all have consequences, their effects vary depending on the circumstance and the environment. Such a framework is necessary to root the rest of the book within equivalent context, and this chapter begins our examination of the responses to political sex scandals.

We continue this examination of response in Chapter 5, when Jan Smith and I take a closer look at the specific constituencies of recognized politicians who have been recently caught in sex scandal. The demographics and characteristics of the constituents combine to create a political climate in which a scandal-struck politician must maneuver. This means that every case may begin similarly, but they all end differently: The political fallout from sex scandals involving elected officials differs from case to case. For example, politicians like Mark Foley and Elliot Spitzer were forced to resign from their positions, yet Larry Craig and Bill Clinton stayed in office until they retired. David Vitter, John Ensign, and Mark Sanford remain in office to this day and, after apologizing, simply moved on as if nothing untoward has occurred. What are the reasons for this disparity? Clearly, some answers may be found in the makeup of the constituents whose capacity for understanding or desire for political retribution may vary by demography. In Chapter 5, we use demographic data to draw some conclusions about the consequence of political sex scandals at the constituency level. We also examine the media's reporting on these scandals at the national and local levels to see whether this coverage plays a part in constituent response. All together, in Chapter 5, we examine the political effects of sex scandals in an attempt to ascertain what factors determine political consequence.

Chapter 6 looks more closely at the media. In 1974, when Congressman Wilbur Mills was caught driving drunk with Argentinean stripper Fanne Foxe in the car, three national television channels and national newspapers were the primary form of news dissemination. When Foxe jumped from the car into the Tidal Basin, setting off a firestorm in Washington, there was no 24-hour cable news station to cover the event, nor were there tourists armed with camera phones, nor were there bloggers calling for Mills to be removed from office. Foxe did not have today's abundant options to make money by selling her story to the press, and the American public was treated to limited coverage of the sex scandal. Times have changed. In today's hyper-mediated political environment, politicians must be concerned not only with their own constituents, but also with a national audience, since their improprieties will be fodder for late-night comedians, websites, partisan news channels, and talk radio outlets. In Chapter 6, Carrie Sipes examines the national news coverage devoted to political sex scandals. As politicians find themselves engaging in extramarital affairs, often labeled as scandals in the media, they soon capture the attention of media personalities. These personalities choose how much to cover the extramarital affair, how to construct and relay messages about it, and which aspects of the affair to emphasize or downplay. This chapter examines framing and agenda setting functions of the media through a content analysis of several recent political sex scandals, and illustrates how the importance of the media in the construction of image and the dissemination of information.

Once the media is on to a scandal, inevitably the scandalous must apologize. And thus, in Chapter 7, Rich Knight examines the political response and the art of the apology, analyzing the responses of politicians who have been caught in such quandaries, in order to better understand political discourse and rhetorical self-defense. He explains the missions of the apology, their construction, and then their success or failure. Since the political apology (oftentimes with the cuckolded wife standing next to the cad who got caught) is the expected and most ubiquitous ingredient of a sex scandal that has definitively unfolded, this chapter sheds light on the immediate aftermath of the "gotcha!" Throughout the chapter, Knight discusses the implications for political rhetoric and apologia, also addressing several directions for future research, including the role of the forum in apologia as well as the fallout for other involved parties.

Breaking the Law

More often than not, the events that produce a political sex scandal violate a marriage or personal partnership. It desecrates the public trust between an elected official and his constituents, but rarely is illegal activity involved. However, when the events that produce a political sex scandal also involves criminal behavior, the scandal becomes something more politically significant. Stephanie Jirard, an attorney and criminal justice scholar, writes in Chapter 8 that the criminal indiscretions that accompany the moral ones in a political sex scandal are largely ignored. Thus, when former New York Governor Elliot Spitzer was caught with a prostitute, taking her across state lines to engage in carnal relations, this was not only a violation of New York law, but was a federal offense, as well. His case involved money-laundering, obstruction of justice, violating the Mann Act, conspiracy to commit interstate travel in aid of racketeering, and wire fraud. Yet Spitzer, while drummed out of office, was not prosecuted for any of these crimes. A review of the resolution of criminal charges against male public servants caught committing consensual sexual offenses reveals that the most severe sanction given is a misdemeanor charge for disorderly conduct, and this is completed without jail time. In homage to the late Huey Long of Louisiana, Jirard argues that the only way an elected male official is going to jail for his sexual misconduct is if he is found "in bed with a dead girl or a live boy." The Foley and Craig cases prove that, even *then*, the politician will likely escape prosecution. Chapter 8 more thoroughly explains this phenomenon.

Finally, in Chapter 9, Cynthia Botteron takes a broad view of politicians around the world and the ways they are chosen for office to examine how some countries place constitutional requirements in their national documents to avoid sex scandal. Different countries view sex scandal differently: Some take such scandals as matters of fact, while some see them as disqualifying. Nearly 15 percent of the world's countries consider a good character or good reputation important enough that it is a constitutional requirement for any candidate seeking to become the Head of State. Eight percent prohibit anyone from seeking elected office if they have been found guilty of the crime of vice or moral turpitude. Additionally, should one be a known violator of the edicts of faith, that person is prohibited from seeking the position of Head of State in 2 percent of the countries. This chapter explores the strategic use of these rather nebulous character credentials within national constitutions to keep the scoundrels out of elected office.

Conclusions

Men and women cheat on their partners, and sometimes—if that person is famous—the cheater garners a significant amount of attention. Often, if the cheater is a famous athlete, entertainer, or rock star, the behavior is excused as part and parcel of the celebrity's talent. If the cheater is a politician, the cheating warrants a different set of standards for discussion and examination.

In this book, we argue that political sex scandals are distinct from other types of sex scandals because the nature of elected office is so different from "civilian" life. To be an American politician today is to serve the public within the never-ending glare of the media's spotlight, which exposes every wrong move and mistake. In the main, our elected officials are tremendously hard working, honest, and important members of our body politic. We need politicians to do democracy's heavy lifting for us, and as a democratic republic we have established a system where is it our responsibility to elect officials and it is their responsibility to lead. It is a daunting profession, and at most times a noble one. Politicians work tirelessly for their constituents and for their countries and often forgo lucrative careers for public service. Yet, since the Watergate scandal, the American public has held an increasingly dim view of politicians, who are often viewed as crooked: loathsome, corrupt creatures who hold less trust among the American public than do used car salesmen. While this is clearly far from reality, the perception prevails. Why? Because the technological developments of the media now allow us to see every facet of our politicians, and some of these qualities inspire damaging opinions of our elected leaders. And, thus, the hysterical and non-stop coverage of political sex scandals feed into our existing biases about politicians, without examining the larger issues that arise from such events. Time and again a news story about a political sex scandal breaks, and the American public collectively clutches at their breast asking: "Why did he do it? What was he thinking? How was he re-elected?" This book attempts to clarify some of the answers to these questions, not only to explain political sex scandals, but also to understand our own responses to this bad behavior.

We will admit up front that we do not solve these puzzles. Instead, we use a multi-disciplinary approach to look both contextually and more broadly at political sex scandals from a wide variety of lenses to help us with our examinations. Each case is independent, each circumstance contextual. Different authors use different case studies to examine their own disciplinary approach, and each chapter individually examines the topic of "scandal" using diverse methods of analysis. But if we gather the varying approaches and examine the different facets that comprise political sex scandals, perhaps we will be closer to understanding more about ourselves as a body politic and about our relationship with our elected officials. It is ultimately the conundrum of government: We elect men to govern us, but men are not angels. And, thus, it is a fact that the scandalous, the corrupt, and the dishonest will sometimes find their way into positions of power. The impact of such scandals can only be determined, at the end of the day, by the citizenry: Which is exactly how government is supposed to work.

Works Cited

Apostolidis, Paul, and Juliet Williams eds. *Politics in the Age of Sex Scandals*. Durham, NC: Duke University Press, 2004; 8.

Brookhiser, Richard. *Alexander Hamilton, American*. New York, The Free Press, 1999.

Cole, C. "Critical Sociology: Visualizing Deviance in Post-Reagan America: Magic Johnson, AIDS, and the Promiscuous World of Professional Sport."*Critical Sociology*, 1994: 123–147.

Goodwin, Doris Kearns. *No Ordinary Time*. New York: Simon and Schuster, 1994.

Houde, Anne. "Sex Roles, Ornaments, and Evolutionary Explanation," *Proceedings of the National Academy of Sciences in the United States,* November 6, 2001. 12857–12859. Accessed July 20, 2010 (www.pnas.org/content/98/23/12857.full).

Rivas, Jorge. "Poll: Americans Think That Television Networks Give Too Much Attention to Celebrity Scandals." *Associated Content*, August 5, 2007. Accessed January 15, 2010 (www.associatedcontent.com/article/337373/poll_americans_think_that_television.html?cat=47).

Sharma, Ashok Kumar. *Clinton Lewinsky Scandal: Most Embarrassing Scandal of American History*. New Delhi, India: Diamond Pocket Books, 1998.

Summers, John, "What Happened to Sex Scandals? Politics and Peccadilloes, Jefferson to Kennedy." *Journal of American History*, December 2000, 87(3): 825–854.

Thompson, John B. *Political Scandal: Power and Viability in the Media Age.* Oxford, UK: Polity, 2000; 8.

Wahl, Grant L., and Jon Wertheim. "Paternity Ward: Fathering Out-of-Wedlock Kids Has Become Commonplace among Athletes, Many of Whom Seem Oblivious to the Legal, Financial and Emotional Consequences." *Sports Illustrated*, May 4, 1998.

Young, Mark S., and Drew Pinksy. "Narcissism and Celebrity." *Journal of Research Personality*, 2006: 1.

Notes

1 Such titles as "Hey Baby," "Ladies of the Road," and "Starstruck," come to mind. Perhaps the most infamous song about a groupie is KISS's "Plaster Caster," which told the tale of a woman who collected plaster casts of rock star penises. The Rolling Stones have three songs alone about groupies, solidifying forever Mick Jagger's reputation as a ladies' man.

CHAPTER 2

Game Changer: The Clinton Scandal and American Sexuality

Cynthia K. Drenovsky

Americans like to think it all began with Clinton.

Prior to President Bill Clinton's affair with White House intern Monica Lewinsky, the personal relationships of our presidents remained strictly personal, and only a seedy few political observers threw innuendo around. But in 1998, President Clinton was caught lying about an extramarital sexual relationship and the nation was thrown into impeachment hearings and breathless 24-hour coverage of accounts of the actual sex itself. Several factors contributed to the way Americans viewed sex scandals starting with Clinton: the ubiquitous presence and coverage by the modern media; the fact that Clinton was actually caught red-handed in the scandal; and the fact that the public was somewhat expecting it. When the *Washington Post* first broke the story about President Clinton and Monica Lewinsky in January 1998, Americans were already desensitized by the accusations of Gennifer Flowers against Bill Clinton that had swirled around his first campaign in 1992. Many Americans rather expected the other shoe to drop at some point. The Gennifer Flowers scandal seemed as if, for at least a moment or two, it might threaten Clinton's 1992 campaign, but it did not. Once Bill Clinton became president, those of us who had our doubts about his marital fidelity gripped onto the same hope that accompanies many brides down the aisle, "He'll change once we are married," or in this case, "Once he is president, he'll know enough not to do this." Like most love-struck brides, by campaign number two, Americans were captivated by the Clinton *je ne sais qua*, his charisma, his economy. We went ahead and renewed our vows with him in 1996, through good times and bad.

By September 1998, Kenneth Starr had given us more details than the reasonable American needed to know about the sexual peccadilloes of the leader of the free world. In 1998, I really wanted to be shocked, and even traumatized, by what I learned from Starr's report on the nightly news, but 30-some years of experiencing both the impact of a baby boomer-induced sexual revolution and a sex-crazed media machine made me cynical about the invincibility of the president to sexual indiscretions. The *Starr Report* is still accessible to the world on the internet (see Starr 1998). Only recently have I actually read the *Starr Report* and it is truly detailed and quite revealing. Baby Boomers are known for being cynics, and I am a Baby Boomer, so perhaps this is why I still do not find the content of the *Starr Report* to be all that shocking.

Of course, political sex scandal did not begin with Clinton, nor did our reaction to such scandals ultimately transform with more modern positions or more reticent ones. American attitudes about sex had been changing for decades, perhaps even centuries. And thus, in this chapter we examine who we are as a sexual nation, to help put our reactions to political sex scandals into historical and sociological context. Then we move forward to examine the impact of the Clinton–Lewinski scandal on our own views of sex and family life, to more clearly ascertain the role that this scandal played in our own understanding of politics and sex.

A Very Brief and Recent History of American Attitudes about Sex

If it is possible for one man to influence the sexual attitudes and behaviors of Americans during the twentieth century, that one man would be Alfred C. Kinsey, pioneer sex researcher and founder of the Kinsey Institute for Research in Sex, Gender, and Reproduction at the University of Indiana. Kinsey's own biography and sexual history are quite complex. Several authors have attempted to chronicle the private and professional life of the most well-known researcher in the study of sex and sexuality (e.g., Gathorne-Hardy 2000; Jones 1997; Pomeroy 1972). What we glean from these accounts of Kinsey's life and work is that Kinsey was serious about the importance of sex in the lives of Americans and he often struggled with various components of his own sexual life. Kinsey was a steadfast researcher, he always thought he was right, and his work reflected his personal experimentation with sexual identity and practices. It is also evident that he was often irritated by the tyranny of America's cultural sexual standards in the 1930s and 1940s. If nothing else, our sexually repressive culture had made it hard for him to get his work supported and completed. Nevertheless, *Sexual Behavior in the Human Male* was published by Alfred Kinsey and his colleagues, Wardell Pomeroy and Clyde Martin, on January 5, 1948. This report of male sexual behavior was based on more than 5,000 interviews and sexual histories. Today, most undergraduate students of social research easily identify the pitfalls of Kinsey's research design (including sampling procedures and research ethics) and his problems with statistical reporting. However, regardless of its methodological errors, the impact of the report on the scientific community and society at large cannot be denied. The book became a bestseller in three weeks (Brown and Fee 2003). Exactly 50 years (to the day) before America heard, "I did not have sexual relations with that woman, Miss Lewinsky," on January 26, 1948, Kinsey's famous study on the incredible frequency and variety of male sexual experiences was the talk of the town, including his finding that more than half of all husbands in his sample had had extramarital sexual experiences.

It would be wrong to say that *Sexual Behavior in the Human Male* effectively lifted the shroud of sexual repression in 1948. Rigid standards on sex and sexuality in American culture continued to be enforced throughout the 1940s and 1950s. What Kinsey's work did accomplish was to expose Americans to the possibility that sex is more than one simple act meant for a strictly and narrowly defined couple. Americans learned from Kinsey that all types of things were happening in American bedrooms, and elsewhere. Unfortunately for Kinsey and his research associates, the 1950s were right around the corner.

The 1950s are a fascinating era for the study of sex and power. Nostalgia is enormously persuasive and even the most sensible among us can fall victim to its charms. Conservative sentimentalists perceive the 1950s as the last decade where family came first, women knew their place, everyone made a good living, and authority was properly respected. The same sentimentalists protest what they see as the absolute moral decay that spread across America from 1960 up until today. Thank goodness for the reason and historical savvy of scholars like Stephanie Coontz who reveal that most of our warm fuzzy feelings about the 1950s are based on nostalgia, not fact:

> Comparisons of contemporary families with those of the 1950s are especially misleading. As many historians and sociologists have demonstrated, the 1950s family was atypical even for the 20th century. For the first time in 80 years, the age at marriage fell sharply, fertility rates increased, and the proportion of never-married individuals plummeted. The values attached to nuclear-family living, including the rejection of "interference" by extended kin and the expectation that family life should be people's main source of personal gratification, were also new—and their hegemony even at the time should not be exaggerated. (Coontz 2000,288)

The authors, politicians, and religious figures who define the family in terms of fictitious 1950s relationships have worked diligently during the past 50 years to encourage a narrow and restrictive definition of sexuality and the family. Given that Kenneth Starr recently argued the case in favor of Proposition 8 (the proposition that eliminates the right of same-sex couples to marry) in the state of California, we can add him to this list of people who defines the family in terms of 1950s nostalgia. If Kenneth Starr had been practicing law in 1953, we can be assured that he would have attacked Alfred Kinsey's research, not on the grounds that it was scientifically flawed, but on the grounds that it was morally flawed.

The 1950s were downright brutal on people like Alfred Kinsey. The impact of these conservative times on Kinsey did not go unnoticed by his biographers:

> After the Second World War, there was a strong feeling in America (especially among Republicans) of getting back to the *true* America. And peace was quite soon under the same general who had won it—in November 1952 Ike was elected

President. For men like these, the same generation as Kinsey (Eisenhower was the last President born in the nineteenth century), America meant the America of their childhood. (Gathorne-Hardy 2000,398)

At the same time, a sexual revolution was stirring, a sexual revolution that Kinsey would never witness because he died in 1956. If sex is a human behavior, then indeed Kinsey was a scholar of human behavior. He was a social scientist, as well as a biologist, and, like any good social scientist, he understood that true social change, revolution, or even sexual revolution is not caused by one human being. Social change occurs as the result of many factors, societal and economic, and Kinsey understood that. However, antecedents to social change were not viewed this way during the 1950s. When Kinsey's report, *Sexual Behavior in the Human Female*, was published in 1953, the social climate was different than it had been just four years earlier. Kinsey's 1953 book was about women and sexuality and it was published during America's baby boom. In 1953, American women were supposed to be having babies, not enjoying sex. The negative response to *Sexual Behavior in the Human Female* has been called a "counterattack" (see Brown and Fee 2003). Newspapers reacted in disapproval and disgust. Scholars drew attention to the report's methodological problems and a congressional hearing eventually led to the termination of funding for the research. For all intents and purposes, the public outcry against his work ruined Kinsey's career and he died only three years later.

Alfred Kinsey's legacy is his research on sexuality. Because of him, sex and sexuality became a legitimate area of scientific inquiry. Today, the standards for ethical behavior and research design have evolved considerably from the quasi-scientific procedures he employed. Kinsey influenced American's awareness of sexuality, but he hardly caused the sexual revolution all by himself. The economic climate of the 1960s, the women's movement, and the prevalence of baby boomers who were at divorcing age when divorce often occurs, are factors often cited as causes of the sexual revolution of the 1960s (Thornton and Young-DeMarco 2001; Reiss 2006). An accurate understanding of the interrelationships between historical events, economic structure, and individual behavior is necessary in order to understand human behavior, especially sexual behavior. Conservative correspondent Susan Brinkmann (2004) sees human behavior differently. In her account of the impact of Kinsey on society, she states:

> The legacy of Alfred C. Kinsey's twisted life and work can be read daily in the ever-worsening moral condition of our country. Since the onset of the sexual revolution, the rates of divorce, abortion, our-of-wedlock births, sexually transmitted diseased, and sex crimes are the highest level ever recorded in the history of this nation. (Brinkmann 2004,69)

Brinkmann's analysis is hardly a social–scientific one. She sees Kinsey's research as the cause of moral and family decline. We are better suited to explain social behavior within a social, economic, and historical context. The American family did change after Kinsey's work was published, not because of Kinsey, but rather the family changed in response to a changing society. Divorce, for example, began to rise in the United States with industrialization (Cherlin 1992). Even though the increase slowed down considerably during the Great Depression and the baby boom of the 1950s, the gradual increase in divorce since industrialization continued during the 1960s and 1970s (Thornton and Young-DeMarco 2001). Women moved into the labor force in the 1960s because they wanted to and because they had to, in order to make sure the needs of their families were met (Coontz 2000). Americans began to practice a wider array of alternative family forms during the 1960s and 1970s in order to adjust in an increasingly complex social and economic environment. Premarital sex, out of wedlock births, non-marital cohabitation, reduced fertility, voluntary childlessness, and gay and lesbian unions have increased since the 1960s. The adjustments families made to their changing society served to transform American values about accepting a diverse and fluid definition of the family.

Not all social scientists and historians agree on the exact causes of family changes in America since the 1950s. Ira Reiss (2006), for example, argues that the introduction of oral contraceptives in 1960 had little effect on the sexual revolution, while other scholars such as Arlan Thornton and Linda Young-DeMarco (2001) list it as an important factor in changing family behavior and relationships. Of course, there are also conservative scholars that still see the family in "decline" because it does not represent the brief, atypical, nostalgic image that we think we remember from the 1950s (e.g., Blankenhorn 2009; Popenoe 2008). It is essential to note here that the debate among scholars on the fate of the American family, whether it is argued in the disciplines of sociology, psychology, history, or other fields, is still a heated one. While organizations that promote scientific research are supposed to be "value free," cultural wars do exist within these fields of inquiry. As in politics, there are different visions in the academic world on what is best for American couples and families.

Like Alfred Kinsey, Kenneth Starr does indeed have a place in our recent history of American views on sexuality. Kenneth Starr is responsible for forcing Americans to peek at the sex life of an American president, even while we suspected that other presidents were deviant in this regard. Because of Kenneth Starr, we know perhaps too much about the private moments of Bill Clinton, and now we have to wonder if it matters.

Did Clinton's Affair Affect Us?

Where should we place President Clinton's scandalous affair with Monica Lewinsky in this history of American views about sex and family life? Would our family lives or our views about sex be different today if not for this scandal of the 1990s? Most sociologists see human behavior and attitudes as the result of the complex economic and social interaction mentioned above. However, a few scholars have delved into the impact of Clinton and Lewinsky on American families and they have not been conclusive studies.

Bonnie Zare (2001) conducted an analysis of "sentimentalism in adultery" in American feature films in order to show that the film industry depicts marital infidelity as an act where "one or more married persons finds phenomenal passion and emotional satisfaction in an affair" (Zare 2001,30). She provides about two lines to the Clinton affair, saying that because of the impeachment trail, the American media is obsessed with adultery. Zare devotes more space to the portrayal of adultery in films like *Shakespeare in Love, Dr. Zhivago*, and *Bridges of Madison County*. She makes no connection to the Clinton scandal and American views whatsoever, but instead she more appropriately suggests an argument inspired by Christopher Lasch, that sexual partners are products in the capitalistic ideology of consumerism and adultery offers Americans the options of "new products." Zare, not a social scientist, but a teacher of English and Women's Studies, offers an interesting take on marital infidelity in American society. She suggests that monogamy is a challenge to Americans, not only because of film portrayals of sentimental adultery, but also because American capitalism offers a distorted gratification system that encourages us to see relationships as products of consumption. Americans see (consume) and enjoy the films that portray sentimental adultery one day, and then criticize the moral weakness of real Americans the next.

In the March/April 1999 edition of *Society*, a journal known for its social commentaries, two sociologists wrote separate essays on the impact of the Clinton–Lewinsky affair on American society. LiahGreenfeld (1999) reminds us that sexual acts, especially the acts of a president, cannot be seen as private acts. The classic distinction between public and private has eroded, especially for a president. She also states that the sexual transgressions of other presidents (she mentions Kennedy and French president Mitterand) were, in their time, private matters, not to be discussed in public. However, sex in the 1990s had become a public matter, especially when the acts were performed in the workplace, in Clinton's case in the Oval Office. Additionally, we note that the growth of the news media contributed to more people knowing more things about more subjects than ever before. That said, some of this certainly is emblematic of the specific time in which it occurred. Greenfeld notes that Clinton, our first baby boomer president, embraced the "personal is political" ideology of his generation. She finds Clinton's conduct unacceptable, not just because he cheated on his wife, but because his actions resembled sexual harassment. Prior to the 1990s, sexual harassment in the workplace had noreal national attention. In fact, several high-ranking politicians were caught in sexual harassment scandals of their own because it was not considered a crime: Oregon Senator Bob Packwood resigned from the Senate after his colleagues voted to expel him following the revelation that he had harassed and abused several female staffers; Supreme Court Justice Clarence Thomas found his Senate confirmation hearings turned into a three-ring circus following accusations that he had sexually harassed a female employee (Anita Hill) while chairman of the Equal

Employment Opportunity Commission. Both were two of the first occasions when the American public (and their elected officials) had to wrangle with the concepts of workplace harassment, equality, and sexual standards. The 1990s began the start of a national discussion about, and a movement against, such discriminatory behavior. As a result, when Clinton was caught with an employee—and a very young one at that—this national discussion was already heated. Greenfeld's analysis is useful because it helps us to see that Clinton was oblivious to the nature of his own position and he was unaware of how he fit into the shifting nature of America's public and private spheres.

Of course, in the months following the breaking news of the affair, there were plenty of media reports on how this situation might affect marriages, or women in the workplace, or the children of America. A study conducted by the Pew Research Center for the People and the Press (1998) does indicate that Americans were responding to the affair within their families during the year that the story captured continual attention from the media (Pew 1998). Based on a survey of 597 parents of children aged 8 to 17, the Pew researchers found in September 1998 that teenagers were more focused on the scandal than were younger children (according to their parents). The researchers also noted that "Children of Republicans talk more about the Clinton scandal to family and friends and are said to be suffering more disillusionment with politics than the average child, while the exact opposite is said to be true of children from Democratic families" (Pew 1998, 1). Later in the report it is revealed that some children did see Clinton's televised address as well as his testimony on his "improper relationship" with Monica Lewinsky. Most interesting is that 10 percent of children aged 8–10, 13 percent of children aged 11–13, and 21 percent of children aged 14–17 actually read parts of the *Starr Report*. While the *Starr Report* is quite damaging to both Monica Lewinsky and Bill Clinton, the report also reveals a conservative traditionalism as reflected in Starr's reporting, so it is not surprising that children of Republicans suffered more disillusionment than did children of Democrats. There were other topics that attracted the attention of children more than Clinton and Lewinsky back in 1998. The Pew report states that schoolyard shootings and the McGwire–Sosa home run race were discussed more than the Clinton–Lewsinsky scandal among parents and their children in all three age categories measured (Pew 1998).

It is important to keep in mind that the Pew researchers collected data from parents, not from the children themselves, and often parents have a limited understanding of how their children (especially teenagers) see or respond to sensitive topics, especially when the topic involves sex. Some error in responses should be assumed when reviewing the results of this study. We also know that there is a strong level of social desirability in a survey that asks parents to report on how they discuss sex, politics, and morals with their children. Few parents, for example, will honestly report that they have little or no knowledge of their own children's moral character. Not surprisingly then, well over half of the parents of younger children and 70 percent of children over age 14 in the Pew study did not think that their children's knowledge of the Clinton–Lewinsky scandal would make a difference in their moral development. Most parents probably felt they had properly instilled morals and values through-out their parenting and even if they did question their ability to socialize morals, they would not reveal this concern on a survey. The report does leave one troubling consequence of the Clinton–Lewinsky scandal for America's children, and that is that children might lose respect for "politicians" after learning about this event. The "politician" is not specified in the report and we can assume a specific political office was not indicated on the original questionnaire, so the political office of children's contempt could be the president of the United States or a Republican White House independent council.

Social scientific researchers have investigated trends in marriage, divorce, cohabitation, premarital sex, and extramarital sex for several decades. Of course, Kinsey's early studies on sexual behavior were the first accounts of premarital and extramarital sex, but as already mentioned, the non-random nature of his sampling procedure make it impossible to generalize his results to the American population in 1948. Social scientists honed their methodology and design during the 50 years since Kinsey's publication, so that the results of studies could be reli-able and generalizable. The 1990s saw some important methodological advance-ments in the scientific study of family life and sexuality, especially in large-scale national studies (Christopher and Sprecher 2000). For example, of the projects listed below, some were started as early as the in the 1960s, most have data from several time periods, and all of them measure indicators of family and sexual behavior and attitudes.

● The General Social Survey (National Opinion Research Center 2009)
● The National Health and Social Life Survey (National Opinion Research Center 1992)
● The National Study of Adolescent Health (Carolina Population Center 2009)
● The Early Years of Marriage Project (Institute for Social Research, University of Michigan 2009)
● Marriage Instability over the Life-course Project (Population Research Institute, Penn State University 2009)
● Monitoring the Future (Institute for Social Research, University of Michigan 2009) National Survey of Families and Households (University of Wisconsin 2008)

When reviewing findings from research reports based on the data from these stud-ies, we see that some areas of family life and sexuality have clearly changed since the 1960s, especially America's increasing tolerance for different family forms such a non-marital cohabitation, single parenting, and gay/lesbian lifestyles (Thorton and Young-DeMarco 2001; Christopher and Sprecher 2000; Treas 2002; Cherlin 2010; Sassler 2010). When it comes to non-marital sex, researchers have noted that sexual activity among never-married adults was high throughout the 1990s (Christopher and Sprecher 2000) and permissive attitudes about premarital sex increased greatly from the 1970s to the 1990s, however the permissive trend did decelerate somewhat from the 1980s to the 1990s (Thornton and Young-DeMarco 2001).

When it comes to extramarital sex, Americans are not tolerant. Thornton and Young-DeMarco (2001) assessed the findings from several studies in the 1980s and 1990s and they conclude that:

> The exclusivity of relationships is thus an exception to the long-running trend toward allowing people more freedom to choose their own behavior. Instead of an increasing norm of tolerance in this area, intolerance has apparently expanded. (Thorton and Young-DeMarco 2001, 1028)

Judith Treas (2002) notes that American's views toward marital infidelity in the mid-1990s were comparable to conservative Catholic populations such as Ireland and Poland. She also notes that a decrease in disapproval of homosexuality is the most revolutionary shift in sexual attitudes among Americans by the 1990s. Similarly, Christopher and Sprecher (2000) note that nonprobability samples yielded poor research results regarding the frequency of extramarital sex in the 1980s, however, studies improved throughout the 1990s and the measures show that extramarital affairs are quite low (Christopher and Sprecher 2000).

The *General Social Survey* (National Opinion Research Center 2009) has collected representative data on American's views and behaviors regarding non-marital sex since 1972. Since 1973, the *General Social Survey* has included an item that asks respondents if they think that sex with a person other than one's spouse is always wrong, almost always wrong, sometimes wrong, or not wrong at all. Specifically, the survey question asks, "What is your opinion about a married person having sexual relations with someone other than the marriage partner—is it always wrong, almost always wrong, wrong only sometimes, or not wrong at all?"(National Opinion Research Center 2009). The trends in the responses to this question are presented in Table 2.1. As the table shows, the proportion of Americans who think that this behavior is always wrong has increased since 1973, but the gradual increase in the disapproval of non-marital sex did not begin in the years following the Clinton–Lewinsky scandal. Rather, as displayed in Table 2.1, the increase in American's opinion that sex with someone other than one's spouse is always wrong began in 1974 (National Opinion Research Center 2009). One artifact of this finding might be that back in the 1970s, many Americans thought of both premarital and extramarital sex as sex with someone other than a spouse, but as premarital sex and premarital cohabitation became more acceptable in the 1970s and 1980s, Americans began to interpret the reference in this item to *only* extramarital sex by the late 1980s and 1990s.

In 1991, the National Opinion Research Center added an item to the *General Social Survey* that specifically refers to *extra*marital sex, by asking respondents to indicate whether they thought extramarital sex was always wrong, almost always wrong, wrong only sometimes, or not wrong at all. Data for this measure was collected in 1991, 1994, and 1998. The greatest increase in disapproval for extramarital sex occurred from 1991, when 73.4 percent of respondents thought it was always

Table 2.1 Percent Who Feel that Sex with Person Other than Spouse is Wrong from the General Social Survey, 1973–2006

Sex with person other than spouse	Always wrong	Almost always wrong	Sometimes wrong	Not wrong at all	Total	N
1973	69.8	14.8	11.7	3.8	100	1491
1974	73.2	12.5	11.8	2.5	100	1463
1976	68.7	16.5	10.7	4.0	100	1479
1977	73.9	13.5	9.9	2.8	100	1508
1980	71.0	16.4	9.6	3.0	100	1446
1982	74.2	13.7	9.7	2.3	100	1482
1984	71.5	18.0	8.7	1.8	100	1450
1985	75.4	13.3	8.4	3.0	100	1514
1987	74.3	16.2	7.4	2.1	100	1446
1988	80.7	12.3	5.1	1.9	100	966
1989	78.5	12.3	7.5	1.6	100	1026
1990	79.0	12.5	6.7	1.8	100	891
1991	77.2	13.5	6.2	3.0	100	969
1993	78.5	13.9	5.2	2.4	100	1044
1994	79.7	12.3	6.0	2.0	100	2001
1996	78.5	14.9	5.0	1.6	100	1882
1998	80.5	11.7	5.5	2.3	100	1861
2000	79.4	10.9	7.3	2.4	100	1827
2002	81.3	12.6	4.1	2.0	100	920
2004	82.1	11.6	4.6	1.7	100	868
2006	82.0	10.9	5.4	1.7	100	1966

Note: Data on this measure was not collected every year from 1973–2006.
Source: National Opinion Research Center 2009.

wrong to 1994 when 80.8 percent of respondents thought it was always wrong (National Opinion Research Center 2009).

Why the increase in attitudes against extramarital sex? A major factor cited in these attitude changes is a cohort turnover (Teas 2002; Smith 1994). A cohort turnover occurs when one age cohort exits from the analysis and another one takes its place. People aged 18 to 25 in the early 1980s were less permissive in their attitudes about sex compared to the young adults who were measured in the 1970s. As this new cohort moved into analyses, the generation gap in attitudes about sexuality began to narrow (Smith 1994). Why would entering cohorts in the 1980s be less permissive in their attitudes about sex than were their age counterparts ten years earlier? First of all, the 18 to 25 year olds of the 1970s were especially liberal in their attitudes about sex because they were socialized with the sexual revolution of that era. Secondly, a factor called *intracohort change* can also influence overall changes in attitudes about sexual behavior (Treas 2002). Intracohort change occurs when individuals enter an adult cohort and change while they are in that cohort. Intracohort change is an indicator of people "changing their minds." In an analysis of attitudes toward nonmarital sex from 1972 to 1998, Treas (2002) finds that intracohort change influenced the attitude changes on extramarital sex from 1972 to 1998. We can't attribute this attitude change to America's reaction to the Clinton–Lewinsky scandal (and Treas doesn't either), mainly because the attitude shifts started to occur in the 1980s.

Modern Behaviors

What about actual behavior, not just attitudes, concerning marital infidelity since the Clinton years? Back in 1948, Kinsey found that more than 40 percent of his respondents had had sex outside of marriage (Kinsey 1948), but we know that his findings are inaccurate and frequently criticized because of sampling problems and measurement error. Today, because the most socially approved setting for sex continues to be marriage (Christopher and Sprecher 2000), respondents are always influenced by a high level of social desirability when responding to questions about marital fidelity on questionnaires and in interviews. We will never know how may people lie about their marital fidelity, but it is more likely that if respondents do lie, they lie to preset themselves as more faithful than they really are. That being said, the *General Social Survey* has measured marital fidelity since 1991 with a question on whether the respondents had sex with someone other than their spouse (see Table 2.2). The percentage of respondents who said "yes" to this question ranges from 11.4 percent in 1991 to 13.4 percent in 2006 (National Opinion Research Center 2009), however, as displayed in Table 2.2, this increase was not incremental. In fact, a clear pattern is not discernible from the data presented from 1991 to 2006. If the Clinton–Lewinsky scandal had any bearing on American's marital fidelity, we should see an increase (or a decrease) in the percentage of people who responded that they had engaged in sex outside of marriage from 1998 to 2000, however there is only a1 percent increase on this measure during the time period.

In June 2010, the *Journal of Marriage and Family,* the premier journal on family issues from a social scientific perspective, published its Decade in Review issue. The research published in this important issue reveals how family attitudes and behaviors have shifted since the 1990s. David Demo, the editor of *Journal of Marriage and Family*, compiled research topics from the past ten years came up with a list of the most important topics for family research, ranging from marriage and divorce patters to the impact of war and terrorism on families. The Decade in Review issue presents the most comprehensive analysis of the most widely studied topics on marriage and family from the past decade (Demo 2010). As most scholars of the family probably predicted, the Decade in Review analyses did indeed reveal that American family life is changing. For example, Americans are waiting even longer to get married. The median age at first marriage for men is now 27.4 and it is 25.6 for women (Cherlin 2010). Also, cohabitation continues to increase, especially among people

Table 2.2: Percent Who have ever had Sex with Someone Other than Spouse while Married from the General Social Survey 1991–2006

Sex with other than spouse	Yes	No	Never married	Total	N
1991	11.4	66.3	22.3	100	1286
1993	13.3	68.3	18.4	100	1443
1994	12.2	67.0	20.9	100	2731
1996	13.8	63.5	22.7	100	2613
1998	12.6	63.4	24.0	100	2413
2000	12.7	62.1	25.2	100	2342
2002	13.2	61.2	25.6	100	2221
2004	11.9	63.8	24.3	100	2177
2006	13.4	60.1	26.5	1-00	2366.

Note: Data on this measure was not collected every year from 1991–2006
Source: National Opinion Research Center 2009.

who have children from previous marriages (Cherlin 2010). While these might seem like statistics that suggest Americans are turning away from marriage, Sharon Sassler states, "Most young Americans have positive attitudes about marriage, believe it will be in their futures, and see it an important life achievement" (Sassler 2010,563). As expected, no scholar in the Decade in Review suggested that the Clinton–Lewinsky scandal, or any political sex scandal for that matter, had any bearing on changes in American coupling practices and family life during the past ten years, because family change occurs within the context of broader social and economic changes. But what can be assured is that the Clinton scandal fit in with the changing norms of sexual acceptance and practice in America, and forced citizens to look at political sex scandals in a new way.

Clinton's Legacy for American Families and the Perception of Political Sex Scandals

On January 19, 2001, on the *News Hour with Jim Lehrer*, Ray Suarez conversed with several historians about how history would assess President Clinton. They carefully avoid the topic of Monica Lewinsky, although she was mentioned once during the segment, as was Linda Tripp. Reflecting on America from 1992 to 2000, and predicting how we would judge Bill Clinton in the future was not easy for these accomplished historians. Doris Kearns Goodwin was not ready to cast judgments as Clinton left office:

[Y]ou know, I think precisely because of what has been said, it is going to take some years before we can get perspective on Bill Clinton. In the sense we know what the elements of his presidency are to be judged. There is impeachment on the one hand. There is the booming economy on the other. There's Kosovo, there's the failed health care, there's squandered opportunities, there's talent, all the things we might be saying now. (*Public Broadcasting System* 2001)

The *News Hour* discussion gives the impression that the historians around the table were suggesting that Americans should step back, take stock, and appreciate the last eight years, despite the wild ride. Haynes Johnson comments on the legacy of the Clinton:

[W]e're at peace. We're not challenged by any enemies, no depression, no world war. The country feels good about itself. He's leaving with the highest job approval rating of any president since they've started taking the poll ratings and all that. And yet there's this other side in the equation of these times, and more people cynical and distrusting of leadership and government. (*Public Broadcasting System* 2001)

Little did they (or we, for that matter) know what the rest of 2001 would bring to us, but as Clinton left office, historians, journalists, academicians, and everyday citizens began to contemplate his legacy. The question at hand here is whether Clinton's sexual affair is part of that legacy.

Are we left having to believe the sociologists, and even Alfred Kinsey—that our sexual attitudes and practices are *not* influenced by *one* book, or *one* scandal? If we are to believe sociologists, we must admit that our current trends in coupling and family life are the products of social and economic trends that began decades ago. However, we also know that our everyday lives are influenced by our interaction with the people around us, and our own consumptive behavior, especially of the media. Who can forget the 24-hour coverage of Bill and Monica in 1998? At the time, I remember one of my anti-television academic friends saying, "I feel like I need to get a television, just to watch all of this history in the making." I told her to save her money, but I watched the history being made. Many of us did. And now when we hear about John Edwards, John Ensign, Mark Sanford, Mark Foley, Larry Craig, or Eliot Spitzer (the actual list can never be complete because it is growing as I write this), we know we have been desensitized. Our desensitization is not from learning about Thomas Jefferson and Sally Heming, or Franklin Delano Roosevelt and Lucy Mercer. Those scandals were not televised and more importantly, there was no Kenneth Starr to write a report about them. Our desensitization to the sexual indiscretions of politician's is attributed to Bill Clinton, and the way his actions were portrayed by the media back in 1998.

Today, when the average American hears about John Edward's affair, or John Ensign's affair, we take the news casually, as we would take the news of any celebrity. We don't think these things affect us from day to day. However, as illustrated by the research on American attitudes cited in this chapter, Americans do have strong feelings about extramarital sex as it applies to our own relationships. And we still care very much about marriage.

The legacy of the Clinton–Lewinsky scandal is found in the boundaries-shattering communal experience of a public official's private life. The tentacles reach into our homes as we address a number of personal questions and into our politics as we grapple with electoral ones.

The personal questions include the most obvious: What is sex? What are "sexual relations?" When asked by White House staffers if he was having improper contact with Ms. Lewinsky, Clinton replied, "There's nothing going on between us." Clinton, in his Grand Jury testimony tried to nuance this:

> It depends on what the meaning of the word "is" is. If the—if he—if "is" means is and never has been, that is not—that is one thing. If it means there is none, that was a completely true statement . . . Now, if someone had asked me on that day, are you having any kind of sexual relations with Ms. Lewinsky, that is, asked me a question in the present tense, I would have said no. And it would have been completely true.(*The Starr Report*, fn. 1,128)

Is sex only penetration, or does fellatio count as sex as well? Is sex found in non-physical communication: Is sexting sex? Is internet pornography sex? Is gaming sex? What is harassment, what is rape, what is right and what is wrong? These are all very personal questions with which we struggle and debate today, in part thanks to the Clinton legacy.

There are political questions to discuss as well. Does the "public" part of a public official mean that he must be held to a higher standard than "average" men? What should the constituencies do when a politician fails so publically? Clinton was impeached—only the second president in American history to be so—because he lied under oath about his sexual promiscuities. But then the Republican-led Congress came under fire by the American public for wasting so much time on the impeachment proceedings. As shall be shown in later chapters, the fate of politicians who are caught in political sex scandals are varied and completely contextual to their own scandal, their constituencies, and their terms. But Clinton did set a standard: One could be caught in a very public and very compromising position and remain in office.

Clinton's own presidential legacy is a mixed one: He led the nation in boom-times, peaceful times, and he was pilloried for a scandal that threatened to break down a presidency but did not. His presidency and his scandal occurred at a time when sexual and familiar norms were changing, which may account for his ability to remain in office *and* for his public skewering. Placed alongside the changes marked by Kinsey first, and other sociologists later, the Clinton scandal helps to explain how we reacted then—and how we react now when our elected officials are caught in disgrace.

Works Cited

Blankenhorn, David. *The Future of Marriage*. New York: Encounter Books, 2009.

Brinkmann, Susan. *The Kinsey Corruption: An Expose on the Most Influential Scientist of Our Time*. Fayetteville, AR: Ascension Books, 2004.

Brown, Theodore M., and Elizabeth Fee. "Alfred C. Kinsey: A Pioneer of Sex Research." *American Journal of Public Health*, 2003; 9(6): 895–896.

Carolina Population Center. *Add Health*. Chapel Hill, NC: Carolina Population Center, 2009. Retrieved March 21, 2009 (www.cpc.unc.edu/projects/addhealth).

Center for Demography, University of Wisconsin. *National Survey of Families and Households*. Madison, WI: Center for Demography, University of Wisconsin, 2008. Retrieved May 21, 2009: (www.ssc.wisc.edu/nsfh/).

Cherlin, Andrew J. *Marriage, Divorce, Remarriage*. Cambridge, MA: Harvard University Press, 1992.

———. "Demographic Trends in the United States: A Review of Research in the 2000s." *Journal of Marriage and Family* 2010; 72: 403–419.

Christopher, F. S., and Susan, Sprecher. "Sexuality in Marriage, Dating, and Other Relationships: A Decade Review." *Journal of Marriage and Family*, 2000; 62: 999–1017.

Coontz, Stephanie. "Historical Perspectives on Family Studies." *Journal of Marriage and Family*, 2000; 62: 283–297.

Demo, David H. "A Decade in Review." *Journal of Marriage and Family*, 2010; 72: 401–402.

Gathorne-Hardy, Jonathan. *Sex, the Measure of all Things*. Bloomington, IN: Indiana University Press, 2000.

Greenfeld, Liah. "Non-Partisan Reflections on the President's Affair." *Society*, 1999; 36(3): 18–21.

Imber, Jonathan B. "American Sexual Morality after 'That Woman.'" *Society*, 1999; 36(3): 29–36.

Institute for Social Research, University of Michigan. *The Early Years of Marriage Project*. Ann Arbor, MI: Institute for Social Research, University of Michigan, 2009. Retrieved May 21, 2009: (http://projects.isr.umich.edu/eym/index.html).

———.*Monitoring the Future*. Ann Arbor, MI: Institute for Social Research, University of Michigan, 2009. Retrieved May 21, 2009: (www.monitoringthefuture.org/).

Jones, James H. *Alfred C. Kinsey: A Public/Private Life*. New York: W.W. Norton, 1997.

Kinsey, Alfred C., Wardell B. Pomeroy, and Paul H. Gebhard. *Sexual Behavior in the Human Female*. Philadelphia: Saunders, 1953.

Kinsey, Alfred C., Wardell B. Pomeroy, and Clyde E. Martin. *Sexual Behavior in the Human Male*. Philadelphia: Saunders, 1948.

The Library of Congress. Bill Text 104th congress (1995–1996) H.R. 3396. ENR, 2010. Retrieved November 29, 2010 (http://thomas.loc.gov/cgi-bin/query/D?c104:1:./temp/~c1044RBeQf::).

———.Bill Text 104th congress (1995–1996) H.R. 3734. ENR, 2010. Retrieved November 29, 2010 (http://thomas.loc.gov/cgi-bin/query/z?c104:H.R.3734.ENR:).

National Opinion Research Center. "National Health and Social Life Survey." Chicago, IL: National Opinion Research Center. Retrieved May 21, 2009: (www.spc.uchicago.edu/prc/nhsls.php).

———. 1992. *General Social Survey*. Chicago, IL: National Opinion Research Center, 2009. Retrieved May 21, 2009: (www.norc.org/projects/general+social+survey.htm).

Pew Research Center for People and the Press. "White House Scandal Has Families Talking." Washington, DC: Pew Research Center, 1998. Retrieved May 15, 2009:(http://people-press. org/report/78/).

Pomeroy, Wardell B. *Kinsey and the Institute for Sex Research*. New York: Harper and Row, 1972.

Popenoe, David. *The War Over the Family*. New York: Transaction Books, 2008.

Population Research Institute, Penn State University. *Marital Instability over the Life Course*. State College, PA: Population Research Institute, Penn State University, 2009. Retrieved May 21, 2009: (www.pop.psu.edu/marinst/).

Public Broadcasting System. *The Clinton Legacy*. Arlington,VA: *Online NewsHour*. PBS, 2001. Retrieved May 21, 2009:(www.pbs.org/newshour/bb/politics/jan-june01/legacy_0119. html).

Reiss, Ira. *An Insider's View of Sexual Science since Kinsey*. Lanham, MD: Rowman and Littlefield, 2006.

Sassler, Sharon. "Partnering across the Life Course: Sex Relationships and Mate Selection." *Journal of Marriage and Family,* 2010; 72: 557–575.

Smith, Tim. "Attitudes Toward Sexual Permissiveness: Trends, Correlates, and Behavioral Connections." In *Sexuality across the Life Course*, edited by Alice M. Rossi. Chicago: University of Chicago Press, 1994; 63–97.

Starr, Kenneth W. "The Full Text of the Starr Report." *Time.com,* 1998. Retrieved May 15, 2009: (www.time.com/time/daily/scandal/starr_report/files/).

Thorton, Arland and Linda, Young-DeMarco. "Four Decades of Trends in Attitudes toward Family Issues in the United States: The 1960s through the 1990s." *Journal of Marriage and Family*, 2001; 63: 1009–1037.

Treas, Judith. "How Cohorts, Education, and Ideology Shaped a New Sexual Revolution on American Attitudes Toward Nonmarital Sex, 1972–1998." *Sociological Perspectives,* 2002; 45(3):267–283.

United States Department of Labor. "Family Medical Leave Act. Wage and Hour Division." 2010. Retrieved November 29, 2010: (www.dol.gov/whd/fmla/).

Zare, Bonnie. "'Sentimentalized Adultery': The Film Industry's Next Step in Consumerism." *Journal of Popular Culture,* 2001; 35(3): 29–41.

CHAPTER 3

The Psychology of Risky Sexual Behavior: Why Politicians Expose Themselves

James D. Griffith

When those holding public office in the United States are caught in sex scandals, their professional careers are often negatively influenced. Mark Foley, Larry Craig, David Vitter, Eliot Spitzer, John Ensign, and Mark Sanford are high profile examples of public officials who were involved in such scandals, resulting in dire consequences for their political careers. The link between such wanton behaviors among politicians and their professions seems obvious and has been documented. For example, scandals decrease regard for government leaders and individual politicians (Clark, Stewart, and Whiteley 1998; Lanoue and Headrick 1994), and scandal has been related to electoral consequences (e.g., Cowley 2002; McAllister 2000; Hetherington 1999; Farrell, McAllister, and Studlar 1998; Banducci and Karp 1994). Welch and Hibbing (1997) reported that incumbents involved in corruption involving issues of morality have seen their support decline by 10 percent. Several researchers (Bowler and Karp 2004; Hibbing and Theiss-Morse 1995) suggested that, regardless of education level, voters lack the necessary understanding to properly evaluate government. Rather than making judgments on the basis of logic, voters often use criteria that are emotional in content. As a further caveat in this equation, McAllister (2000) showed that voters had higher expectations from politicians than the expectations politicians had from themselves. In summary, voters have high expectations of their elected officials, involvement in a sex scandal is damaging to political careers, and judgments regarding politicians are often made on the basis of emotionality. These relationships seem fairly straightforward. Why then, would a politician risk his career for a sexual tryst?

Before attempting to answer why a politician might have a sexual affair, one might ask a more general question of how often it happens. That question would be difficult to answer. The instances that surface are the ones that are discovered and made public by the media. Thus, we could reason that any known number is an underestimate, because there are probably sexual affairs that occur that do not become public knowledge. High-level politicians, celebrities, and professional athletes are groups that gain clear media attention, and because they are they are public figures, their private lives often become public events. The sexual affairs that we know about are the ones that become public, and we have no way of accurately determining the rate of which sexual affairs occur among public officials. Therefore, it would be difficult to compare rates of sexual affairs among politicians to other groups or to the general public. There is some general information we know about infidelity that may be applied to politicians. Even though they have different occupational roles than Americans, the behavior of sexual infidelity is similar regardless of vocation and entails the same factors.

As stated in Chapter 2, the vast majority of Americans believes in the institution of marriage and feels that extra marital affairs are wrong. Sexual infidelity research has focused on three factors related to engaging in these sexual affairs. These factors include personal values of the individual, opportunities for a sexual affair, and the nature of the couple's relationship. With regards to personal values, permissive sexual attitudes are associated with a greater likelihood of engaging in an affair. Smith (1994) reported that 76 percent of respondents who believed that having an extramarital affair was not at all wrong actually had an affair, compared to 10 percent who believed that an extramarital affair was always wrong. So, who tends to have permissive sexual attitudes? Research has shown that permissive sexual attitudes are attributed to being male, being African-American, having high levels of education, living in a large city, and having liberal political and religious ideologies. Opportunities typically take the form of potential partners and circumstances that offer secrecy. Blumstein and Schwartz (1983) reported that couples that live separate lives have more opportunities for and are more likely to have sex partners outside their marriage or committed relationship. Further, individuals who are married and perceive alternative partners to be available are more likely to have a sexual affair (Maykovich 1976). Also related to participating in an extramarital tryst are factors related to dissatisfaction with the current relationship (Brown 1991). Those who practice infidelity report being unhappy in their marriage (Greeley 1991), with men citing sexual dissatisfaction in their marriage (Maykovich 1976). Based on this summaryhigh risk profile of our elected officials may begin to emerge. Those who fit the profile include highly educated males who live in Washington, DC, away from their families, and who experience some degree of marital dissatisfaction and permissive sexual attitudes.

Because some elected officials have been caught having sexual affairs, we know that such behaviors do in fact occur, since the political environment provides ample opportunities for sexual encounters. Do elected officials have a higher level of moral fiber compared to the general public that would prevent them from engaging in a sexual encounter? Or perhaps the consequences come into play when they decide to pursue an affair. The personal consequences may be similar to those in the general public, but it could be argued that the professional consequences would be more severe for a politician. Perhaps the difference is that those in public office are more likely to believe that they will not get caught. These rationale are certainly speculative, but they do raise interesting points. In any case, the fact of the matter is that sexual affairs do occur among elected officials. Most politicians have many of the same needs and desires as non-politicians. Some of those desires involve having sexual needs met, and those needs can be met in a variety of ways, but the mechanisms or processes of decision-making seem to be consistent across individuals, regardless of their careers. Therefore, why might a politician have a sexual affair with someone he is not married to or with someone he does not intend to marry, at the risk of being caught and that indiscretion becoming public knowledge?

Well, one explanation may be—because they can. That reasoning is not a very illuminating rationale as to why politicians engage in such behaviors, but it does serve as a starting point. Some say that the field of psychology attempts to describe, explain, and predict human behavior. Providing explanations as to why those in public offices engage in behaviors that put their careers at risk is not clear because data has not been collected in any empirical fashion addressing this particular issue for this specific group of individuals. However, there are theories that do attempt to explain such behaviors, which will be applied to those in public office to serve as a framework for future work. These theories will be applied to the most common political sex scandals. Those are a male politician who has a sexual encounter with a female or another male. It is certainly true that other types of indiscretions which occur could include a female politician with a male, a female politician with a female, a male politician with a male and female, etc. The point is that the possible iterations are many and interesting. However, the focus of this chapter will focus on the most common scenario, which involves a male politician and female partner, and a related caveat discussing male–male encounters.

In addition to their political careers, many public servants who have been part of sex scandals have also been married, which significantly affects their personal life. As might be expected, infidelity is the most common reason for divorce (Betzig 1989). So again, with apolitical (and sometimes married) life on the line, why would a politician engage in such risky behavior? There are two explanations that will be offered to account for these behaviors among high-profile politicians. Additionally, there is some degree of overlap between the theories, although they certainly are different perspectives of the same behavior. The first is rooted within evolutionary psychology and is largely derived from the work of Buss (2003). This evolutionary account of behavior provides predictions as to who would be more likely to engage in various kinds of sexual behaviors and why. This theory often has different names but will be referred to here as the Sexual Strategies Theory. The second explanation is based on the work of Baumeister and Vohs (2004),in which the act of sex is considered a female resource and it is applied to social exchange theory. This is not a case study of a particular politician who had an affair with a particular individual. Rather, it is an examination of how and why individuals make decisions regarding sexual behavior. Human sexual behavior is an incredibly complex behavior and it is not practical to provide a simple explanation for a specific behavior. A more valuable perspective might be to provide competing theories on the factors and processes involved in human mating and consider how these theories might be applied to gain a better understanding of political sex scandal.

Sexual Strategies Theory

Darwin (1859) suggested that natural selection was the key to evolutionary change. These changes or adaptations are linked to differential reproductive success. And these adaptations can be either physiological or behavioral. Because reproduction is so central to the evolutionary process, sexuality should be a process that has been subjected to many selection pressures. In other words, some characteristics became more prevalent due to the advantages they offered for an ancestral individual's mating success. It seems as though sexual selection involves two processes: intrasexual competition and intersexual selection (Darwin 1871). Intrasexual or same-sex competition is when members of one sex compete with one another and the winner of the competition gains sexual access to those mates. Then, the characteristics leading to success will be selected and can evolve over time. We may think of the size of an elk's antlers as an example from the animal kingdom. For male humans, these characteristics may be bulging biceps, nice teeth with a nice smile, intelligence, and economic security. Intersexual selection, on the other hand, involves the selection of particular members of the other sex as partner, or mate choice. If there is reasonable consensus among members of a given sex regarding the desirable characteristics in potential mates, then those individuals who have those qualities have a preferential mating advantage. Thus, preferences and the desired characteristics may evolve over time.

So, is there a difference with regards to which process is operative for each sex? There is much data to suggest that there is a difference. Specifically, males engage in intrasexual competition and females in intersexual selection. Trivers (1972) is given credit in providing the first explanation as to why there is a gender difference with regards to the two processes, indicated that parental investment of the offspring in determining which of the two components was more important for each sex. Parental investment can be defined as the effort expended to aid the survival and reproduction of an offspring. Because women have the greater obligatory parental investment, they should be more involved with mate selection (Buss 1996). As an example, consider the gestation term of a woman. Even before the child is born, the woman invests nine months of carrying and caring for the fetus, whereas the man invested only a few minutes during the insemination process. During those nine months, the woman will be infertile and is committed to obligatory parental investment. The man, on the other hand, may be able to fertilize many other mates during that time period, each fertilization session. To put this in perspective, consider research that has shown that typical male intercourse duration is from two to eight minutes (Miller and Byers 2004; Hunt 1974; Kinsey, Pomeroy, and Martin 1948). We will give males the benefit of the doubt and assume the higher estimate of eight minutes per act. Using that value, a man would have to fertilize approximately 48,600 women (assuming an eight-minute obligatory parental investment) to equal one term of pregnancy investment by a woman. It must be pointed out that this simply concerns the prenatal time period. After the child is born, if the man–woman pair separates, the woman would typically care for the infant. However, those estimates are not part of the calculation. The point is that the woman's parental investment far outweighs that of the man, in each and every instance. Because of this enormous obligatory parental investment differential, the lower-investing sex (males) should be more competitive with members of their own sex to gain access to the more selective women and take advantage of seemingly low-risk opportunities for short-term trysts (Buss and Schmitt 1993).

Over time, successful women (those who were able to reproduce healthy offspring, who, in turn, reproduced their own healthy offspring) were careful in selecting their mates and allocated their limited reproductive resources wisely. Because of women's selectivity, males tended to be those who competed successfully with rivals to obtain and maintain access to those selective women and were able to take advantage of low-risk opportunities for short-term mating (Buss and Schmitt 1993). Thus, one aspect to take into consideration involves the difference between long-term and short-term mating. Because of different selection pressures, men and women have evolved different mating strategies and mate preferences (Buss 2006). Further, these strategies may differ, depending on the type of relationship desired. For example, kindness may be more important for men when they are seeking a long-term mate, because cooperation with that mate will be more extensive (Botwin, Buss, and Shackelford 1997).

Clearly, men experience far fewer risks compared to women when pursuing short-term mating. This is directly related to the obligatory parental investment concept that was previously mentioned. Men's minimum investment is a single act of sexual intercourse lasting a few minutes, whereas women must endure the risk of the burden of a nine-month pregnancy and may be left to raise the child as a single parent. Men who seek short-term mates look for women with high reproductive value even though they do not desire reproduction. The types of women tend to be young and physically attractive, since they are perceived to be more fertile than older less attractive women (Buss 1989). Other preferred characteristics related to a woman's future reproductive success include breast and buttock symmetry (Li and Kenrick 2006), low waist-to-hip ratio (Marlowe, Apicella, and Reed 2005), low body mass index (Kurzban and Weeden 2005), and unmarried with no casual sex partners (Shackelford et al. 2004). For women, the preferred characteristics related to short-term mates include men who are physically attractive and muscular (Li and Kenrick 2006), and unmarried with no casual sex partners (Shackelford et al. 2004). Although both genders prefer an attractive mate for short-term mating, men exhibit a stronger desire for perceived attractiveness (Li and Kenrick 2006). Characteristics associated with short-term mating have been identified for men, but why might women engage in this potentially costly strategy? There are two possible reasons that have been offered. First, women may want to gain material resources or replace a current long-term partner (Greiling and Buss 2000). Second, they may engage in short-term mating in order to acquire the perceived good genes of the target male (e.g., Gangestad, Thornhill, and Garver-Apgar 2005). In fact, there is some support for the good gene acquisition explanation. Women in the fertile phase of their ovulatory cycle are more likely to pursue short-term mating and prefer more muscular men (Provost, Troje, and Quinsey 2008). Interestingly, women who are ovulating tend to prefer men who are more creative (Haselton and Miller 2006) and who engage in intrasexual competitiveness (Gangestad et al. 2004).

Long-term preferences tend to be more straightforward because consideration of having a mate for a long period of time is important. There does not seem to be much of a gender difference with regards to how selective each gender is in choosing a long-term mate, although they do look for some different characteristics. Women tend to prefer men who are high in social status, have expendable resources, are older and have greater financial capacity, ambition, and industriousness, whereas men prefer women who are attractive and young (Buss 1989). It has also been found that both genders prefer mates with high levels of kindness and intelligence (Buss 1988). In addition, it turns out that homosexual mate preferences are similar to preferences found among heterosexuals. For example, homosexual men place high priorities on attractiveness and youth (Gobrogge et al. 2007). The characteristics of high-level male politicians align with these preferences seems to fit the preferential mold quite nicely. Many congressmen could be considered to possess many, if not all, of those aforementioned characteristics, making them attractive potential mates for many women. Even though some may not possess the desired physical characteristics sought after in short-term mating, they do possess the desired characteristics for long-term mates. The assessment of potential mates begins by determining whether a potential mate has acceptable levels of the most important characteristics, then considers the less important ones, such as a sense of humor (Li et al. 2002). In each situation (i.e., short-term and long-term), the woman has more factors to consider and has the more complicated decision, because of the potentially great parental obligation that may need to be fulfilled. The stability of these desired characteristics have been looked by scholars across time in a fairly systematic manner.

There was an ambitious study conducted by Buss et al. (2001) that looked at the importance of characteristics of potential mates over a six time periods with a 57-year interval, ranging from 1939 to 1996, across various regions of the United States. Individuals rated the importance of 18 different mate characteristics in an attempt to assess the cultural evolution of values over time. There were several relevant findings. First, the United States was considered to be a single culture, as there were minor regional differences throughout the country. One of the domains examined that appears throughout the literature is that of physical attractiveness. Over time, physical attractiveness became more important for both genders. In 1939, women ranked physical attractiveness 17th, whereas it was ranked 13th in 1996 (note that a lower number reflects a more important characteristic in rankings, 1st is most important and 18th is least important). For men, it was more pronounced, as the ranking jumped from 14th to 8th. The study was not causal in nature but there is a clear pattern over time. One might speculate on the different reasons accounting for the change. One may be the effect of media and how that may be related to expectations. By seeing more attractive individuals on various forms of media, individuals may increase their expectations of potential mates. Financial resources were also examined, and within an evolutionary perspective, it follows that these are an important characteristic for men to possess such that women desire that characteristic in men. Among women, the ranking changed from 13th to 11th, which was regarded as interesting because it was predicted that it would have an overall higher ranking. The more striking finding on this dimension occurred among men, where the ranking changed from 17th to 13th. Perhaps because of women having more opportunities in the workplace, men placed a higher value on a partner who can increase his resources because once married, they are shared. The dimension with the largest change over time for both genders was that of chastity. For both genders, the ranking importance declined over time from 10th to 17th. It is speculated that the availability of birth control methods and sexual revolution of the late 1960s and early 1970s may be related to the observed shift in importance of chastity. The last domain that showed significant change was that of mutual attraction and love. For women, it increased from a low of 6th to 1st, whereas for men it increased from 4th to 1st. The change clearly shows the escalated importance of love in a marriage over time. Buss et al. (2001) speculated that, over time, access to extended family members might be more limited, due to migration patterns following work or moving for other reasons. The family unit may have become much smaller; thus, more importance may have been given to mutual attraction and love. Although there were observed gender similarities, the predicted patterns were observed across all time periods in which males assigned more importance of physical attractiveness than did women, and women assigned more importance to financial resources than did men.

Individuals assess potential mates on the basis of prioritized characteristics and assign some type of value on that individual, even though this may occur at an unconscious level. This assessment is often termed "mate value" (e.g., recall the movie *10*). This term refers to one's attractiveness as a prospective mate. There is ample evidence that demonstrates that mate value is related to mate selection (e.g., Smith et al. 2009; Buss and Shackleford 2008). These mechanisms are in place in order to efficiently and effectively identify appropriate potential partners. Assume there are two identical male twins, with all characteristics being similar except for their salaries. Both work in sales, with one earning $25,000 annually and the other $125,000; the latter twin would have a higher mate value than would his lower-earning brother because he has more resources available. As another example, highly attractive women show preferences for men who are willing to invest highly in them, compared to less attractive women rating the same men. What often occurs is that men and women tend to pair with others of a similar mate value (Buss 2003).

Once one has a mate, how does one keep a partner? This is referred to as mate retention and the behaviors that ensure such retention are performed to ensure the continued relationship and fidelity of the partner. If these behaviors do not occur, a sexual affair outside of the established relationship is more likely to occur. Each gender expends effort toward mate retention that is proportional to the potential costs and benefits, which take into account the likelihood of effectiveness of those behaviors (Buss 1988). These retention strategies occur when there is a perceived risk of infidelity on behalf of one's partner. In other words, if one believes that his or her partner is likely to stray, one is more likely to put more efforts in certain mate retention behaviors believed to be most effective(Buss and Shackelford 1997). It has been found that men spend more time with mate retention behaviors when they have spent a greater time period away from their partner, since the couple's last time they had sexual intercourse, compared to shorter periods of time (Starrat et al. 2007). There are two categories of mate retention strategies.

The first strategy involves behaviors that offer benefits to the partner, while the other cause costs to the partner (McKibbin et al. 1976). Men with a low mate value (i.e., ugly men who are poor) are more likely to engage in cost-inflicting behaviors. These behaviors may include insulting remarks (e.g., telling his mate that she is over-weight or ugly). High mate-value men (i.e., good looking men who are wealthy) typically offer benefits to their partner (e.g., giving his partner an expensive gift). Women tend to use more benefit-related strategies, such as enhancing their beauty by dressing in a sexy manner or having their hair styled. Each gender performs mate retention behaviors that advertise the important characteristics to their partner's gender, such that men display their resources and women try to improve their appearance by looking more youthful (Buss 1988).

Sometimes the costs of retaining a mate outweigh the benefits of attempting to retain the partner, so mate expulsion is another strategy followed. As one would predict, the most common reason for marital termination is infidelity. Infidelity can be either sexual or emotional in nature. Compared to men, women are more likely to forgive a sexual infidelity than an emotional one, and are more likely to end a relationship following an emotional infidelity compared to a sexual one (Shackelford, Buss, and Bennett 2002). It has also been found that women are less likely to stay in a marriage without children than are men, and more likely to initiate a divorce earlier in the relationship, compared to men. Furthermore, it has been found that following a divorce, men are more likely to remarry compared to women. Men with no children from a prior marriage tend to marry women who have never been married and have no children, whereas men with children from a prior marriage tend to remarry to women who have been married (Buckle, Gallup, and Rodd 1996). Following a divorce, women are more likely to engage in behaviors to enhance their appearance prior to seeking a new mate (Perilloux and Buss 2008). Although both genders need to deal with a change in their mate status following the dissolution of a relationship, each follows a different pattern.

What would the Sexual Strategies Theory predict as behavior for male politicians? First, it would predict that more indiscretions occur among male politicians compared to females. Although this has not been empirically tested, there do seem to be more reports of indiscretions among men relative to women, even when taking into consideration the relative percentage of each gender. There are relatively few reports of sexual scandals involving female politicians compared to their male counterparts. Second, most male politicians should have elevated mate values, based on their high-status occupations and access to a wide variety of economic, legal, and political resources, and would be considered powerful individuals by potential mates (i.e., senators have big antlers). A fair number of politicians certainly do have financial wealth, which is a desirable characteristic, but they all have a powerful position of status. That is, they are most likely to be perceived to be socially powerful individuals because of their profession and rank high in that important category. Third, sexual affairs among male politicians should be with younger, attractive females, and males in the cases of homosexual encounters. This would be accomplished by examining the characteristics of the sexual partners of the politicians. Again, this would be a study that would be very difficult to generalize because the data would be on only the reported cases that may not be representative of what actually does occur.

Social Exchange Theory

Implementing an economic perspective by examining the costs and benefits of interactions between two parties is central to Social Exchange Theory. Within each interaction, a person gives something to the other and, in turn, gains something from the other, and the interactions are likely to continue if each party gains more than it loses over time. The value of what is gained or lost depends on various factors, including the preferences of the individual and the broader market (i.e., society's value). Using this approach, Baumeister and Vohs (2004) provided a framework where sex is a resource in a marketplace. Here, men and women represent buyer and seller, respectively, and the value is affected by other buyers and sellers..In this view, the act of sex is not viewed as an equal exchange as dictated by cultural systems. Female sexuality is given value, whereas male sexuality is largely worthless. If a man and woman have sexual intercourse, the exchange is not equal; thus, the man must provide something to the woman beyond his participation. How much he gives will be dictated by the individual involved in the exchange and market forces and will most often be in the form of affection, material gifts, commitment promises, time, and other similar "goods."

Baumeister and Vohs (2004) provided a summary of factors related to the price fluctuation of sex and separated it on the basis of individual and market level factors. When present, the following individual level factors increase the price of sex: the man has a higher sex drive, the man does not have a much higher status than the woman, other men desire the woman, the woman has a reputation for having few partners, the woman is attractive, the woman is in young adulthood, the woman wears sexy clothing, other women do not want the man, and the woman does not lack alternate access to resources. Likewise, the following market level factors also increase the price of sex: there is a larger of pool of men than women, men have few opportunities for sexual satisfaction, and there exists restrictive sexual norms. These factors will be examined to show patterns related to the cost of sex.

Individual factors

A crucial point of this account suggests that sex is a female resource, although both members engage in this behavior. If this were to be true, then one could predict that men would offer women non-sexual resources in exchange for sex, whereas women would generally not offer such resources in exchange for having sex with a man. In addition, characteristics such as virginity, fidelity, and a virtuous reputation would be of higher value among women. An explanation as to why sex is a female resource may be deduced from a classic explanation provided by Waller and Hill (1951), referred to as the "principle of least interest." This principle suggests that in a dyad, the one with the most power is the one who wants the connection less. The application is that men want sex more than do women, therefore, women have more power in that context, suggesting more value. Is there evidence to support the notion that men want sex more than do women?

Prostitution provides one perspective by which we can explore sex as a female resource. It is the most straightforward form of sexual exchange. In most cases, the buyer is quite certain that sexual activity will occur following payment, an event that is not as certain in non-prostitution scenarios. If sex is a female resource, the theory would predict that the majority of prostitutes are female and the majority of clients are male, which is the case. Although not specifically examining prostitution, Loewenstein (1987) conducted a study that attempted to put a monetary value on a kiss. It can be argued that a kiss is not sexual activity, but it is often a precursor and may have sexual connotations associated with it. Participants were asked to identify their favorite opposite-gender movie star and were asked how much they would be willing to pay for a kiss from that person. As social exchange theory would predict, males were willing to pay more.

There is ample evidence suggesting that males want sex more than do women. Buss and Schmitt (1993) asked individuals how many different sex partners they desired through various time periods. Over the course of a lifetime, men hoped to have 18 partners, while women desired slightly fewer than five. Baumeister, Catanese, and Vohs (2001) provided a detailed review of gender differences on a variety of behavioral measures of sex drive. The evidence was quite compelling. With regards to cognitive behaviors, compared to women, men are more likely to think about sex, fantasize about sex, desire sex, have more permissive sexual attitudes, and rate their sex drive as higher. Sexual behaviors show a similar pattern, as men are more likely to be sexually aroused, masturbate, enjoy more varied sexual practices, engage in goal directed behavior to get sex, and have more partners. In a clever study by Clark and Hatfield (1989), men and women at a college campus were approached by an attractive member of the opposite sex and asked if they would go out on a date, go back to the confederate's apartment, or have sex. Among the female participants, none agreed to have sex and only 6 percent agreed to back to his apartment. In contrast, 75 percent of male participants were willing to have sex with the female confederate, and 69 percent were willing to go to her apartment. For both genders, about 50 percent agreed to go on a date. This study was able to clearly demonstrate the contrasts between genders. Not a single woman agreed to have sex with the confederate, whereas three out of four men were willing to engage in this type of activity. Similar patterns have been reported in studies of couples or those with a mate. Byers and Lewis (1988) found that half of the couples in their study had arguments about sex at least once a month. In all the cases, males wanted more sexual activity. The data on gender differences on sex drive is so compelling that, in fact, there were no studies that reported women having a stronger sex drive than men. Based on these data, there is a strong argument to consider sex as a female resource and, within an economic context, to view female sexuality as more valuable than a male sexuality.

Other individual level factors that have been examined simultaneously include the reputation and physical characteristics of the woman. There are two resources that a woman can consider with regards to sex (Baumeister and Vohs 2004). First is actual sexual activity, which can be considered a renewable resource. In other words, her ability to engage in sexual intercourse is not strongly related to her prior sexual experiences. Another related resource is her reputation, which is a non-renewable resource. In other words, once a bad reputation is in place, it is often permanent or difficult to adjust, unless one relocates. So, a woman may be more concerned about how she is perceived by others regarding sexual activity than how she feels about it. Why is this an important consideration? The value of a good can rise and fall, dependent on the distribution of that resource. Thus, sex would have a high value if a woman had few partners or is reluctant to give sexual favors. In contrast, the same activity would possess less value if a woman has a reputation of having had many lovers or is willing to have sex with many different people. Therefore, a man's perception of a woman's sexual history is related to the amount he is willing to pay to have sex with her. It is to her advantage that if she does have multiple partners, to do so in secrecy and to maintain a perception that she is selective in those to whom she chooses to provide sexual favors. In line with this thinking, the more a man desires a particular woman, the higher price he is willing to pay. Consider three recent scandals and how they might fit into this category:[1] Eliot Spitzer spent in excess of $80,000, much of which was on 22-year-old Ashley Dupré; David Vitter paid an undisclosed amount to a prostitution service over a three-year period; and Mark Sanford made frequent trips to Argentina to visit his lover. In each of those cases, the men were with younger women and they were willing to spend considerable resources (e.g., time and money) to have sex with those women. They certainly took measures to ensure secrecy, as two were with professional call girls where secrecy is assumed and the other traveled to a different continent–all of which were costly routes to have sex. Each of these men chose women who were able to demand a high price for sex. A more attractive woman can demand a higher price than might a less attractive woman. There is ample evidence that men prefer young, attractive women as short-term partners (Li and Kenrick 2006; Kurzban and Weeden 2005; Buss and Schmidt 1993). In addition, attractiveness is often culture specific. How a woman might advertise could include wearing certain clothing, flirting, derogating competitors, and creating the perception of how satisfying it would be to be with her. Essentially, this is her way of increasing demand. And, as there are more men interested in her, the price of having sex with her increases. In sum, women would focus on maintaining or enhancing their perceived beauty, while maintaining a good reputation, in order to stay competitive in the marketplace.

Yet another individual level factor to consider is the socioeconomic status of the woman in a given society, which is related to her access to alternate resources. There are societies in which women have limited options in which to gain resources. This lack of opportunities may be in the political, legal, educational, economic, and occupational areas. In these types of societies, the price of sex must remain high in order for a woman to be able to acquire these alternative resources through men. However, the more dire the circumstances of the women, the greater the decrease in the price of sex. Those in middle- and upper-class levels can more easily increase the value of sex, whereas those women in the lower strata often find themselves in situations in which sex is devalued. An historical account of Victorian society offers some support for this notion. Bullough and Bullough (1998) provided an analysis of data from the Victorian era and found that approximately 10 percent of women in the lower economic strata engaged in prostitution. In contrast, during the same time period, it was commonplace for middle-class women to have sex only if they were married or engaged to be married. There is also evidence in prostitution that further supports this socioeconomic phenomenon. Although wealthier Western countries seem to have more permissive sexual attitudes, sex tourism tends to occur in poorer countries, such as Southeast Asia, Eastern Europe, and Central America. Men from rich countries travel to poor countries to pay lower prices for sex relative to their own country. The women in the poor countries charge low prices (from the perspective of the wealthy tourists), but these prices are actually higher than they would commonly get locally.

The final cluster of individual level characteristics to consider involves those related to the man. As discussed in the Sexual Strategies Theory, women prefer men who are high in social status, have expendable resources, are older, and have greater financial capacity, ambition, and industriousness (Miner and Shackelford 2010). Many male politicians can be viewed as possessing some, and often all, of those desirable characteristics. In addition, there are two other factors that should be taken into consideration. First is the issue of unequal status. The male politician often is regarded as having a higher status than most women in the pool of available partners. The status differential may be even more marked in short-term sexual relationships compared to long-term ones. As an example, consider the situation where groupies are able to interact with celebrities whose status is much higher. This means that one of the only possible ways to spend time with a celebrity is if sex is proffered as an enticement.(Des Barres 1987). It is true that both genders fantasize about having sex with celebrities, but in the case of politicians it is predominantly a male "celebrity" in the power position. Some examples include Wayne Harris, who had an affair with his secretary, as well as Dan Crane and Gerry Studds, who had affairs with congressional pages. In each case, there was a definite status differential providing the male politicians a situation in which the price of sex was lowered for those serving in lower-level occupational roles. Also contributing to this male opportunity is media exposure, which is a relatively new phenomena (from an evolutionary perspective). Several studies by Kenrick and his colleagues (Kenrick et al. 1994; Kenrick, Gutierres, and Goldberg 1989; Kenrick and Gutierres 1980) indicated that both gender are exposed to an unrealistic distribution of highly attractive people in the media, which may be related to individuals believing that highly attractive and desirable mates may be more accessible than reality would dictate. In fact, data shows that women with high rates of media exposure are less satisfied with their current partners and less willing to engage in relationships they perceive to be less desirable. It is not unreasonable to assume that because politicians are often in the media women find them to be a most desirable potential mate while. These factors all contribute to male politicians typically being able to pay less for sex.

Market factors

If sex can be considered a female resource and we are viewing this behavior from an economic perspective, then the topic of supply and demand must be discussed. With regards to sex and gender, females represent the supply and males the demand. Variations in the ratios of supply and demand should be related to sexual activity. What is assumed is that the price of sex will favor the gender in the minority. It has been found that the more numerous gender will lower its standards in order to gain access to a partner of the less numerous gender. So, if the pool of eligible women is substantially larger than the pool of eligible men, the price of sex should decrease (supply is greater than demand). Men have to offer fewer resources to women for sex in politics, compared to areas where men outnumber women. Gender behavioral differences have been found in unbalanced sex ratio societies. For example, in societies where women outnumber men, there are higher rates of female promiscuity (Schmitt 2005), women wear shorter skirts (Barber 1999), and there are higher rates of illegitimate births (South and Trent 1988) and teenage pregnancies (Barber 2001). In contrast, in societies where men outnumber women, women have greater interest in commitment cues (Buss 2003), divorce rates are lower (Pederson 1991; Secord 1983), and first marriages occur at an earlier age (South and Trent 1988). Evaluating data from the 2000 Census, is it possible to determine what areas are best for each gender? The highest price of sex would be in the state of Alaska, where men have competition from others in a small pool of women. The lowest price of sex would be in the District of Columbia, based in it having the lowest male-to-female ratio. So, male politicians working in Washington, DC, are in the best market for sex, based on the gender ratio.

Related to supply and demand are low cost substitutions (e.g., such as a generic brand of a product). With sex, two substitutions may be prostitution and pornography. Males may pay money to have sex with prostitutes or spend many hours watching pornography on a DVD or on the internet. In general, females have a more negative view of pornography and prostitution, compared to men. For example, two studies (Lottes, Weinberg, and Weller 1993; Weiss 1991) reported that women were more opposed to pornography than were men, and another study found that women are much less supportive of prostitution compared to men (Klassen, Williams, and Levitt 1989). In fact, more than three times the number of men compared to women indicated that there is nothing wrong with prostitution. This is as the Social Exchange Theory would predict, because the more men pay for prostitutes and use pornography, the less the demand for women in general, resulting in a lower price. Interestingly, the only state in which prostitution is legal (i.e., Nevada) has the second highest male-female ratio. Males may be more likely to be supportive of measures that would devalue sex, such as prostitution or pornography, whereas women would most likely have opposing views, in order to reduce the supply of sex alternatives, which increases the value of sex.

The price for goods also has to take into consideration the local marketplace (Baumeister and Vohs 2004). For example, in a given large city, real estate prices vary considerably depending on the specific neighborhood where a given unit is located. So how much sex costs is related to the sexual norms of a given area. Those norms can be thought of as a standard rate. And, it should be noted that this can vary greatly across time and cultures. For example, consider the late 1960s and early 1970s in some parts of California where many advocates of the "free love" movement were present. This was a buyer's market and men were doing well. Consider that same geographic region in the 1950s. There were different cultural expectations where it was not uncommon for women to wait until they were married to have sex. This time period was a seller's market. The point being is that the local marketplace can change fairly quickly depending on cultural influences stemming from political and social forces. Regardless of the time period and location, each gender strives to get the best deal. Men want to pay as little as possible, whereas women want to get a high price. During this sexual negotiation, men will try to convince women that many couples have sex at a low price and that they may exaggerate their own sexual activity to try and convey the impression of the norm. Women, on the other hand, may emphasize the norm of sex within committed relationships and she may underestimate her sexual experiences in order to keep the price higher. By men claiming to have many female partners, they devalue the price of sex, while women underestimating their number of partners, appreciate the price. Thus, in a scenario with a male politician and a younger female, the man may exacerbate his sexual experience while the woman may act more innocent than she actually is.

Sexual negotiations between a man and woman require each party to eventually make a decision. The role of men seems to be straightforward in that they compete against other buyers by offering more to a desired woman for sexual favors.

The female has a more complicated decision-making process, similar to the Sexual Strategies Account. The woman must balance conflicting forces such as her own sexual desire, her aim to get a good price, how much she would be willing to lower her price to attract a given man, the resulting depreciation of her resource if she decides to be with a given man, and others (Baumeister and Vohs 2004). Men do not have such an array of competing forces to deal with. Another name for this sexual negotiation may be referred to as courtship, which can be viewed as a man's attempt to have sex with a woman. In this view, the woman determines when sex will occur. Cohen and Shotland (1996) conducted a study in which they asked men and women in a given relationship when they should have first had sex and when they actually had sex. Based on these results, it was very clear that women determine when sex will occur. Other evidence can be found in the complaints of couples over partners who did not keep their part of the deal. Buss (1989) asked both genders their primary complaint about partners. As would be predicted, men were most upset about women who accepted resources and yet rejected sexual advances. In contrast, women's primary complaint involved men who offered a relationship but backed out after having sex.

So, what does this theory say about male politicians? For the most part, it is a buyer's market at the federal level. These men are in the most favorable sex-ratio geographic region in the nation, their jobs they are perceived to be of high status with an array of resources, they are in demand as many women are interested in them, their media exposure assists by improving their status while decreasing the desirability of competitors (i.e., women's current partners), they have direct access to many lower-level employees, and the overall market price for sex should be favorable because of the current environment. In essence, male politicians working in the District of Columbia have many opportunities to access willing female mates. From an investment perspective, an advisor would probably recommend to buy, buy, buy as prices are low, particularly if you are representing Alaska. There are, however, potential political consequences that could be described as dire at best.

The purpose of this chapter was to offer some possible explanations as to why male politicians might engage in risky sexual behaviors. In this context, risky sexual behavior, rather than concern safe-sex practices, are political and professional in nature..There are two theoretical accounts that provide frameworks describing factors and situations associated with sexual behavior. Studies can be conducted to evaluate these theories on predicting the scandalous sexual behaviors of public servants. As mentioned before, it would be a daunting task to accurately assess the occurrences and rates of sexual affairs among politicians. Efforts are made to keep these trysts as secretive as possible because of the consequences. Even so, men routinely engage in these behaviors, knowing full well the risks involved and putting their careers on the line for a sexual encounter. If nothing else, one needs to appreciate the incredibly strong motivating forces behind such behaviors. Logic and reasonable decision-making are somehow overridden by passion and desire. Why are some politicians more likely to engage in these behaviors, while others resist? Are politicians inherently different compared to the general public or other groups, based on their status? How well do the theoretical models predict the known sexual affairs? And to the degree to which they do or do not predict indiscretions, how representative is that of all our public officials? These are just a few of the many questions that may someday be addressed.

Works Cited

Banducci, Susan A., and Jeffrey A. Karp. "The Electoral Consequences of Scandal and Reapportionment in the 1992 House Elections." *American Politics Quarterly*, 1994; 22: 3–26.

Barber, Nigel. "Women's Dress Fashions as a Function of Reproductive Strategy." *Sex Roles*, 1999: 40: 459–471.

———. "On the Relationship between Marital Opportunity and Teen Pregnancy—The Sex Ratio Question." *Journal of Cross-Cultural Psychology*, 2001; 32: 259–267.

Baumeister, Roy F., Kathleen R. Catanese, and Kathleen D. Vohs. "Is There a Gender Difference in Strength of Sex Drive? Theoretical Views, Conceptual Distinctions, and a Review of Relevant Evidence." *Personality and Social Psychology Review*, 2001; 5: 242–273.

Baumeister, Roy F., and Kathleen D. Vohs. "Sexual Economies: Sex As a Female Resource for Social Exchange in Heterosexual Interactions." *Personality and Social Psychology Review*, 2004; 8: 339–363.

Betzig, Laura. "Causes of Conjugal Dissolution: A Cross-Cultural Study." *Current Anthropology*, 1989; 30: 654–676.

Blumstein, Phillip, and Pepper Schwartz. *American Couples*. New York: Morrow, 1983.

Botwin, Michael D., David M. Buss, and Todd K. Shackelford. "Personality and Mate Preferences: Five Factors in Mate Selection and Marital Satisfaction." *Journal of Personality*, 1997; 65: 107–136.

Bowler, Shaun, and Jeffrey A. Karp. "Politicians, Scandals, and Trust in Government." *Political Behavior*, 2004; 26: 271–287.

Brown, Emily M. *Patterns of Infidelity and Their Treatment*. New York: Brunner Mazel, 1991.

Buckle, Leslie, Gordon G. Gallup, and Zachary A. Rodd. "Marriage As a Reproductive Contract: Patterns of Marriage, Divorce, and Remarriage." *Ethology and Sociobiology*, 1996; 17: 363–377.

Bullough, Bonnie, and Vern L. Bullough. "Introduction: Female Prostitution: Current Research and Changing Interpretations." In *Prostitution: On Whores, Hustlers, and Johns*, edited by J. E. Elias, V. L. Bullough, V. Elias, and G. Brewer. Buffalo, NY: Prometheus, 1998.

Buss, David M. "From Vigilance to Violence: Tactics of Mate Retention in American Undergraduates." *Ethology and Sociobiology*, 1988; 291–317.

———. "Sex Differences in Human Mate Preferences: Evolutionary Hypotheses Tested in 37 Cultures." *Behavioral and Brain Sciences*, 1989; 12: 1–49.

———. "Paternity Uncertainty and the Complex Repertoire of Human Mating Strategies." *American Psychologist*, 1996; 51: 161–162.

———. *The Evolution of Desire* (2nd ed.). New York: Basic Books, 2003.

———. "Strategies of Human Mating." *Psychological Topics,* 2006; 15: 239–260.

Buss, David M., and David P. Schmitt. "Sexual Strategies Theory: An Evolutionary Perspective on Human Mating." *Psychological Review*, 1993; 100: 204–232.

Buss, David M., and Todd K. Shackelford. "From Vigilance to Violence: Mate Retention Tactics in Married Couples." *Journal of Personality and Social Psychology*, 1997; 7: 346–361.

———. "Attractive Women Want It All: Good Genes, Economic Investment, Parenting Proclivities and Emotional Commitment." *Evolutionary Psychology*, 2008; 6: 134–146.

Buss, David. M, Todd K. Shackelford, Lee A. Kirkpatrick, and Randy J. Larsen. "A Half Century of Mate Preferences: The Cultural Evolution of Values." *Journal of Marriage and Family*, 2001; 63: 491–503.

Byers, E. Sandra, and Kim Lewis. "Dating Couples' Disagreements over the Desired Level of Sexual Intimacy." *Journal of Sex Research*, 1988; 24: 15–29.

Clark, Russell D., and Elaine Hatfield. "Gender Differences in Receptivity to Sexual Offers." *Journal of Psychology and Human Sexuality*, 1989; 2: 39–55.

Clarke, Harold D., Marianne C. Stewart, and Paul F. Whiteley. "New Models for New Labour: The Political Economy of Labour Party Support, January 1992–April 1997." *The American Political Science Review*, 1998; 92: 559–575.

Cohen, Laurie L., and R. Lance Shotland. "Timing of First Sexual Intercourse in a Relationship: Expectations, Experiences, and Perceptions of Others." *Journal of Sex Research*, 1996; 33: 291–299.

Cowley, Philip. *Revolts & Rebellions—Parliamentary Voting Under Blair*. London: Politico, 2002.

Darwin, Charles. *On the Origin of the Species by Means of Natural Selection, or Preservation of Favoured Races in the Struggle for Life*. London: Murray, 1859.

———. *The Descent of Man and Selection in Relation to Sex*. London: John Murray, 1871.

Des Barres, Pamela. *I'm with the Band: Confessions of a Groupie*. New York: Jove, 1987.

Farrell, David M., Ian McAllister, and Donley T. Studlar. "Sex, Money and Politics: Sleaze and Conservative Incumbency in the 1997 British Election." In *British Elections and Parties Review*, edited by David Denver et al., Vol. 8. London: Frank Cass, 1998.

Gangestad, Steven W., Jeffry A. Simpson, Alita J. Cousins, Christine E. Garver-Apgar, and P. Neils Christensen. "Women's Preferences for Male Behavioral Displays Change across the Menstrual Cycle." *Psychological Science*, 2004; 15:203–207.

Gangestad, Steven W., Randy Thornhill, and Christine E. Garver-Apgar. "Women's Sexual Interests across the Ovulatory Cycle Depend on Primary Developmental Instability." *Proceedings of the Royal Society of London* B, 2005; 272: 2023–2027.

Gobrogge, Kyle L., Patrick S. Perkins, Jessica H. Baker, Kristen D. Balcer, S. Marc Breedlove, and Kelly L. Klump. "Homosexual Mating Preferences from an Evolutionary Perspective: Sexual Selection Theory Revisited." *Archives of Sexual Behavior*, 2007; 36: 717–723.

Greeley, Andrew M. *Faithful Attraction*. New York: A Tom Doherty Associates Book, 1991.

Greiling, Heidi, and David M. Buss. "Women's Sexual Strategies: The Hidden Dimension of Extra Pair Mating." *Personality and Individual Differences*, 2000; 28: 929–963.

Haselton, Martie G., and Geoffrey F. Miller. "Women's Fertility across the Cycle Increases the Short-Term Attractiveness of Creative Intelligence." *Human Nature*, 2006; 17:50–73.

Hetherington, Marc J. "The Effect of Political Trust on the Presidential Vote, 1968–96." *American Political Science Review*, 1999; 93: 311–326.

Hibbing, John R., and Elizabeth Theiss-Morse. *Congress as Public Enemy: Public Attitudes toward American Political Institutions*. Cambridge: Cambridge University Press, 1995.

Hunt, Morton. *Sexual Behaviour in the 1970s*. New York: Dell, 1974.

Kenrick, Douglas T., and Sara E. Gutierres. "Contrast Effect and Judgments of Physical Attractiveness." *Journal of Personality and Social Psychology*, 1980; 38: 131–140.

Kenrick, Douglas T., Sara E. Gutierres, and Laurie L. Goldberg. "Influence of Popular Erotica on Judgments of Strangers and Mates." *Journal of Experimental Social Psychology*, 1989; 25: 159–167.

Kenrick, Douglas T., Steven L. Neuberg, Kristin L. Zierk, and Jacquelyn M. Krones. "Evolution and Social Cognition: Contrast Effects as a Function of Sex, Dominance and Physical Attractiveness." *Personality and Social Psychology Bulletin*, 1994; 20: 210–217.

Kinsey, Alfred C., Wardell B. Pomeroy, and Clyde E. Martin. *Sexual Behaviour in the Human Male*. Philadelphia: Saunders, 1948.

Klassen, Albert D., Colin J. Williams, and Eugene E. Levitt. *Sex and Morality in the U.S.: An Empirical Enquiry under the Auspices of the Kinsey Institute*. Middletown, CT: Wesleyan University Press, 1989.

Kurzban, Robert, and Jason Weeden. "Hurry Date: Mate Preferences in Action." *Evolution and Human Behavior*, 2005; 26:227–244.

Lanoue, David J., and Barbara Headrick. "Prime Ministers, Parties, and the Public: The Dynamics of Government Popularity in Great Britain." *Public Opinion Quarterly*, 1994; 58: 191–209.

Li, Norman P., and Douglas T. Kenrick. "Sex Similarities and Differences in Preferences for Short-term Mates: What, Whether and Why." *Journal of Personality and Social Psychology*, 2006; 90: 468–489.

Li, Norman P., J. Michael Bailey, Douglas T. Kenrick, and Joan A. W. Linsenmeier. "The Necessities and Luxuries of Mate Preferences: Testing the Tradeoffs." *Journal of Personality and Social Psychology*, 2002; 82: 947–955.

Loewenstein, George. "Anticipation and the Valuation of Delayed Consumption." *The Economic Journal*, 1987; 97: 666–684.

Lottes, Ilsa, Martin Weinberg, and Inge Weller. "Reactions to Pornography on a College Campus: For or Against?" *Sex Roles: A Journal of Research*, 1993; 29: 69–90.

Marlowe, Frank., Coren Apicella, and Dorian Reed. "Men's Preferences for Women's Profile Waist-to-Hip Ratio in Two Societies." *Evolution and Human Behavior*, 2005; 26: 458–468.

Maykovich, Minako K. "Attitudes versus Behavior in Extramarital Sexual Relations." *Journal of Marriage and the Family*, 1976; 38: 693–699.

McAllister, Ian. "Keeping Them Honest: Public and Elite Perception of Ethical Conduct among Australian Legislators." *Political Studies*, 2000; 48: 22–37.

McKibbin, William F., Aaron T. Goetz, Todd K. Shackelford, Lucas D. Schipper, Valerie G. Starratt, and Steve Stewart-Williams. "Why Do Men Insult Their Intimate Partners?" *Personality and Individual Differences*, 1976; 43: 231–241.

Miller, S. Andrea, and E. Sandra Byers. "Actual and Desired Duration of Foreplay and Intercourse: Discordance and Misperceptions within Heterosexual Couples." *The Journal of Sex Research*, 2004; 41: 301–309.

Miner, Emily J., and Todd K. Shackelford. "Mate Attraction, Retention and Expulsion." *Psicothema*, 2010; 22: 9–14.

Pedersen, Frank A. "Secular Trends in Human Sex Ratios: Their Influence on Individual and Family Behavior." *Human Nature*, 1991; 2: 271–291.

Perilloux, Carin, and David M. Buss. "Breaking Up Romantic Relationships: Costs Experienced and Coping Strategies Deployed." *Evolutionary Psychology*, 2008; 6: 164–181.

Provost, Meghan P., Nikolaus F. Troje, and Vernon L. Quinsey. "Short-Term Mating Strategies and Attraction to Masculinity in Point-Light Walkers." *Evolution and Human Behavior*, 2008; 29: 65–69.

Schmitt, David P. "Sociosexuality from Argentina to Zimbabwe: A 48-Nation Study of Sex, Culture, and Strategies of Human Mating." *Behavioral and Brain Sciences*, 2005; 28: 247–311.

Secord, Paul F. "Imbalanced Sex Ratios: The Social Consequences." *Personality and Social Psychology Bulletin*, 1983; 9: 525–543.

Shackelford, Todd K., David M. Buss, and Kevin Bennett. "Forgiveness or Breakup: Sex Differences in Responses to a Partner's Infidelity." *Cognition and Emotion*, 2002; 16: 299–307.

Shackelford, Todd K., Aaron T. Goetz, Craig W. La Munyon, Brian J. Quintus, and Viviana A. Weekes-Shackelford. "Sex Differences in Sexual Psychology Produce Sex-Similar Preferences for a Short-Term Mate." *Archives of Sexual Behavior*, 2004; 33: 405–412.

Smith, Finlay G., Benedict C. Jones, Lisa L. W. Welling, Anthony C. Little, Jovana Vukovic, Julie C.Main, and Lisa M. DeBruine. "Waist-Hip Ratio Predicts Women's Preferences for Masculine Male Faces, But Not Perceptions of Men's Trustworthiness." *Personality and Individual Differences*, 2009; 5: 476–480.

Smith, Tom W. "Attitudes Toward Sexual Permissiveness: Trends, Correlates, and Behavioral Connections." In *Sexuality Across the Life Course*, edited by A. S. Rossi. Chicago: University of Chicago Press, 1994; 63–97.

South, Scott J., and Katherine Trent. "Sex Ratios and Women's Roles: A Cross-National Analysis." *American Journal of Sociology*, 1988; 93: 1096–1115.

Starratt, Valerie G., Todd K. Shackelford, Aaron T. Goetz, and William F. McKibbin. "Male Mate Retention Behaviors Vary with Risk of Female Infidelity and Sperm Competition." *Acta Psychologica Sinica*, 2007; 39: 523–527.

Trivers, Robert L. "Parental Investment and Sexual Selection." In *Sexual Selection and the Descent of Man: 1871–1971*, edited by B. Campbell. Chicago: Aldine, 1972; 136–179.

Waller, W., and R. Hill. *The Family: A Dynamic Interpretation*. New York: Dryden, 1951.

Weiss, Daniel E. *The Great Divide: How Females and Males Really Differ*. New York: Poseidon, 1991.

Welch, Susan, and John R. Hibbing. "The Effects of Charges of Corruption on Voting Behavior in Congressional Elections, 1982–1990." *Journal of Politics,* 1997; 59: 226–239.

Notes

1   These case studies are examined more thoroughly in Chapter 5, along with three others: Mark Foley, Larry Craig, and John Ensign.

CHAPTER 4

A Framework for Understanding: Sex Scandals in Comparison

Mark Sachleben

It is mysterious to many Americans that what is considered scandalous to the American public is often seen as blasé to foreign press. The French press, in particular, was mystified by the focus on President Bill Clinton's affair with intern Monica Lewinsky. Similarly, there is a disconnect between how the European press and the American press cover an American sex scandal. These differences point to the necessity to understand deeper issues at work. This chapter creates a framework to understand sex scandals. While such scandals generate prurient interest and water cooler gossip, the effects can be predicted. . . even if we cannot predict which politician might get caught up in a scandal.

Growing up in Louisville, Kentucky, I was always baffled by the case of William Stansbury, the mayor of my hometown. Today, there is a park named after him across the street from the University of Louisville; however, when he was in office, no one in their right mind would have guessed any honors would have been posthumously bestowed upon him. During a paralyzing 1978 firefighters strike, Stansbury was out of town, ostensibly on business, when the city newspaper, the *Courier-Journal*, discovered that he was actually in a hotel in New Orleans with his administrative assistance, who had become his mistress. A political fury ensued, but calls for the mayor to step down went unheeded. An attempt by Louisville's Board of Aldermen to impeach the mayor collapsed when a state court refused to grant the aldermen the power to call witnesses. After the political firestorm died down, Stansbury retreated from public sight and he gave few interviews, but he remained in office and continued to pursue his mayoral agenda. By the time he left office in 1982, downtown revitalization had taken hold and the city was enjoying a love affair with their new minor league baseball team, the Louisville Redbirds, which the mayor was instrumental in bringing to the city (Kleber 2001, 848–849).[1]

Three years after he left office, in 1985, Stansbury and his mother were struck and killed by an automobile while crossing a street as they returned home from Maundy Thursday services.[2] There was an outpouring of grief and sympathy for the former mayor, probably in part because of the tragic nature of his death, but it does raise a question: How does the mayor of a mid-sized city leave town during a major crisis to have a tryst with his secretary and still manage to retain his job afterwards? To me, as a child growing up in Louisville, the prospect that Stansbury would keep his job seemed preposterous. A review of Stansbury's *Wikipedia* entry in September 2010 helps to illuminate the story of his rehabilitation. The only reference to the scandal reads, "Stansbury became unpopular during a firefighters' strike in 1978 and was the object of an impeachment attempt in 1979" (*Wikipedia*n.d.).[3]There is no mention of the reasons why he became unpopular, or of the implications. Sex scandals are major news events and they have the ability to publicly humiliate public officials. Yet, the lasting effects might not be what we initially think. To understand the impact of sex scandals on politics is the purpose of this book, and this chapter helps to establish a framework for this understanding.

Understanding Sex Scandals Systematically

Sex scandals can be understood as exogenous shocks to a system; like other scandals and crises, as sex scandal is a time in which the public can examine the performance of all involved. Scandals can test the political skills of those involved; however, scandals do not exist in a vacuum. If sexuality is viewed as commonplace and a part of daily life, then sex might not be solely seen as scandalous. However, if sex is seen from a chaste point of view, something that is exotic, profligate, and hidden from sight, then a public discussion of sex, especially when the behavior is outside the norms of a perceived chaste society, can be seen, in and of itself, as a scandal. Thus, a key point to understanding the impact of sex scandals is to appreciate how a public views sexuality in a society. The American public's attitude toward sex was examined in Chapter 2. Here we look at the political culture, as well.

One of the key actors in any sex scandal is the media. Without the active participation of the media a scandal does not become a scandal. BBC journalist Gerald Priestland once argued, "Journalists belong in the gutter because that is where the ruling classes throw their guilty secrets" (Andrews 1993, 486). Media outlets often receive derisive comments because of their coverage of the salacious activities of the common and the powerful. While we can debate the effect of sex scandals among non-politicians, and a commitment to celebrity culture, there is no doubt that sex scandals among politicians have an impact on politics. Yet calculating what that impact might be is a little trickier. It is difficult to calculate the effects of a particular sex scandal on an individual politician, or a specific political system, without considering the context from which it occurs.

Woody Allen once opined, "Love is the answer, but while you are waiting for the answer sex raises some pretty good questions." Indeed, when it comes to politics, Woody Allen's quote helps to explain differences in views of sex, sexuality, and scandals. To understand why sex scandals have different impacts in different societies, we must first have an understanding of the broad phases of a scandal. First, we must differentiate between various types of scandals. A simple office fling is vastly different from an abuse of power or of sexual bribery. What made Mayor Stansbury's affair particularly damning was that it was uncovered in the midst of a crisis (in some quarters, the affair would have been enough). Second, we must take into account the political environment in which the scandal occurs. Societies have different standards to which they hold their public officials; what may seem normal for one society may be completely inappropriate in another. In the midst of the environment, we must be cognizant of how the press covers a scandal. Further, what might be seen as a liability in one context might be seen as a positive in another. Third, the ability or skill of a politician, and his staff, to overcome or "spin" such a scandal is particularly important, as well. The skill of said politician will go a long way in determining the impact of such a scandal. Finally, in examining the impact of the transgression, it must be determined what effect the scandal had on the politician's career, and on the political body, in order to judge the future ramifications. We can chart how scandal will impact politics. It will be argued here that differences in the three variables of the scandal will impact the outcome of the scandal; that is, the type of scandal, the political environment in which the scandal takes place, and the skill of the politician to maneuver during and after the scandal. Thus, Table 4.1 outlines the different component variables:

If we are to understand the impact of sex scandals on politics, then we must evaluate the constituent components of a scandal. In the remainder of this chapter, we differentiate and establish characteristics of the variables involved in political sex scandals to deduce impacts. This chapter will provide references outside the United States, and outside the book's time frame, to help illustrate different political environments. It stands to reason that while political scandals, by definition, might be scandalous, their effects are different. For example, taking sexual advantage of underlings is much different than a collegial romance between consenting adults.

Table 4.1 Variables Associated with a Sexual Scandal

Type of Sex Scandal	Independent variable	Is the scandal simply an extramarital affair? Does the scandal point to other issues, such as, abuse of power, or contain illegal activities?
Political Environment	Independent variable	Is the public willing to tolerate (or look beyond) the issues of a single event? Is the public willing to forgive an indiscretion?
Skill of the politician	Independent variable	Does the politician have the political skill (charisma and charm) to survive a sex scandal?
Impact of scandal	Dependent variable	What is the ultimate effect of the scandal? Does the politician go to jail, be forced to resign, permanently lose his/her political status?

A Typology of Political Sex Scandals

A typology helps us to isolate factors to assess the impact of such scandals. These categories are not necessarily discrete; there can be overlap between categories. As most social scientists will attest, measurement sometimes can be difficult. As time moves on and more information is revealed, scandals might move from one category to another. This typology is an attempt to distinguish between different levels of scandalous behavior. I will argue that there are five major categories of sex scandals: (1) non-scandalous dalliances, (2) personal failures, (3) ironic scandals, (4) professional failure, and (5) abuse of power. Each can have varying impacts on the body politic. Similarly, engaging the services of a sex worker is different from sleeping with a foreign agent who potentially compromises state secrets. Tracking different types of scandals allows us to systematically analyze impacts and assess the public's reaction to events.

Sexual Dalliances That Are Not Scandals

The first category is one in which there is an affair or sexual impropriety that might on the surface cause a political impact, but eventually does not. There are two main reasons why this might be the case: First, the scandal is not a scandal because, although the dalliance might be known in elite circles, the story is not widely circulated in the press. The affair may be generally known in the public, through whispers and innuendo, but the effects are negligible for a wide possibility of reasons, one being its irrelevancy to politics. An example from outside the United States is that of Francois Mitterrand. After the death of French President Mitterrand, his wife, Danielle, invited his mistress, the art historian Anne Pingeot, and their daughter Mazarine, to the funeral. Most French people, even Mitterand's political opponents, deemed this a personal matter, outside the affairs of state.

Second, are the discoveries of affairs after the fact? While political office holders might have had affairs in the past, most often, they were not discovered until after the politicians left office. While the stories are salacious and make for interesting reads in memoirs and biographies, there is often little, if any, impact on the political system. Examples include Franklin D. Roosevelt's relationship with Lucy Mercer; Dwight D. Eisenhower's affair with Kay Summerby; John F. Kennedy's encounters with a number of women, including Marilyn Monroe; and British Prime Minister John Major's relationship with Edwina Curry. In each case, because the adulterous affair did not rise to the level of scandal, it did not impact politics or the political system.

Sex Scandal as a Personal Failure

A sex scandal is usually one of indiscretion; as noted in Chapter 8, there are few, if any, criminal implications. This type of scandal is one in which the politician is exposed for a sexual relationship outside marriage or a committed partnership. Depending on the political environment and the ability of the politician, the impact of the affair might be more greatly affected. In some societies, the political figure who has engaged in the scandal could be seen as unfit to carry out his duties because the personal capacity is morally bankrupt and, therefore, the politician's ability to lead is called into question. In other societies, such an act is considered (perhaps) as undesirable, but not necessarily a disqualification from office. Yet, even if the politician is not forced from office, the politician might be wounded. Therefore, although the politician might not pay the price of losing his job or serving jail time, there is still an impact. Examples include: San Francisco Mayor Gavin Newsome, Los Angeles Mayor Antonio Villaraigosa, former New York City Mayor Rudy Giuliani, Italian Prime Minister Silvio Berlusconi (with an 18-year-old woman), and the heir apparent to the British throne, Prince Charles. In each of these cases, such a scandal can tarnish a reputation, but does not necessarily destroy it.

The reasons for such a public dismissal can range from a perceived right of privacy to a cultural understanding along the lines of "boys will be boys."[4] In less permissive societies, there is sometimes an assumption that men *need* to engage in multiple sexual activities because women might not have the same sexual drive. Thus, a man who engages in such activity is seen as normal, even healthy. A woman who does so is viewed less charitably.[5] While the dearth of female politicians has meant there are far fewer sex scandals that involve female politicians, the treatment of the women involved in sex scandals with male politicians is instructive. The treatment of women, such as Deborah Jeane Palfrey (the so-called "DC Madam") and Ashley Dupré (the escort at the center of the Eliot Spitzer scandal), demonstrates that punishment, especially in legal terms, often falls on the female involved in the scandal, even if they are not a public official.

Sex Scandal as Irony

When a politician builds his career as a family-oriented person or a person of moral standing, then a scandal establishes the opposite of what the politician has stated. Such a scandal is devastating to the politician in question because his career is built on the presumption that he is above the dirt of normal political life. The prominence of such a scandal is due to the person in question being the one who was a champion of morality or piety, and who is now caught in a sex scandal that undermines his claims to legitimacy. Such a scandal feeds the salacious appetite of the press and of the public. It also calls into question the ability of a political system to produce virtuous leaders. A result of such a scandal is a societal cynicism about politics and political leaders. The outcome not only applies to sexual indiscretions, but to corruption, as well.

Because former New York Governor Eliot Spitzer built a reputation on going after corruption and malfeasants, the revelation that he frequented a high-priced brothel, engaged the services of an escort, and participated in an alleged illegal transfer of funds meant that his scandal had significant impacts.[6] Upon discovery of such a scandal, supporters of the politician are disillusioned. One could argue that the effect on the public is important, as well; the public becomes even more cynical about its political leaders.

Americans are familiar with these types of scandals among officeholders and those who comment on politics. This type of scandal has the ability to unseat powerful individuals and derail up-and-coming politicians. The irony need not be overt. In 2004, the Republican senatorial candidate from Illinois was Jack Ryan; his opponent was Democratic State Senator Barack Obama. During the campaign, Ryan's divorce proceedings revealed that his former wife, actress Jeri Ryan, claimed that Ryan had taken her to sex clubs and asked her to have sex in front of other patrons. After this admission, Republican leaders encouraged Ryan to withdraw from the race (Chase and Ford 2004). Because the Republican Party had cast itself as a party of family values and moral leanings, it found it distasteful that a candidate such as Ryan could represent the party in Illinois.[7] Such scandals are not limited to politics and are particularly damaging to religious figures. One also is reminded of the scandals involving Jimmy Swaggart; Swaggart systematically revealed personal indiscretions of other ministers (including Marvin Gorman and Jim Bakker) and publicly commented on what he saw as the evils of society. In a retaliatory move, Gorman hired a private investigator to follow Swaggart and eventually photographed him in a hotel room with a prostitute. The ensuing scandal became a major story because of Swaggart's prior crusading zeal.[8] In each case, the credibility of the ministers was severely undermined.

Sex Scandal as a Professional Failure

Some scandals are more than just family matters; in the pursuit of sexual activity, the politician in question could have violated his fiduciary duties. The affair in question is not simply a personal peccadillo, but the action results in the compromise of one's personal duties. The scandal becomes even more scandalous because the action involves not only sex, but includes the failure of the individual to carry out his professorial responsibilities or even endangers innocents. The implications of such a scandal are direr, so that even the most permissive of polities will find it hard to be forgiving in such a situation. Drawing from the international arena, the archetypal example of this type is the Profumo Affair, which broke in Britain in 1963. Secretary of State for War John Profumo's mistress, Christine Keeler, was also carrying on an affair with a known Russian spy. Matters were made worse when Profumo lied in Parliament about the affair. The case was seen as sensitive when revealed because of the security risks that might have come into play. The case of South Carolina Governor Mark Sanford fits this category as well, since he disappeared for a period of time to visit his mistress in Argentina. The Stansbury case from Louisville fits here, as well.

Sex Scandal as an Abuse of Power

This category is different from the previous categories in that the person in question is using his position to acquire sex. Rather than the scandal causing a politician to fail to fulfill a duty, the person in question in this type of scandal actively uses his power to pursue sexual conquest(s). Alternatively, the press and public perceive that the issue at the core of the scandal is the politician is using his position to acquire sexual favors. The best example may be of the casting couch in Hollywood, when it is alleged that directors or producers have lured young actresses with the promise of a role in a film in exchange for sex; or, similarly when professors have sex with a student in exchange for better grades.[9] Clearly, the sexual relationship in this category is a power relationship in which a person in a position of authority uses his power to have sex with an underling.

It is difficult to verify this type of scandal, although there are several instances that support this case. Clearly, the situation of President Clinton and Monica Lewinsky raised a number of eyebrows because she was an intern at the White House. Nevertheless, there are several other instances that appear to fit the criteria; one case in Europe that had significant political implications was that of Polish Deputy Prime Minister Andrzej Lepper. Aneta Krawczyk accused Lepper of abuse of power because she said that she had sex with him in order to get a political job. Subsequently, to retain her job, she was required to have sex multiple times with another party figure, Stanislaw Lyzwinski, over several years. Krawczyk claimed that Lyzwinski had fathered her daughter (*BBC News* 2006).[10] In the United States, officials at the Mineral Management Services (MMS), an agency that collects royalties on behalf of the Interior Department, were accused of frequently engaging in sexual relationships with representative of oil and gas companies (as well as other familiar acts), the entities from which they were to collect revenues. Such activities raised the possibility that officials at MMS might be abusing their power or, at the very least, not providing diligent oversight (Savage 2008).

In the United States, the Mark Foley scandal serves as this type of scandal. Foley was forced to resign his seat in Congress after it was reported that he had sent sexually suggestive emails to teenage boys who previously had been Congressional pages. Among the accusations lodged against Foley was that he improperly used his position of authority and power to solicit sexual gratification from underlings (or at least he had attempted to do so). Even if he did not misuse his power, which seems like a dubious argument given the age of Foley's contacts, the press and public opinion clearly believed he did so.

The charge of improper use of power can be a substantial tool, to use in reverse, against powerful politicians. Government leaders in Malaysia accused Anwar Ibrahim, a political reformer and the leader of the opposition, of being a homosexual and a "serial sodomite." The evidence given in trial was graphic and contradictory; whether true or not, the allegations and charges, most analysts agree, were introduced to the public in order to undermine Ibrahim politically. The charge of sexual indiscretion or preference can be used by political opponents to undermine the power for many political figures.[11]

Perhaps because the lack of open political dialogue in many countries, whispering campaigns about sexual dalliances or perceived deviancies help to undermine the power or popularity of individuals. Before and during the French Revolution, Marie Antoinette and King Louis XVI were both the subject of many rumors, which were intended to cast doubt on their ability to lead (Fraser 2001, 146–48, 161, 193, 209, and 225).[12]

Contextualizing Scandals: Different Political Environments

It is erroneous to assume sex scandals will have similar impacts across different types of societies. Indeed, there are several studies that suggest that permissive attitudes toward sexual issues are more prevalent in urban settings because of the population of these areas (Weis and Jurich 1985).[13] While the notion of political culture is abstract and vague, it can be a helpful concept to tease out differences within the cultures. Simply put, political culture is the emotional and attitudinal environment in which a political system operates (Kavanagh 1972, 10–11; Norton 2001, 23). An examination of political cultures might be helpful because of its importance in understanding different political environment. In their classic study, Almond and Verba (1963) argued that political culture is the bedrock of understanding the politics of a society; it gives us a shorthand understanding of the rules of the road, what is acceptable, and what is to be expected. While what is expected politically varies from country to country, the environment in which politics operates can vary within a country, as well; what might be expected from the political structure in one part of the United States, for example, might not be what was expected elsewhere. We will argue that the distinctions between political cultures can be extended to discuss the political implications of the scandalous sexual activities of politicians, as well. Thus, understanding a political environment helps us to understand the impact of sexual scandals on politics.

Philosopher A. C. Grayling (2008) has argued that Anglo-Saxon culture, which includes Britain and the United States, is adolescent and apprehensive in its attitude towards anything sexual. Grayling further argues that puritanical Christianity moved sex from the category of natural to vice (Grayling 2003, 46–49). Political environments, in which religion plays a major role in political discussions, are more likely to view sexual issues as problematic to discuss publicly. Thus, attitudes about sexual behavior vary drastically from country to country. For example, a 1998 survey found that the acceptance of premarital sex (agreeing that premarital sex was "not wrong at all") varied from a high in Sweden of 89 percent to a low in the Philippines of 11 percent; the percentage of those who agreed with the sentiment was 41 percent in the United States, as opposed to 69 percent in Canada. The same survey had similar findings with regard to extramarital sex. The percentage of people surveyed who thought extramarital sex was always wrong varied, as well;

from 36 percent agreeing in Russia to 88 percent in the Philippines. In the United States, 80 percent of those surveyed thought that extramarital sex was always wrong (Widmer, Reas, and Newcomb 1998). There is a strong body of evidence to suggest that there is a strong variation on the acceptance of non-marital sexual behavior across even Western countries (Buss 1989; Christensen and Carpenter 1962; Christensen and Gregg 1970; Jones et al. 1985; Jones et al. 1986; Ross 1985). This information points us to the idea that the context in which a sex scandal takes place is important. Thus, according to such an argument, the American polity will be more fixated on sexual improprieties than would the Czech Republic or Germany. For example, when Czech President Vaclav Klaus revealed that he had an affair with a flight attendant half his age (behind his wife's back), Czech citizens largely ignored the affair and seemed not to care (Charter 2008). One should note that, on the other hand, in the German state of Bavaria, broadcasts that promote the "glorification of violence. . . shall be prohibited."[14] By contrast, American broadcasters must be very careful in broadcasting any nudity whatsoever, for fear of a hefty fine from the Federal Communication Commission (FCC), while allowing gruesome crime scenes to be shown with virtually no editing. I have a German friend who wryly asked, "Why would you not allow something that is natural (sex/nudity) to be broadcast, while something that is decidedly not natural (murder and violence) to be shown with impunity?" His argument posits that this dichotomy leads Americans to believe sex and nudity are not normal, but murder and violence are. If this is the case, then it would stand to reason that a politician having an extramarital affair in Germany might face less scrutiny than one in the United States. Further there also might be differences with a polity's relationship with their politician. A polity that regards their politician as simply a representative of their interests in probably more inclined to view a politician's personal life as private; however, a polity that regards their political leaders as moral leaders as well will consider such conduct as an offense.

Clearly, culture varies from country to country, but there are also variations within countries. In his classic study, political scientist Daniel Elazar noted that there were different political sub-cultures in the United States that created different relationships between local communities and the federal government. Elazar speculated that traditionalists, for example, believe that prestige in politics is particularly important. Therefore, one can extrapolate that anything that might damage the prestige of the system, such as a sex scandal, should be avoided (Elazar 1966, 85–94 and 96–97; Kincaid 1982). Studies of political cultures have evolved and are probably not as deterministic as once thought. Additionally, the realities of a modern economy means the internal movement of people have diminished the regional effects described by Elazar. Nevertheless, there is no doubt that different regions in the United States expect different things from politicians and government. Thus, a careful consideration as to the political base of a politician is important in the aftermath of a sex scandal. (This is more carefully addressed in Chapter 5.)

Finally, an important component of the environment in any modern polity is the media. As a gatekeeper of information, if the press deems a story insignificant, then marriage infidelity, for example, is not likely to be a problem for the politician. If, however, the press covers the story heavily, such a scandal might resonate more with viewers. As a significant part of the political environment, understanding how the press might react is key to understanding the impact of a sex scandal (a point that is addressed in Chapter 6).[15]

The Skill and Resources of Politicians

Missed in many of the reflections of a sexual scandal are the skills and resources a politician might bring to a crisis. Because of the way politicians acquire their jobs, most have a charismatic personality that connects with voters (some might add that a politician's charisma is often the reason they get into sex scandals in the first place). No doubt that the skills of a magnetic personality will serve a politician well in the midst, or after-effects, of a scandal. Some would attribute President Clinton's political survival to his ability to admit fault, his general likeability, and his empathetic nature; similarly Eliot Spitzer's post-scandal career as a political commentator for CNN is a testament to his personal charisma. Yet, skill will only take a politician so far; if the scandal is so scandalous that most constituents are repulsed, no amount of charisma is likely to save the politician's career. If, on the other hand, the damage of a scandal can be minimized, then the personality and charisma of a politician can mitigate some of the damage of a scandal.

Politicians also have other considerable resources to limit the damages of a sex scandal. Politicians not only have their own personalities to rely on, but also have staffs that can be an excellent resource in any crisis situation. To be sure, the staff of a politician varies in talent and size, particularly depending on the level of the office; nevertheless, a staff can shield a politician from answering embarrassing questions directly (or on camera) and provide a dispassionate appraisal of the situation. After all, it is the politician who would have been in an intimate situation—not the staff. For example, White House spokesperson Mike McCurry was a stoic face who answered intimate and potentially embarrassing questions about President Clinton's affair with Monica Lewisnky. His demeanor of calmness in the face of an all-consuming scandal lent credence to an administration mired in serious trouble (Kurtz, 1998a). A long-serving politician has another resource at his disposal: a track record. If a political has been successful in his job(s), then the politician has established a track record of service and accomplishments that will stand in contrast to a scandal.

Taken together, a politician's ability to position himself in the public's mind as a likeable and capable person prior to a scandal can help him weather a scandal. Other resources, such as a capable and organized staff, can help the politician weather a political firestorm. These resources have limitations; they cannot fix everything a scandal might damage. Nevertheless, a politician that has these resources can mitigate some of the damage of a sex scandal.

Toward a Framework for Understanding

To put each of these factors together, it helps to think about the eventual outcome of a sex scandal. Scandals are never exactly the same; they exist in different contexts. Thus, while most voters would not approve of an extramarital affair, it is not as

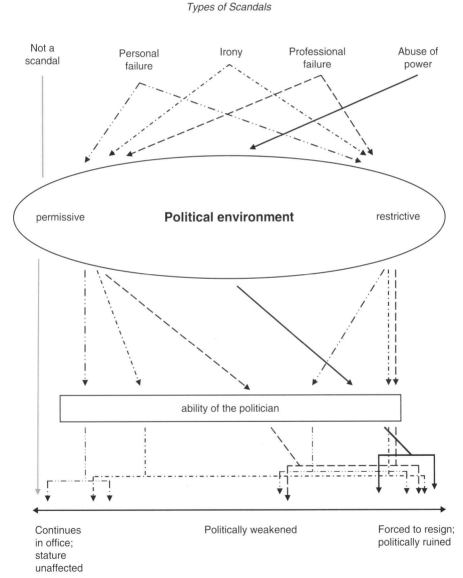

Figure 4.1. Impact of Political Sexual Scandals.

serious, most people would argue, as forcing an underling into a sexual relationship. After the incident is exposed, less sexually permissive polities might be inclined to sack a politician, while more permissive polities might see the politician in a diminished light but allow him to retain his job. Finally, politicians can use their considerable personality skills and resources to mitigate the effects of a scandal. All of these factors can be summarized in Figure 4.1.

Figure 4.1 illustrates the causal mechanism through which a political sex scandal evolves. Depending on the type of scandal, the impact on politics must be viewed through the lens of the political environment, the more restrictive the political environment on the subject of sex, the more likely the politician will experience substantial damage to his career. The resources available to the politician, including charisma, an established political record, and a competent and supportive staff, can mitigate the political effects a politician might face. Ultimately, the effects a politician might face can be described as a continuum; on one side only marginal effects on the politician's career to the other side of the continuum, which would represent a completely devastated political career including possible imprisonment.

All scandals have impacts, but the effects vary depending upon the situation. Impacts can be limited or wideranging. Other chapters in this book explore different factors of scandals and the outcome of them. While initial public reactions may demand justice in the form of resignation, impeachment, or even jail time, seldom do politicians face such consequences as with the case of Mayor Stansbury. Some politicians, again like Stansbury, might be able to recover enough to resume a productive career. Yet, politicians rarely get off scot-free, either. No matter how little the tangible impact, the politician always suffers some loss of stature and respect among constituents and colleagues.

The next chapter utilizes this framework to help explain the political outcomes of six well-known political scandals.

Works Cited

Almond, Gabriel A., and Sidney Verba. *The Civic Culture: Political Attitudes and Democracy in Five Nations.* Princeton, NJ: Princeton University Press, 1963.

Andrews, Robert. *The Columbia Dictionary of Quotations.* New York: Columbia University Press, 1993.

Baum, Matthew A. *Soft News Goes to War: Public Opinion and American Foreign Policy in the New Media Age.* Princeton, NJ: Princeton University Press, 2003.

Baum, Matthew A., and Samuel Kernell. "Has Cable Ended the Golden Age of Presidential Television?" *American Political Science Review*, March 1999; 93(1): 99–114.

BBC News. DNA Twist in Polish Sex Scandal. December 9, 2006. Accessed November 30, 2010 (http://news.bbc.co.uk/2/hi/6165847.stm).

Buss, David M. "Sex Differences in Human Mate Preferences: Evolutionally Hypotheses Tested in 37 Cultures." *Behavioral and Brain Sciences*, 1989;12: 1–4.

Charter, David. "President Admits to Affair with Airline Attendant Number 3." *The Times (London)*, April 9, 2008: 34.

Chase, John, and Liam Ford. "Ryan File a Bombshell: Ex-Wife Alleges GOP Candidate took Her to Sex Clubs." *Chicago Tribune*, June 22, 2004.

Christensen, Harold T., and George R. Carpenter. "Timing Patterns in the Development of Sexual Intimacy: An Attitudinal Report on Three Modern Western Societies." *Marriage and Family Living*, February 1962; 24(1): 30–35.

Christensen, Harold T., and Christina F. Gregg. "Changing Sex Norms in America and Scandinavia." *Journal of Marriage and the Family*, November 1970; 32(4): 616–627.

Dagnes, Alison. *Politics on Demand: The Effects of 24-Hour News on American Politics*. Santa Barbara, CA: Praeger, 2010.

Elazar, Daniel J. *American Federalism: A View from the States*. New York: Thomas Y. Cromwell, 1966.

Epstein, Daniel Mark. *Sister Aimee: The Life of Aimee Semple McPherson*. New York: Harcourt Brace Jovanovich, 1993.

Fischer, Claude S. "Toward a Subculture Theory of Urbanism." *American Journal of Sociology*, May 1975; 80(6): 1319–1347.

Fisher, Max. *Why So Few Female Politician Sex Scandals?*. April 1, 2010. Accessed November 29, 2010 (http://www.theatlanticwire.com/features/view/feature/Why-So-Few-Female-Politician-Sex-Scandals-995).

Fraser, Antonia. *Marie Antoinette: The Journey*. New York: Doubleday, 2001.

Grayling, A. C. *Life, Sex and Ideas: The Good Life Without God*. New York: Oxford University Press, 2003.

———. "Who Are You Calling a Hypocrite?." *The Times*, March 15, 2008: 23.

Jones, Elise F., et al. "Teenage Pregnancy in Developed Countries: Determinants and Policy Implications." *Family Planning Perspective*, 1985; 17: 53–63.

———. *Teenage Pregnancy in Industrialized Countries*. New Haven, CT: Yale University Press, 1986.

Kavanagh, Dennis. *Political Culture*. London: Macmillan, 1972.

Kincaid, John. *Political Culture, Public Policy and the American States*. Philadelphia: Institute for the Study of Human Issues, 1982.

Kleber, John E. *The Encyclopedia of Louisville*. Lexington, KY: University Press of Kentucky, 2001.

Kurtz, Howard. "Mike McCurry, Poised Under Pressure." *Washington Post*, February 3, 1998a: B1.

———. *Spin Cycle: How the White House and the Media Manipulates the News*. New York: Simon & Schuster, 1998b.

New York Times. "William Stansbury, Ex-Mayor Of Louisville, Is Killed by Car." *New York Times*, April 6, 1985.

Norton, Philip. *The British Polity, Fourth Edition*. New York: Longman, 2001.

Pittsburgh Post-Gazette. "Targeting the Clinton White House." *Pittsburgh Post-Gazette*, July 1996.

Ross, Michael W. "Actual and Anticipated Societal Reaction to Homosexuality and Adjustment in Two Societies." *The Journal of Sex Research*, February 1985; 21(1): 40–55.

Savage, Charlie. "Sex Drug Use and Graft Cited in Interior Department." *New York Times*, September 11, 2008: A1.

Shepard, Alicia C. "The Incredible Shrinking News Cycle." *The World & I*, June 1998; 13(6): 80–85.

Sutton, Matthew Avery. *Aimee Semple McPherson and the Resurrection of Christian America*. Cambridge, MA: Harvard University Press, 2007.

Tripathi, Ashish. "Sex, Crime and Politics." *The Times of India*, January 02, 2009.

Weis, David L., and Joan Jurich. "Size of Community of Residence as a Predictor of Attitudes Toward Extramarital Sexual Relations, 47 (1): 173–178 (February 1985)." *Journal of Marriage and Family*, February 1985; 47(1): 173–178.

Widmer, Eric D., Judith Reas, and Robert Newcomb. "Attitudes toward Nonmarital Sex in 24 Countries." *The Journal of Sex Research*, November 1998; 35(4): 349–358.

Wikipedia. "William B. Stansbury." *Wikipedia.* Accessed September 9, 2010 (http://en.wikipedia.org/wiki/William_B._Stansbury).

Notes

1 See also, *The Louisville Courier Journal* 2 January 1982 and 4 April 1985. (Not in Works Cited)

2 Also injured in the crash was Stansbury's wife, the woman who was previously his mistress and the one who was found with him in New Orleans; they married in 1983.

3 Also, Stansbury's obituary in the *New York Times* makes no mention of the scandal that precipitated the impeachment proceedings (*New York Times* 1985).

4 Clearly there is a double standard between male and female politicians (as well as people in general) when it comes to sexual behavior. Although there are relatively few instances of female politicians who have been caught in sex scandals, it is difficult to imagine an easy time for such politicians based upon the societal norms that govern sexual perceptions (Weis and Jurich 1985).

5 Around the world it is typically men who are politicians. Thus, the sample size to measure the effect of women politicians and political sex scandals is relatively small and it is difficult to draw substantive conclusions (Fisher 2010).

6 The Spitzer scandal is addressed in greater detail in Chapter 5.

7 Ryan would be forced to eventually relinquish the nomination. Alan Keyes would take Ryan's place on the ballot and was defeated handily by Obama.

8 One also can point to a similar, albeit less salacious, story of Sister Aimee Semple McPherson in 1926. Sister Aimee, as she was famously known, became an influential person, especially in the realm of politics and religion, during the 1920s. In the summer of 1926, she mysteriously disappeared claiming she had been kidnapped. A grand jury was convened, but it concluded there was no substantial evidence to warrant further investigation. Most people assumed that she had a tryst and ran off with a married man by the name of Kenneth G. Ormiston (Epstein 1993; Sutton 2007).

9 A similar case would be the abuse of power that is at the heart of the Roman Catholic Sex abuse scandal. Priests have been accused of using their position of authority and power to procure sex with adolescents in their parishes.

10 For other instances, see (Tripathi 2009).

11 This seemed to be a tactic of political opponents of the Clinton Administration. While President Clinton engaged in a sexual relationship with Miss Lewinsky, his wife, Hillary Clinton, was the subject of a whispering campaign that characterized her as a lesbian bent on securing power for herself through her (sham) marriage to the president (*Pittsburgh Post-Gazette* 1996).

12 We should not be blind to the use of sexual imagery and language in commenting or evaluating a political regime; it is common to use words such as "impotent" to describe

politicians or the casual use of "rape" to describe unwanted consequences. This use of sexual imagery was quite common among opponents of the monarchy in France. Pamphlets, rhymes and cartoons questioned the fatherhood of the Dauphin (the heir apparent), portrayed the queen as harlot and sexually adventurous and her library as pornographic (actually her books were romance novels). This was an attempt to undermine her legitimacy by suggesting she was deviant.

13 Fischer (1975) argued that population concentration creates subcultures. The interaction among subcultures fosters reinforcing acceptance in these urban areas. Thus, it stands to reason that urban areas might be more forgiving to politicians involved in a sex scandal.

14 Constitution of the Free State of Bavarian, Article 111A. (Not in Works Cited)

15 Given the nature and pressure of a 24/7 news cycle, it seems a safe bet that news media would find any such story of infidelity or sexual scandal of a significant political figure as "newsworthy." The media must find stories and controversies to keep viewers tuned in to their programming (Dagnes 2010;Shepard 1998). The advent on cable and internet news sources has several impacts. Baum and Kernell (1999) have argued that it has dramatically changed presidential campaigns in the United States. Baum (2003) also examined the effect of "soft news" on American politics and one of the finding was that because entertainment programs often covered political events and figures (especially scandals), the public erroneously believe they were more informed. Kurtz illustrates how the pressure of the news cycle and competition creates an increasingly antagonistic media, which ultimately leads to more manipulation and deception of the American public (Kurtz 1998b, ix–xxii).

CHAPTER 5

The Politics, Geography, and Constituencies of Political Sex Scandals

Alison Dagnes and Janet Smith

The most essential ingredients in a political sex scandal are found in the politics that surround the scandalous. Often politicians retain their offices after being caught, while just as often they are forced to resign: The political factors combine to determine the outcome of a political sex scandal. There are several important political units that always play deciding roles in a continuously evolving political environment; these include political parties, interest groups, religious groups, and state and local political organizations. Since all politics is contextual, these groups provide the context that influences the political outcomes of scandal. As mentioned in Chapter 4, other important factors that determine the political conclusion of a sex scandal are found in the details surrounding the scandal itself, such as whether the affair included an abuse of power or included "deviant," amoral, or illegal behavior. Also as noted, the political climate and the skill of the politician matter greatly. Undoubtedly, all of these components are crucial in concluding the consequence of a political sex scandal, but we argue here that the politics of place matter, too: Put another way, the different dynamics of race, class, economics, religion, and place of the constituencies make a difference in how these scandals are acknowledged and how the politicians are dealt with politically.

Some of these regional differences have been negated by the modern 24-hour media, which reports with breathless judgment and conclusion every time a political figure becomes ensnared in scandal. The voters of South Carolina certainly heard about their governor, Mark Sanford, when he was caught in an especially jarring sex scandal, but so, too, did the rest of the country because of the jaw-dropping nature of the affair and the manner in which Sanford was caught. In the constancy of our media-drenched political environment, where entertainment matters as much (if not more) than real information, political sex scandals at all geographic scales are nationalized and reported upon because of their salacious nature. What differs is not whether the media cover a scandal but rather the constituent response when elected official gets caught in a compromising position. Much has to do with the education level, religiosity, race, marital status, and income levels of the constituencies. And thus, we examine the geography of place to further examine the politics of people.

In 1960, Angus Campbell and three other political scientists wrote one of the most influential books on voting behavior called *The American Voter*, which examined the decision to vote and the ensuing candidate choice. What Campbell and his colleagues determined was that the factors that went into such decisions varied widely among sociological and demographic lines. The psychological factors that Campbell and his colleagues addressed focused on the decision-making involved in choosing a presidential candidate. They wrote that there were three factors involved: (1) Political party identification; (2) Public policy adherence and concern; and (3) Candidate attraction. Political scientists have endeavored to build on Campbell's research, and several important studies (to include Knoke, 1974) have augmented these three factors to include a number of variables that affect party identification: (1) Race; (2) Religion; (3) Occupation; (4) Social class membership; and (5) Education attainment (Knoke 1974). Since *The American Voter* was written in 1960, there was special attention paid to party identification and the point was made that independent voters—those without a strong partisan attachment—were less likely to vote, since they had so little involvement in the political process. In the past 50 years there has been a dramatic drop in party allegiance and a concurring drop in voting rates. Yet at the same time, those inclined to participate politically are doing so with even more fervor. Bafumi and Shapiro (2009) addressed the changing characteristics of the American voter and found that increases in ideological devotion have led to strong party devotion, even as the number of independent voters has increased. (Bafumiand Shapiro 2009) Bafumi and Shapiro demonstrate that this has much to do with the issues being debated today and their lasting consequence in American politics. Write Bafumi and Shapiro:

> [T]here have been real changes among a portion of the electorate consisting of liberals and conservatives as well as Democrats and Republicans who have continued to sort themselves on racial, social, and religious values issues. These changes in public opinion and the electorate have occurred over a very extended period, have fed back into party politics, and show no sign of reversing. (Bafumiand Shapiro 2009)

This means that throughout the country there is a widening gap between those interested and active, and those apathetic and unresponsive. Additionally, these two sides are being pulled in dramatically different directions, where those who engage in politics now do so loudly and fervently while those uninterested lump all political actors into one pool of bums, dismissing the sex scandals as part of the system they choose to ignore. Thus, when a politician is caught in scandal, his voters may react especially passionately or not at all, depending on their own political awareness and activity. Consequently, any analysis of constituent reaction to a political sex scandal must be measured by party identification, along ideological lines, and via social and economic demographic factors. We argue that all of these features combine to create a larger dynamic that can help explain voter reaction and political consequence resulting from political sex scandal. In other words, all of these factors combine to create the political climate discussed in the last chapter: Whether the climate is permissive or restricted is, at least in part, determined by the demographic characteristics of the constituents. This chapter will examine the following elements of constituent make up and political geography to more fully address these voter reactions and the resulting political environment. Taken together, we can more completely establish a "sense of place" that helps determine how voters respond when their elected officials get caught with their pants down.

A Sense of Place

Much has been written in the field of political science about regional differences in voting and voter turnout. Class, race and ethnicity, marital status, and gender have all been identified as contributing elements to the political landscape in the United States (Shafer 1991; Miller and Shanks 1996; Stonecash 2000). Recently, Mellow (2008) argued that to conceptualize a region, it is prudent to examine material and economic characteristics as well as the demographic factors outlined above. This prominence of regions in U.S. electoral behavior has a long history dating from Reconstruction. The regional nature of recent elections, depicted using red states and blue states, suggests that a sense of place may still play a role in American politics. Indeed, regional boundaries have sometimes been closely aligned with voting behavior and party identification patterns.

The prominent cultural geographer Yi Fu-Tuan promoted consideration of the concept "sense of place" (1992), describing that places are given meaning by those who reside in them. Further, people share a particular collective identity of place despite their difference in individual experiences. So, although a place is inhabited by a diverse group of individuals, the place itself can be characterized. This idea of characterizing places has long been adopted in the U.S. vernacular culture through the acceptance of monikers such as the "frugal New Englander," the "tea-sweet Southerner," the stoic Midwesterner, and the "independent Westerner." This common characterization of regions within the United States made us question whether this sense of place might influence constituent response to political sex scandals. A major theme in the book *Place and Politics*(1987) written by geographer John Agnew, is that political behavior is, by its nature, geographic and that to truly understand political behavior one must have a place-based perspective. Thus, this is the framework adopted for our examination. As Mark Sachleben noted in Chapter 4, there are certain qualities that define us nationally as "Americans." And yet we are not a monolithic entity, so we investigate whether the moral tenor of a place influences the political consequences of scandalous behavior.

Our study examines the facts of six case studies, the national and local news coverage of the scandal, and the demographics of the constituencies of the politician in question. We use a 2008 Gallup poll to help determine the partisanship of the constituency, as well as election results from 2008 to 2010 in order to illustrate the partisan divide of the representative community. The national media coverage of political sex scandals can be categorized in three primary ways: Through humor (late night television); through procedure (serious news coverage of the process following scandal); and through partisan outrage (bloggers, talk radio, and cable news punditry). Local news coverage tends to be more careful and thorough, examining the politician, his transgression, the players involved, and the consequences of his actions. We capture a national snapshot of each case study first, using the *New York Times* as the national paper of record. We then very briefly mention one or two blogs covering the scandals to provide color, and then move on to local news coverage in order to contrast that to the national reporting. Our colleague and collaborator, Carrie Sipes, delves into media framing in greater detail in Chapter 6, but we use the national and local press to help illustrate the circumstances of the scandal.

Data

The data used in our examination of constituent characteristics were drawn from the 2006–2008 American Community Survey (3-Year Estimates) conducted by the United States Census Bureau. Data were collected from the Selected Social Characteristics, Selected Economic Characteristics, and Selected Demographic and Housing Estimates on marital status, highest level of education attained, race, urban/rural composition, types of households, and labor force participation..

Additionally, data were collected by state and by county in order to determine the degree of religiosity of the constituents. These data were derived from the 2003 National Survey of Children's Health conducted by the U.S. Department of Health and Human Services and from data collected by the Association of Statisticians of American Religious Bodies (ASARB) in 2000 (Jones, *et al.* 2002). These datasets focus on: (1) children who attend religious services weekly; (2) all adherents in the denominations counted by the ASARB; and (3) estimates of adherent totals for the historically African-American denominations and other religious groups not listed in the ASARB totals. These data were downloaded from Social Explorer, an online research tool designed to support demographic analysis, and compiled in a GIS (Geographic Information System) by the authors. Our study examines six politicians caught in very public sex scandals, and we move on to them now.

Our Case Studies

We examine here six politicians who were caught in sexual scandals from 2006 to 2009, and examine them in chronological order. Their offices vary, but all have constituencies at the scale of the state or congressional district level. Here we focus on each of these political actors specifically according to their scandal, and contrast the national description to the local perception of the scandal. We also characterize the composition of the constituencies and describe the sense of place of each politician, and to try and establish a pattern for political outcome once a politician is caught.

Mark Foley

Scandal: Republican U.S. House member Mark Foley is caught sending sexually explicit electronic messages to underage boys working on Capitol Hill.

Mark Foley was born in Massachusetts but moved to Florida when he was a child. He graduated from high school in Lake Worth, Florida, and attended classes at Palm Beach Community College. He was elected first to the Florida State House, then to the Florida State Senate, and in 1995 he moved to Washington as a member of the United States House of Representatives, where he served for a decade. Considered to be a moderate Republican, Foley served on the House Ways and Means Committee and gained some national attention in 2000 when his congressional district was the epicenter of the presidential election recount between Al Gore and George W. Bush. He was considered a front-runner to replace a retiring Republican U.S. Senator from Florida in 2004 but rumors of his homosexuality began to emerge from the gay press outside Florida. One article was titled: "Being gay in the GOP: Congressman Mark Foley: A model of political hypocrisy and personal cowardice," and another was called: "Liberace Candidate: Mark Foley's glass closet." These articles helped squash Foley's senatorial run, but he stayed in his House seat until 2006 when he was caught sending sexually suggestive e-mails and instant messages to teenage boys serving as Congressional Pages. Although the investigation was closed due to insufficient evidence, the scandal led to Foley's resignation from the House of Representatives in September of 2006.

The sword fell pretty quickly. Foley was confronted on September 29, 2006, by an ABC news reporter about the suggestive instant messages he had sent from his AOL account to male Congressional Pages who were 16 years old. Using the screen name Maf54, Foley made "repeated references to sexual organs and acts" (Ross 2006). Three hours later, Foley sent his resignation letter to then-House Speaker Dennis Hastert. Once the flood gates were opened by *ABC News*, past Congressional Pages began to surface with similar stories, many of who provided damning evidence of Foley's predatory behavior. There was evidence that the House Republican knew of Foley's behavior and did nothing to stop it. All of this would be generally horrific, but it was made even more so because of Foley's earlier denials of his homosexuality and because he was the Chair of the House Caucus on Missing and Exploited Children. Add to that the fact that he was considered safe for re-election two months later, which put the Florida Republican Party into trouble when trying to find a replacement candidate, and the political story became enormous.

National and Local Narratives

The good news? Florida Congressman Mark Foley has entered rehab. The bad news? Rehab is a 14-year-old boy from Pakistan.

—Jay Leno

The news accounts of the Foley scandal focused first on the materialization of the instant messages and of Foley's resignation. But as the story continued to unfold, the national news began to more closely investigate the House Republican leaders who knew of Foley's behavior but did nothing to stop it. The *New York Times* wrote two stories about this quickly, the first on October 1, the second on October 3: "Top G.O.P. Aides Knew In Late '05 Of E-Mail To Page," and then "Pressure Grows For Republicans Over Foley Case." Also on October 3, the Times ran an editorial condemning the congressman:

> The news about Mr. Foley should have set off alarm bells instantly, even if the messages the leaders saw were of the "inappropriate" variety rather than the flat-out salacious versions that surfaced last week. But there was certainly no sense of urgency in their response, which seemed directed at sweeping the matter under the rug rather than finding out precisely what was going on. The obvious first step—notifying the bipartisan committee that oversees the page program—was never taken, presumably because that would have meant bringing a Democrat into the discussions. . . . It's astonishing behavior for a party that sold itself as the champion of conservative social values. (Editors 2006)

Throughout October, the Times ran more stories about the political process surrounding the Foley scandal, with special attention on the Congressional Page program. Editorials from readers universally condemned Foley but went in two directions after that: Either criticizing Republican leaders for their part in the problem or arguing that the leadership did nothing wrong. In the national press, Mark Foley was continually disparaged, his reputation in tatters.

On the political blogs, it was worse. The outrageous sexual nature of the instant messages made them catnip for bloggers who printed the absolute worst of them with great delight. It was how the blogosphere trumped television, after all: In their ability to print material not even remotely family friendly. The blog "Technorati" posted more than 8,000 postings about Foley in the week after the scandal broke. The "Blogosphile" column from CBS News posted a story titled "Foley Scandal a 'Perfect Blogstorm.'" The DC media blog "Fishbowl" covered how the blogs and the media covered the Foley case.

The local press from Florida covered the story thoroughly, especially the Palm Beach Press, which is the largest paper in Foley's district. The paper printed 18 news articles about the Foley scandal in the one month following the initial ABC News story, starting with the text message revelations and then moving on to Foley's claim he was molested by a priest as a child. Every story run by the Palm Beach Press, even the ones strictly committed to describing the situation, had an element of condemnation in them: "Foley Secluded, Said To Be Wreck; As Ex-Congressman's Career Crumbles, Republicans Vent Over Betrayal" and then "Foley's Case Tragic, But Boys Victims."

The paper also ran nine opinion pieces, all of which denounced Foley, many moving on to the question of the Catholic Church's alleged involvement in Foley's mental problems. No one rushed to Foley's defense, since the crime was generally regarded as indefensible.

Table 5.1 Foley-16th Congressional District-Florida

Highest Education Level Achieved		Race (reporting one race 98.6%)		Types of Households	
Less than 9th Grade	6.0	Two or More Races	1.4	Married Couple	54.8
Some High School	10.1	Other	3.7	Male-Headed Household	4.5
High School Graduate	33.2	Hawaiian/ Pacific Islander	0	Female-Headed Household	9.1
Some College, no degree	20.9	Asian	1.6	Non-Family	5.6
Associates Degree	7.9	Native American	.4	Householder living Alone	25.9
Bachelor's Degree	14.4	Black	8.3		
Graduate or Professional Degree	7.6	White	84.6		

Constituency

Of the residents in the 16th Congressional District (110th Congress) of Florida, only 29.7 percent are natively Floridian. Most of these residents live in urban areas (84.5%), in family-based households (68%), have graduated from high school (84%), are younger than 45 (52.2%, median age 43.4), and are employed in either management/professional (29%) or sales/office (27%) occupations. They, generally, adhere to a religion (45.5%), while nearly one-fifth speak a language other than English at home (18%). Racially, this district is 85.9 percent White, 8.9 percent African American, and 1.9 percent Asian. Fifteen percent of this district self-declared to be either Hispanic or Latino. The average household income is $68,747, with 11 percent of the district's population living in poverty. This percent increases for female-headed households with children (21%), particularly for children under the age of five (30.7%). Although the majority of people own their own homes (80%), nearly 23 percent of all housing units are vacant, 4 percent of all households did not have telephone service, and 4 percent of households lacked access to a vehicle for private use.

Analysis

Florida is a swing-state that recently elected a Tea Party candidate two years after voting in Obama to the White House. In the Foley case, party politics played little role in his fate: The predatory nature of his crime against children was indefensible. Rooney won re-election in 2010 and was elected to a leadership position in the House. The House Republican leadership did not investigate the Foley affair after the fact. Foley now lives as an openly gay man in Florida and is in the real estate business.

Larry Craig

Scandal: U.S. Senator Caught trying to solicit prostitute in airport bathroom.

Larry Craig was born and raised in Idaho, served in the state Senate, and then as one of the state's two members of the U.S. House. He served in the House for ten years, served on the House Ethics Committee, and also on the National Rifle Association's Board of Directors. He was elected to the United States Senate in 1990 and ran successfully for re-election twice after that, thus accruing 17 years of seniority. He was a reliably conservative Republican, consistently voting in favor of legislation promoting small government and fiscal responsibility. He was also an outspoken social conservative, opposed to gun control, abortion, and gay rights, and the American Conservative Union consistently rated Craig highly for his performance. He spoke out against President Clinton during his impeachment trial, and gave the following statement after the closed-door Senate proceedings:

> On the first day of this trial, as I watched the Chief Justice take the chair, I was angry—profoundly angry that this president had brought this nation to this point because of his own self-gratification, setting what was good for himself above what was good for the nation. (Craig 08/28/07)

Craig was in his third term in the Senate when the congressional newspaper *Roll Call* reported that he had been arrested for lewd conduct in a men's bathroom at the Minneapolis International Airport. The charges alleged that Craig was trying to solicit sex from an undercover policeman, and in August 2007 he pled guilty to the lesser charge of disorderly conduct. Once this was made public, Craig vehemently denied the charges and asserted his innocence:

> First, please let me apologize to my family, friends, staff, and fellow Idahoans for the cloud placed over Idaho. I did nothing wrong at the Minneapolis airport. I regret my decision to plead guilty and the sadness that decision has brought to my wife, family, friends, staff, and fellow Idahoans. For that I apologize. In June, I overreacted and made a poor decision. While I was not involved in any inappropriate conduct at the Minneapolis airport or anywhere else, I chose to plead guilty to a lesser charge in the hope of making it go away. I did not seek any counsel, either from an attorney, staff, friends, or family. That was a mistake, and I deeply regret it. Because of that, I have now retained counsel and I am asking my counsel to review this matter and to advise me on how to proceed. . . . Let me be clear: I am not gay and never have been. (Craig, Sen. Larry Craig's statement 2007)

Initially, Craig said he would resign immediately, but then decided instead to fill out the remainder of his term. His constituents tacitly consented to his decision by not demanding his removal from office. He did not run for re-election the following year, which ended his political career. He was succeeded by former Governor Jim Risch and is now a political consultant.

National and Local Narratives

> The airport bathroom where Senator Larry Craig was arrested is now being reno-
> vated, and the new bathroom will have stall dividers that go all the way down
> to the floor. When he heard about the new stall dividers, Senator Craig said, "It
> doesn't matter. Love will find a way."

> —Conan O'Brien

The *New York Times* began running the Larry Craig arrest story in late August, 2007
with the news report headlined: "Senator, Arrested in an Airport Bathroom, Pleads
Guilty." The next day, the headline read "Idaho Senator Says He Regrets Guilty Plea in
Restroom Incident." The *Times* opinion piece that ran two days after the initial news
report chided the Republican Party for their further embroilment in scandal, and
then the news articles that followed chronicled Craig's fall from his party's political
grace, which led to another opinion piece along the same lines: "Disowning Senator
Craig." Further opinion pieces questioned the fiscal and judicial efficacy of arresting
men who solicit sex in bathrooms, but then moved back to the political questions surrounding Craig's possible resignation and his eventual decision to remain in office.
The national *news* narrative of Larry Craig's arrest focused on the political consequences of his actions, and rarely varied from this line of inquiry. The blogosphere,
however, went dirtier and got off topic pretty quickly. Leftist bloggers denounced the
apparent hypocrisy of Craig's stand against gay marriage with his bathroom behavior. Right-wing bloggers declared their annoyance with the lefties, writing that if a
Democrat had been caught they would be given a free pass. But all of the blogosphere
had a lot to say on the subject since it was about a senior politician and cruising for gay
sex. "Wonkette," the snarky and sexual blog about DC life, posted it most clearly:

> We've been having loads of fun with gay restroom goblin Larry Craig over the
> past couple of months, haven't we? What we've been missing, though, is an
> on-the-record account from a source willing to come forward and tell what it's
> like to have an actual romantic liaison with the Idaho Republican. Meet David
> Phillips, a local IT geek and bear-about-town. (Phuestis 2007)

The blog posting went on to interview Phillips, who chronicled his sexual encounters
with Craig, the over-arching narrative being Craig's apparent history of secret sex.
    The late-night jokes about Craig's bathroom arrest were seemingly endless, as
were the political cartoons. Craig's assertion that he was not tapping the foot of his
bathroom stall neighbor to solicit sex, but instead tapped because he had a "wide
stance" brought an onslaught of mockery and made Craig a national joke. Back at
home, however, the *Idaho Statesman* did a thorough job of chronicling the sex scandal in specific and the senator's career in broader terms. Craig clearly had no love
lost for the *Statesman* and blamed the newspaper (at least in part) for the scandal,

stating: "For eight months leading up to June, my family and I had been relentlessly and viciously harassed by the *Idaho Statesman*." (Craig, Sen. Larry Craig's statement 2007) The *Statesman* responded with an editorial rejoinder:

> As our story today demonstrated, we followed leads and asked questions. We worked hard and behaved responsibly, not publishing a story until it was ready. We didn't print anything until the senator pleaded guilty. Our story outlined what we've done and it speaks for itself. (Manny 2007)

Craig went on to allege, through his attorney, that the investigative pressure from the *Statesman* led him to plead guilty in the first place. The *Statesman*, through their editor and vice president, Vicky Gowler, responded:

> The *Statesman* has taken great care in investigating these serious allegations about Sen. Craig. From the start, it was important to us to do a thorough and responsible investigation, outside of deadline pressures. We did that. Because of the allegations made last fall, a necessary part of a thorough investigation did include trying to determine whether the senator was regularly cruising restrooms for anonymous sex. The length of the investigation was due in large part to difficulties we encountered getting information from the senator. (Gowler 2007)

The *Statesman* ran 44 news stories about Craig, his career, the scandal, and the fall-out from his arrest from August 28 to September 11: 44 stories in two weeks worth of newspapers. The paper examined his role in state party politics, his lengthy political career, and his legacy in Idaho, among the other articles about the arrest, the practice of soliciting sex in bathrooms, and the other men who came forward to allege sexual

Table 5.2 Idaho-Craig

Highest Education Level Achieved		Race (reporting one race 97.7%)		Types of Households	
Less than 9th Grade	4.5	Two or More Races	2.3	Married Couple	57
Some High School	7.6	Other	2.2	Male-Headed Household	4.3
High School Graduate	29.2	Hawaiian/Pacific Islander	.1	Female-Headed Household	9.0
Some College, no degree	26.1	Asian	1.1	Non-Family	6.1
Associates Degree	8.6	Native American	1.2	Householder living Alone	23.6
Bachelor's Degree	16.5	Black	.6		
Graduate or Professional Degree	7.4	White	94.2		

encounters with the senator. Amidst all that was written, the *Statesman* called for Craig's resignation. He did not resign, and more importantly, the Idaho Republican Party did not call for his termination.

Constituency

The majority of Idahoans live in family-based households (70%), while nearly a quarter (24%) live alone. Some 46 percent of those living in Idaho are natives of the state and can be characterized as white (94.7%), married (57.6%), with at least a high school degree (87.9%), under the age of 45 (64%), attend church regularly (53.6%) although not particularly evangelical; additionally, Idahoans are urban (65.6%), employed in the service industry (56.9%), predominantly in management and professional occupations (32%). The mean household income in Idaho is $60,460, with just over 12 percent of people living in poverty. This number rises dramatically for Idahoans living in female-headed households with children (30.9%), with more than half of children under the age of five residing with a single mother (52%) living in poverty. The majority of Idahoans own their own homes (71%), while 4 percent lack access to a vehicle for private use and 4 percent of households do not have telephone service.

Analysis

Idaho is a solidly Republican state, with Gallup ranking the Republicans as having a 15-point advantage over their Democratic counterparts. The homogenous nature of the Idaho constituency and its reliably conservative political climate helped to form Craig's apology and created an environment for the aftermath of his scandal. The seemingly obvious lie that Craig was not gay and the hypocrisy of his anti-gay rights attitude went largely unchallenged by the voters of Idaho, who allowed Craig to remain in office until the next election. The national understanding and criticism of Craig's untruth was echoed in his isolation from the Republican Party on Capitol Hill. Because Craig had been such an important figure in Idaho politics for so long, it should not be surprising that the voters there continued to maintain at least a degree of support for him.

The fact that the vast majority of Idahoans are from family units who own their own homes lends credence to Larry Craig's apology with his wife by his side. The religiosity of his constituency and their rock-solid Republican adherence also helps to clarify how Craig stayed in office even after the scandal broke nationally. While the national media mocked Craig's "wide stance," his constituents remembered his devotion to Idaho. They, essentially, gave him a pass.

This does not make Idaho a permissive state—on the contrary, it holds a quite restrictive political environment. However, because the constituency viewed Craig's scandal as a personal one, as opposed to an abuse of power or professional failure, they allowed him to remain in office—politically weakened but not destroyed.

David Vitter

Scandal: Republican Senator caught in DC prostitution scandal.

David Vitter is a native Louisianan with a remarkable educational pedigree. He graduated from Harvard, went to Oxford as a Rhodes Scholar, and earned his law degree from Tulane. He served in the Louisiana State House for most of the 1990s, was elected to the U.S. House in 1999 where he served three terms, and then he was elected to the United States Senate in 2004. He is a self-described conservative whose policy positions include strong support for a balanced budget Constitutional amendment, abolition of the estate tax, and reforms aimed at shrinking the size and scope of the federal government. His social stands include vocal opposition to abortion and gay rights, strong opposition to gun control, and support for a crackdown on illegal immigration. Vitter was re-elected in 2010 as a Republican Senator from Louisiana, despite the fact that in 2007 he was named as a former client of Deborah Jeane Palfrey, known thereafter as the "DC Madam." David Vitter's connection to the DC Madam scandal came after *Hustler* magazine called his office telling him they had found his office phone number in Palfrey's records. Said *Hustler* magazine publisher Larry Flynt: "We called him for comment and he left through the back door" (Marszalek 2007). The *New Orleans Times-Picayune* followed up on the story and reported on the phone calls from Palfrey to Vitter.

Vitter phone calls to Palfrey's escort service occurred between 1999–2001, when he had been a U.S. House member. Because so much time had lapsed, and the statute of limitations had expired, Vitter was not charged with a crime, but Palfrey was found guilty of federal racketeering charges in connection to her prostitution business and she committed suicide before she went to jail. The scandal rocked both Washington, DC, and Louisiana, and the predictable calls for Vitter's resignation came from Democrats. But the problem for Republicans in Washington was that the governor of Louisiana at the time was a Democrat, so if they pushed hard for Vitter to resign, he would undoubtedly be replaced with someone in the opposing party. After the Washington story had broken, more stories about Vitter's escort servicing broke as well, and a prostitute from a Louisiana brothel alleged that when Vitter saw her for sexual services, he liked to dress in diapers.

Vitter weathered the storm. He first went into hiding with his family in a vain attempt to avoid the reporters camping out on his lawn and the places he frequented in Louisiana. He finally resurfaced to hold a news conference, and stated:

> I want to again offer my deep, sincere apologies to all those I have let down and disappointed with these actions from my past. I am completely responsible. And I am so very, very sorry. No matter how long ago it was, I know this has hurt the relationship of trust I've enjoyed with so many of you, and that I have a lot of work to do to rebuild that. I will work every day to rebuild that trust. . . . I confronted it in confession and marriage counseling. I believe I received forgiveness from God. I know I did from Wendy, and we put it behind us. (Moran 2007)

And put it behind him he did. He kept his head down for a while and ran successfully for re-election in 2010, beating the Democratic House member who tried to use the scandal against him.

National and Local Narratives

> And this madam says that Vitter was not only having sex with the prostitutes— this is unbelievable— he would also pay them to dress him up in a diaper. See, that's what you call a pampered politician. And she also said today in an interview that he sometimes paid $300 an hour just to have the hookers talk to him because his wife didn't listen to him. Well, I bet she's all ears now.
>
> —Jay Leno

Clearly, the attraction of a conservative politician being serviced by prostitutes, perhaps wearing diapers at the time, was simply too sensational a story to pass up and the late-night comedians made hay of Vitter. The *New York Times*, however, wrote only three news articles about the affair at the time, starting with Vitter's admission to using prostitutes: "Senator Admits Use of an Escort Service," moving to "A Senator's Moral High Ground Gets a Little Shakey," then ending with "Senator Apologizes Again for Link to Prostitution." One opinion piece, written by *Times* writer Frank Rich, hit Vitter hard for his tough stand on other people's morality at the same time he was lax on himself: "I Did Have Sexual Relations with That Woman." The Rich piece moves on to criticize the Republican Party more broadly for their hypocritical stands on sexuality, and ends by calling GOP officials "preacher politicians" (Rich 2007). The blogosphere had a field day with the diaper aspect and went mostly for the salacious details that made it a fun topic to post about. From "Wonkette": "A Disgusted Nation Begs Wendy Vitter Not To Chop Off Diaperman's Dick." But some bloggers looked more seriously at the case and at the Republican Party amidst scandal. Wrote one blogger for *The Atlantic* named Ross Douthat posted:

> The real hypocrites in this scandal are the Republican senators who have called for Craig's resignation but not for the resignation of Sen. David Vitter, Republican of Louisiana, who admitted to using the services of an escort: "from any social-conservative calculus (or at least my social-conservative calculus) prostitution has to be considered a greater social evil than cruising for gay sex in bathrooms. (Douthat 2007)

The local coverage of Vitter's prostitution scandal was extensive and the Times-Picayune, like the Idaho Statesman did to Craig, exhaustively detailed Vitter's political career amidst the sexier prostitution discussion. Beginning with the very start of the story, the Times-Picayune chronicled the events surrounding the senator: "Vitter on 'D.C. Madam' list; Senator says he's sorry for 'very serious sin in my past,'" then moved on to the story of the Louisiana prostitute who said she was a client of Vitter's, as well. All in all, the Times-Picayune printed 14 news articles from July 5, 2007 to August 10, 2007, and 17 opinion pieces during the same time period. The preponderance of opinion was remarkable, and although the paper tried to represent both sides of the arguments surrounding David Vitter, the majority of the op-eds spoke out in favor of the senator: "Tainted Vitter shouldn't preach family values," "Keep out of a good man's life," "Can this senator's career be saved?" "Standing by a bright official," "In fact, Vitter represents conservatives perfectly." One editorial included the following statement:

> However, as long as [Vitter] continues to represent my values and the state of Louisiana without compromise and not be proven a liar with regard to other accusations, I will continue to support him in future elections. (Bourg 2007)

As the Vitter scandal died down, so, too, did the press attention, but one would expect it to rise again once the senator ran for re-election. Not so. In the end, the Times-Picayune even got tired of the hooker scandal, writing an opinion piece before the 2010 midterm elections that brought Vitter another term in the Senate:

> [T]he Democrats continue to bang on about Vitter's history of whore-mongering, which long ago lost all shock value. The attacks are now merely tedious. . . . In any case, prostitution is a picayunish crime and laws against it might be seen as a restraint on free enterprise. Vitter was a very willing buyer, and the high-end girls who worked for the D.C. madam evidently had their heads screwed on all right. Plenty of congressmen might have escaped serious censure in similar circumstances, but Vitter's embarrassment caused whoops of delight because it meant he

Table 5.3 Vitter-Louisiana

Highest Education Level Achieved		Race (reporting one race 98.8%)		Types of Households	
Less than 9th Grade	7.2	Two or More Races	1.2	Married Couple	46.9
Some High School	12.6	Other	1.0	Male-Headed Household	4.7
High School Graduate	35.3	Hawaiian/ Pacific Islander	0	Female-Headed Household	16
Some College, no degree	19.9	Asian	1.4	Non-Family	4.9
Associates Degree	4.7	Native American	.6	Householder living Alone	27.5
Bachelor's Degree	13.7	Black	31.5		
Graduate or Professional Degree	6.7	White	64.3		

could no longer drone on about family values and his own spotless character. But there cannot be a single voter out there who doesn't know Vitter is a humbug, and we have had our fun. (Gill 2009)

David Vitter remained in office, his marriage intact, and appeared to suffer no political consequences for his scandal.

Constituency

A typical Louisianan was born in the state (80%), has at least a high school degree (80%) (See Table 5.3),is an adherent to a specific religion (85.7%), and lives in an urban area (75%) in a family-based household (68%). Racially, the state is 31 percent African American and 64 percent White. Slightly over half (56%) of those employed in the state are either in professional/management or sales/office occupations. The mean household income (2006–2008) is $58,911. However, 18.5 percent of the entire state's population lives below the poverty line, with female-headed households (39%), and specifically children under the age of five living with single mothers (54.3%), being the most impacted. Slightly more than two-thirds of Louisianans own their own home (68%), while the majority of individuals are under the age of 45 (63%), with the median age 35.1. Of all Louisiana households, 6 percent do not have telephone service and 8 percent lack access to a vehicle for private use.

Analysis

Louisiana is a solidly Republican state, and Gallup gives Republicans a 9-point advantage over the Democrats. More diverse than Idaho, Louisiana is also more prone to poverty. One of the great economic supports of the state is tourism in New Orleans, which was hit especially hard after Hurricane Katrina. Standard anti-government conservatism does not work well in Louisiana because of the state's dependence on the federal government for economic support and emergency management assistance. However, because the government has botched so much of the post-Katrina recovery efforts, anti-government sentiment takes different forms, explaining Republican Vitter's popularity and his ability to ride the storm of his prostitution scandal.

But perhaps in this case, party plays less of a role than timing: The Vitter scandal gives great credence to the theory that time heals all wounds, because three years after the scandal hit, the voters not only re-elected Vitter but eschewed the discussion of the prostitution humiliation. Perhaps it is because Louisiana has a long and storied history of political sex-scandals or because New Orleans is known as the "Big Easy," but the voters there were more than happy to give Vitter a pass on his indiscretion. Perhaps Vitter's religiously based apology played well enough with the voters to afford him another term in Washington. Most likely, all of these combined to forgive Vitter and allow him to maintain his position in his party and in office.

Vitter viewed and framed his scandal as a purely personal one and, given Louisiana's demography, the state can be seen as a permissive one. Thus, Vitter was able to ride the storm and stay in office, his stature unaffected.

Eliot Spitzer

Scandal: Democratic governor of New York caught by the FBI in a prostitution sting.

Eliot Spitzer was born in the Bronx, New York, and went to Princeton for his undergraduate education and Harvard for Law School. He joined the Manhattan District Attorney's office in 1986 and was elected as State Attorney General in 1998, winning re-election in 2002. He was well known as a crusader against corruption, and earned the nickname the "Sherriff of Wall Street" for his aggressive examination of the banking industry. In the Attorney General's office, he brought down the Gambino crime family, *The Nation* endorsed him for vice president in 2004 because of his anti-corruption efforts, and he was a serious player in American politics. Spitzer was the Democratic Governor of New York and widely considered to be a national political powerhouse when he was caught in a prostitution scandal in 2008. He was known as a hard-hitting champion of integrity, but he was also known as "Client #9" to the prostitute he transported across state lines when Spitzer attended meetings in Washington, DC. The situation was revealed to the public and Spitzer resigned from office.

The Spitzer saga occurred amidst the 2008 presidential race and was one of the most watched dramas of the Spring season. Spitzer's wife, Silda, stood by his side as he apologized to the people of New York and resigned from office, which spawned a veritable cottage industry of popular culture material in response. The long-running television show *Law and Order* ran a show based on the Spitzer affair, a new TV series was created called *The Good Wife* (ostensibly based on the Spitzers), and several fiction books about cuckolded political wives were published, including *Fly Away Home* by best-selling author Jennifer Weiner. The scandal was so big, unexpected, and fabulous it captured the attentions of Americans around the country, even as it shocked the most jaded New Yorkers.

National and Local Narratives

"The New York Times was able to find Kristen, the 22-year-old prostitute who Spitzer allegedly paid $1,000 an hour. Her real name is Ashley Dupré. . . . Her MySpace page says her first love is music, she wants to be a singer, and then her second love is having sex with governors for money."

—Jimmy Kimmel

The *New York Times* probably had a difficult time covering this story, since they cater to a national, state, and local audience, but they devoted a great deal of ink to the Spitzer affair. Immediately after the nature of the scandal was uncovered, Spitzer hid in his New York City apartment and refused to deal with the matter. It took several days for him to resign, and in that time the papers were covering his crime, the prostitute with whom he was caught, and the inevitable political fallout from the disgrace. Finally, the *New York Times* asked for his resignation in an editorial:

> Governor Spitzer has now twice violated his obligations to the people of New York. He violated their trust when, according to law enforcement officials, he patronized a prostitution ring. He compounded that violation Tuesday by hiding in his Fifth Avenue apartment and refusing to explain his actions or his future plans.
>
> To put it bluntly, Mr. Spitzer must either resign immediately or explain why he deserves to continue in office. It is almost impossible for us to imagine how he can survive this scandal and provide the credible leadership that his state needs. (Editors, Waiting for Mr. Spitzer 2008)

But this played more as a local editorial than a national narrative. The *Times* was so full of editorials from New York readers they had a special section of the paper devoted to the scandal. The *Times* national coverage began in print after Spitzer had apologized with Silda by his side. The *Times* ran a story about the immediate reaction to the news of Spitzer's humiliation:

> The idea that Gov. Eliot Spitzer, the square-jawed crusader who promised to bring ethics to Albany, the former prosecutor who chased corruption on Wall Street so ferociously that people nicknamed him Eliot Ness—was somehow involved in a prostitution scandal was too much. New Yorkers who thought they had heard everything were, for a change, dumbfounded. (Barron 2008)

The *Times* coverage appeared on the front page of the newspaper, in its editorial pages, in its Arts & Entertainment section (for coverage of the unfolding drama on television) and in its Metropolitan section. In the first 24-hour period, the Spitzer saga was the subject of 31 stories in the *New York Times*, including two "Quotes of the Day."

The blogs had their own orgy of coverage, focusing entirely on the prostitution aspect of the scandal because that was simply the most interesting and jaw-dropping part. Before the actual story even broke, there were parts of it leaked around the media. A "Wonkette" posting titled "Gov. Eliot Spitzer is a Whoremonger," Ken Layne wrote before the announcement:

> Hey, the Governor of New York runs a prostitution ring of sex prostitutes! The *New York Times* says this is true! This is funny because Eliot Spitzer was supposedly Mr. "I will crack down on the prostitution rings," but he apparently really meant "I will destroy the competition." Speculate wildly as to what this is all about, if you like! (Layne 2008)

The political blogs went on to compare Larry Craig with Spitzer, since Craig's affair had broken the previous year ("How Big is Your Hypocrite?"), they examined the

"Emperor's Club," the brothel that Spitzer used ("So You Want to Open a Brothel"), and Ashley Dupré, the prostitute he was caught with. They examined the cover story he used ("A Shonda for the Quakers") and the effect Spitzer's arrest would have on those he had prosecuted ("Spitzerfreude"). They examined the current state of his career ("Will Spitzer Lose His Superdelegate Vote?") and his legacy ("Spitzer Gets Spitzered"). In other words, they left no stone unturned.

In Albany, the *Times Union* newspaper covered the story as extensively as the *New York Times* did, but they addressed the political fallout more than Spitzer's past performance as a regulator. During the two weeks following the Spitzer press conference and resignation, the *Albany Times Union* ran 34 stories about Spitzer, and finally concluded with one called: "Enough, Already, With Stories About Spitzer." Even they had had enough. Spitzer was quiet for two years until he began his redemptive roll-out, first with a series of lush profile interviews (including one in *People* magazine), followed by the launch of his own show on CNN ("Parker-Spitzer").

Constituency

Most New Yorkers were born in the state (64.3%); however, 21.7 percent of the population is foreign born (See Table 5.4). Overwhelmingly, New Yorkers claim to be religious adherents (76.7%), with the majority being Catholic (39.8%); there is a very small Evangelical Protestant presence (2.95%) in the state. For the most part, New Yorkers have attained at least a high school degree (84%), live in family-based households (64%) in urban areas (92.1%), and own their own home (56%); in those homes, 28.9 percent speak a language other than English. Four percent of households do not have telephone service, and 28 percent of households lack access to a vehicle for private use. Well over three-quarters of New Yorkers are employed in

Table 5.4 Spitzer-New York

Highest Education Level Achieved		Race (reporting one race 98.1%)		Types of Households	
Less than 9th Grade	7.1	Two or More Races	1.9	Married Couple	45.2
Some High School	8.8	Other	8.6	Male-Headed Household	4.8
High School Graduate	29.0	Hawaiian/Pacific Islander	0	Female-Headed Household	14.5
Some College, no degree	15.4	Asian	6.9	Non-Family	6.0
Associates Degree	8.1	Native American	.4	Householder living Alone	29.5
Bachelor's Degree	18.1	Black	15.6		
Graduate or Professional Degree	13.6	White	66.7		

service (19%), sales/office (26%), or management/professional (37%) occupations. The mean household income is $80,425, although 14 percent of the state's population lives in poverty. These percentages rise dramatically for female-headed households with children (26.7%), particularly with children younger than five (40%). Some 66.7 percent of New Yorkers are White, with 15.6 percent African American, 6.9 percent Asian, and 16.4 percent of the population of Hispanic or Latino descent. The median age for a New Yorker is 37.7, with nearly two-thirds of the state's population younger than 45 (60.7%).

Analysis

The Empire State is extremely diverse, and while many think of New York as consisting only of Manhattan, the state includes wide varieties of communities that thrive happily six hours away from New York City. Upstate New York along the Canadian border is home Fort Drum, to one of the largest U.S. Army divisions (the 10th Mountain Division) and three hours west of Fort Drum is Lake Placid, home of the 1980 Winter Olympics. Syracuse, Rochester, and Albany are not only immensely different from New York City, but also different from one another. Being Governor of New York means being adherent to a wide and diverse swath of constituents.

Despite pockets of GOP districts throughout the Empire State, New York is a solidly Democratic state, and the 2008 Gallup survey showed a 28-point advantage over the Republicans. Because of the criminal nature of his scandal, Spitzer resigned from his position as governor and fellow Democrat David Patterson was sworn in after him. Following the scandal, Spitzer used a similar tactic to David Vitter and remained quiet for a period of time. As mentioned, he went on to repair his reputation and re-emerge into the public eye. In one interview, Spitzer answered the question "does he still kick himself" for his behavior? His response: "It will never stop. That I don't think will *ever* stop. Nor should it . . . This is now part of my life story" (Cotliar 2010). It is, therefore, certain that Spitzer will use his scandal as a way to construct his own narrative. When asked if he would run again for public office, Spitzer responded: "You never rule things out in life" (Cotliar 2010).

The Spitzer scandal was a stew of scandal types. Certainly, it was a personal failure but there were also significant elements of irony (Sherriff of Wall Street nabbed in illegal behavior) combined with a sprinkling of professional failure (he brought Dupré to DC for a conference) and a heaping teaspoon of power abuse. Spitzer did immediate resign but has re-emerged. Thus weakened and not ruined, Spitzer's future will depend on the benevolence of a largely liberal New York and his own skills as a charismatic leader.

John Ensign

Scandal: Republican U.S. Senator caught in extramarital affair that led to bribery.

John Ensign was born and raised in Nevada, went to college in Oregon and veterinary school in Colorado. He returned to Nevada where he worked as a veterinarian until his election first to the U.S. House of Representatives in 1994 and then to the United States Senate in 2000. He was re-elected to the Senate in 2006 and has established a reputation as an animal rights advocate, thanks to his experience as a veterinarian. A conservative Republican, Ensign has traditional small-government stands on business and fiscal responsibility. He has been an outspoken opponent of abortion rights and gay marriage, and released the following press statement after he spoke in favor of a Constitutional ban on gay marriage in 2004:

> "Marriage is the cornerstone on which our society was founded. For those who say that the Constitution is so sacred that we cannot or should not adopt the Federal Marriage Amendment, I would simply point out that marriage, and the sanctity of that institution, predates the American Constitution and the founding of our nation." (Ensign, July 13, 2004)

In 2009, Ensign admitted to an extramarital affair with the wife of one of his top staffers, a man named Douglas Hunter. In the course of the affair's revelation, Ensign arranged for Hunter to leave his office staff and join a lobbying firm in Nevada, despite federal laws that prohibit lobbying for one year after leaving public service. Additionally, Ensign's parents gave Cindy Hunter, Doug's wife and the woman with whom Ensign had the affair, a gift of $96,000. There were additional accusations of settlement offers brokered by other Republican senators. Thanks to this scandal, Ensign was named as one of the most corrupt officials in Washington by the citizen watch group called Citizens for Responsibility and Ethics in Washington (Spillman 2009).

Ensign is a member of a Christian society known as "the Family" or "the Fellowship." The group was founded in 1935 in opposition to FDR's New Deal and its adherents subscribe to a conservative Christian fundamentalist and free market ideology. The Family has a connection to house on C Street in Washington, DC, just a few blocks from the Capitol, and Ensign lives in this house when in Washington. Officially registered as a church, the C Street house serves as a meeting place and residence for conservative politicians. According to Jeff Sharlet, who wrote a book about the group, the Family's philosophy is based on "a sort of trickle-down fundamentalism," that believes that the wealthy and powerful, if they "can get their hearts right with God . . . will dispense blessings to those underneath them." It was this religiosity that appeared to be hypocritical when Ensign was caught cheating on his wife.

According to a *New Yorker* article about C Street (titled "Frat House for Jesus"), the affair between Cindy Hampton and Ensign was first discovered by the Fellowship in 2008, and members of the C Street house (including fellow lawmakers Senator Tom Coburn and Representatives Bart Stupak, Mike Doyle, and Zach Wamp) confronted Ensign. They made him write a letter to Cindy ending the affair and reaffirming his commitment to God, and they made Ensign send the letter to Cindy by Fed Ex that day. According to *The New Yorker*, many in the C Street house thought this was not only the end of the story but also a victory for their group:

Some in the C Street group wanted Ensign out of the house, but the prevailing view was that he should stay. Dealing with the affair seemed to pose a test of the group's very purpose: in the fevered atmosphere of an election year, could the men of C Street cope with the situation privately? Looking back, Coburn believed that the Ensign case was a C Street success story. A year after that midnight confrontation, word of Ensign's affair had not leaked, and Ensign and his wife, Darlene, had reconciled. (Boyer 2010)

But in 2009, Doug Hampton (the cuckolded husband of Cindy) was still angry, and he leaked the story about the affair to *Fox News*, which then led to a media feeding frenzy. After almost two years of investigation in which time Ensign remained in office, the events of the affair and the cover-up that ensued became public. Ensign resigned from office immediately before a Senate Ethics Committee report recommended his possible expulsion from the U.S. Senate. The Ethics Committee referred the case to the U.S. Department of Justice where it stands today.

National and Local Narrative

Sen. John Ensign of Nevada had to resign as chairman of the Republican Policy Committee because he admitted to having an affair. It was an unusual affair for a senator—it was with a woman.

—Craig Ferguson

Perhaps it was because John Ensign was not a nationally well-known figure, or perhaps because the scandal lacked the craziness of the scandals that came before this one, but the *New York Times* devoted only five stories to the Ensign affair, and every single one of them was a staid procedural piece about what happened, the political fallout, and the post-disclosure events. Beginning with "Senator Says he Had Affair with an Aide" the *Times* covered Ensign's admission after Doug Hampton revealed the affair. The next two stories were titled: "After Affair, Senator Resigns Leadership Job" and "After an Affair, a Bid for Cash," and then the *Times* wrote "Senator Apologizes." The final story dealt with the financial dealings: "Senator's Parents Gave Mistress Thousands." And that ended their coverage of the Ensign affair.

The bloggers were at first dulled by the nature of the Ensign affair, but as the details dripped out they caught on, as evidenced by "Wonkette:" "Lame Ensign Scandal Getting Super-Funny In a Hurry:"

It was bad enough for sex person John Ensign when his mistress' husband (his friend Doug Hampton!) claimed that Ensign paid Cindy Hampton $25,000 in severance when she left his PAC, because this may have been a campaign finance violation of some sort. Damn you, John McCain! But NOW, in the necessary legal response Ensign's lawyer has had to issue, we are provided with high comedy: it was actually $96,000 . . . and Ensign *had to ask Mommy and Daddy pay it*. Did Ensign have to mow the lawn in return? . . . This is a whole new level of loserdom.

Sure, David Vitter wore diapers, but he didn't make his mother change them. (Newell 2009)

Not surprisingly, the local coverage of the Ensign scandal went into greater depth and detail. The *Las Vegas Review-Journal* wrote 20 stories about Ensign in the month following his affair admission, including three editorial pieces that all criticized his behavior as unethical and corrupt. As in the *New York Times* coverage, the *Review-Journal* news stories addressed the technicalities of the affair, but went into greater detail about the affair, about Cindy Hampton, and about the financial aftermath of the scandal. Several addressed his political future, including one story titled: "Ensign could be re-elected—if all adulterers and hypocrites vote for him." Most stories were reproachful in their tone, including one titled: "Something funny is going on with Ensign, but it really isn't laughable." In all, the Las Vegas paper seemed to hold Ensign in high contempt, but fell short of calling for his resignation. In fact, an editorial from the Review-Journal allowed Ensign's continuation as senator even as it expressed disappointment:

Sen. Ensign **Sen. Ensign**-Search using: must now demonstrate to Nevadans that he can learn from his mistakes, rebuild his reputation for steadiness and straight talk, and most of all be an effective leader in the currently outnumbered resistance to big government and the systematic looting of the storehouses of private capital that have made America prosperous and great. He starts from square one. He had better start right now. (Editors, "Ensign Woes" 2009).

Ensign was unable to start at square one, although he did remain in office for many months after the affair was uncovered. This was because the cover up, the planned pay-off, and the possible illegality of Ensign's dealings with Hampton were finally

Table 5.5 Ensign-Nevada

Highest Education Level Achieved		Race (reporting one race 96.9%)		Types of Households	
Less than 9th Grade	6.5	Two or More Races	3.1	Married Couple	47.3
Some High School	9.8	Other	6.9	Male-Headed Household	6.0
High School Graduate	30.4	Hawaiian/Pacific Islander	.5	Female-Headed Household	11.7
Some College, no degree	24.8	Asian	6.0	Non-Family	8.1
Associates Degree	7.2	Native American	1.2	Householder living Alone	26.9
Bachelor's Degree	14.2	Black	7.4		
Graduate or Professional Degree	7.2	White	74.9		

released to the public in 2011 in a scathing Senate Ethics Committee report that dredged it all up once again. Because of the possible criminal nature of the cover-up and the fact that the case is now within the jurisdiction of the Justice Department, Ensign's political future has been destroyed.

Constituency

Slightly more than three-quarters of those employed in Nevada work in service (25%) (See Table 5.5), management/professional (27%), or sales/office (26%) occupations; the mean household income is $73,223. Most of the people in Nevada are not native to the state, with slightly fewer than a fourth born in Nevada (23.2%). Nevadans can be characterized as mostly urban (90%), with at least a high school degree (84%), living in family-based households (65%), and owning their own home (61%). While not a particularly religious state, 41.4 percent claim to adhere to a religious tradition. White (74.9%) is the main racial characteristic, although nearly one-fourth declare Hispanic or Latino ethnicity; 7.4 percent of Nevadans are African American and 6 percent are Asian. Some 27.3 percent speak a language other than English in their homes. The median age in Nevada is 35.8, with 64 percent of the population younger than 45. Poverty levels in Nevada are 10.8 percent for all people, with higher rates for female-headed households with children (21.5%), and for those same households with children under the age of five (34.1). Four percent of households do not have telephone service and 7 percent of households lack access to a vehicle for private use.

Analysis

Obama won Nevada in 2008 and Democrat Harry Reid narrowly won Senate re-election in 2010, but Nevada is divided politically, and trends more conservative than not. While most voters are willing to forgive the personal failure of their lawmaker, they are far less willing to forgive criminal behavior that illustrates a grand abuse of power. The Senate Ethics Committee took pains to state that the Special Prosecutor in charge of the investigation did not spend too much time on the extra-marital affair, because these matters are deemed private. However, when a private matter involves violation of election law, bribery, and official deceit, it becomes far less private. The Ensign affair began as a simple personal failure story but gained momentum as the stories about the Family and the C Street house unfolded and became fodder for media attention. As the Special Prosecutor investigated and the Senate Ethics Committee reported, it became a story that was far less about a sex scandal and instead about pure political corruption.

Mark Sanford

Scandal: Republican governor of South Carolina disappears for almost a week and returns to admit a passionate love affair with a foreign woman.

The Mark Sanford scandal is notable among all others for several reasons: First, the start of the scandal occurred because Sanford was actually deemed *missing* during Father's Day weekend in 2009, which led many to worry for his safety; second, his wife Jenny left him after the revelation of his affair(rather than play "good wife" and stick around for the public apology and reputation regeneration); and lastly, Sanford made national headlines for his affair but was then bumped from the national spotlight thanks to the death of pop sensation Michael Jackson. Sanford then *re-emerged* in the public limelight after losing the glare, thanks to a completely optional (and slightly crazy) news conference that saw Sanford loudly weeping and pledging his love for his mistress. This was one of those cases that kept coming back to the public's attention—and unnecessarily so.

National and Local Narratives

> Several weeks ago, South Carolina Governor Mark Sanford disappeared without explanation for five days. Now of course, as it turns out, he didn't really disappear. It turns out he was hiking on the Appalachian Trail. Which is a trail that starts in Maine and ends in an Argentine woman's vagina."
>
> —Jon Stewart

The *New York Times* first covered Sanford's disappearance with the article titled "A Governor Goes Missing," which was printed on June 23. Two days later, the *Times* followed up with "Ending Mystery, A Governor Says He Had an Affair." Further *Times* articles reported the effect of the fallout on the Republican Party, on the frequency of disappearing lawmakers, on the status of Jenny Sanford, and finally ending with their coverage with the story of the state Party's Censure motion against Sanford. All in all, the *Times* printed ten news articles about the scandal and a slew of opinion pieces, to include a scathing piece by Maureen Dowd who compared "Mark" the Senator to "Marco," the lover of an Argentinean goddess:

> Mark was the self-righteous, Bible-thumping prig who pressed for Bill Clinton's impeachment; Marco was the un-self-conscious Lothario, canoodling with Maria in Buenos Aires, throwing caution to the e-wind about their "soul-mate feel," her tan lines, her curves, "'the erotic beauty of you holding yourself (or two magnificent parts of yourself) in the faded glow of night's light." Mark is a conservative railing against sinners; Marco sins liberally. Mark opposes gay marriage as a threat to traditional marriage. Marco thinks nothing of risking his own traditional marriage, and celebrates transgressive relationships. He frets to Maria in e-mail that he sounds "like the Thornbirds—wherein I was always upset with Richard Chamberlain for not dropping his ambitions and running into Maggie's arms." (Dowd 2009)

Another *Times* opinion piece about Sanford addressed the South Carolina governor in relative terms with Illinois Governor Rod Blagojevich and New York Governor

Spitzer: "On behalf of the people of Illinois and New York, I'd like to thank South Carolina for giving us Mark ("I've been unfaithful to my wife") Sanford. Finally, a governor who's weirder than Rod Blagojevich and less responsible than Eliot Spitzer." (Collins 2010) This neatly summarizes the national press coverage of Mark Sanford, seen not as a mean-spirited hypocrite but instead as a truly barmy politician.

Generally, the national coverage of Sanford's affair began rather tamely and then escalated, thanks to his public and peculiar admission of guilt at a press conference where he actually took reporters' questions and went into lurid detail about his affair. Sanford gave a tear-filled statement to the press that lasted almost 20 minutes: he apologized to his mistress before his family, and then spoke of God's law and morality, without a shred of irony. Even veteran newspersons such as Cokie Roberts and Sam Donaldson noted the oddity of the apology, stating on *ABC News* that Sanford was a "cooked goose" and that the press conference was "bizarre to say the least" (Frias 2009). Sanford was spared the public excoriating normally devoted to such situations by the surprising death of Michael Jackson, which occurred on the same day as his long and emotional affair explanation.

The political blogs had focused on Sanford's rejection of stimulus money earlier in the year, and so when Sanford was caught cheating, they had fun merging the two stories. Posted Josh Fruhlinger on "Wonkette", "Man-Whore Mark Sanford Takes Obama's Dirty Money, Like A Prostitute:"

> South Carolina Governor Mark Sanford was a guy with a future in politics, and if there's one thing guys with futures in politics do, it's go in for dumb grandstanding stunts that score points with ideologues but do real, actual damage to the people who elected them. That's why 2012 sleeper political candidate Mark Sanford bravely told Chairman Obama that he didn't want to use the money allocated to his state by the stimulus package to "stimulate" the economy in the intended Keynesian (Kenyan?) fashion, but rather to pay off this guy he owed money to. What happened to that strong, principled conservative of yore, anyway? Well, obviously he *betrayed* those principles, by having a consensual sex affair with an adult woman who doesn't even speak English natively. And that was the end of his political career, pretty much. But he still has to/gets to be governor of South Carolina for several more months! And now that he doesn't have to worry about what Iowa caucus-goers think about his conservative credentials, he's just up and taking that Obama money, stained red with blood and communism, and giving it in greasy handfuls to South Carolina's laziest unemployed. (Fruhlinger 2010)

These national narratives contrasted with the local ones, if only because the people of South Carolina took closer attention to the whereabouts of their missing governor than the national press did. The Charleston *Post and Courier* first called attention to the missing governor on June 22:

Thirty-year lawman Sen. Jake Knotts said he got wind of news over the weekend that Gov. Mark Sanford had taken a SLED vehicle Thursday night and told his security detail to stand down. "Ain't nobody seen from him or heard from him since," Knotts said this afternoon. Knotts is a West Columbia Republican and a retired law enforcement officer. (Wenger 2009)

After the Governor's office released a statement that Sanford was hiking the Appalachian Trail, the paper printed an article two days later titled: "Sanford expected back at work today; Details remain scarce about governor's 5-day trail hike." That same day, the Post and Courier's Editorial page opined: "While the governor ought to be given some space to clear his head and put things in perspective, he also should be available in an emergency. That apparently wasn't the case during his recent foray in the mountains." These tame editorials gave way to outraged writings once Sanford's transgressions were made public. Later stories were titled "Shocker" and "Another One Bites the Dust," seemingly annoyed by yet another sex scandal to the Republican Party. Yet again, the paper restrained from calling for Sanford's resignation, instead opting to chide him on his behavior and letting the citizens of South Carolina write in that they thought he should resign. Although the state legislature officially censured Sanford, he remained in office until 2011.

Table 5.6 Sanford-South Carolina

Highest Education Level Achieved		Race (reporting one race 98.7%)		Types of Households	
Less than 9th Grade	6.1	Two or More Races	1.3	Married Couple	48.3
Some High School	11.7	Other	1.4	Male-Headed Household	4.2
High School Graduate	32.1	Hawaiian/Pacific Islander	0	Female-Headed Household	14.9
Some College, no degree	18.7	Asian	1.1	Non-Family	10.0
Associates Degree	8.2	Native American	.3	Householder living Alone	27.7
Bachelor's Degree	15.1	Black	28.3		
Graduate or Professional Degree	8.2	White	67.5		

Constituency

The majority of South Carolinians have been born in the state (60.4%) and regularly exercise their religious traditions (67.2%), with nearly a third declaring adherence to an Evangelical Protestant tradition (29.4%). A South Carolina resident can be characterized as having at least a high school degree (82%), living in a family-based household (67%), owning their own home (70%), and being under the age of 45 (60.9%—the state's median age is 37.3). South Carolinians are either White (68.7%) or African American (29%) and are employed in either management/professional (31%) or sales/office (25%) occupations. The mean household income is $59,602, although 15.5 percent of all South Carolinians live in poverty. This percent increases dramatically for female-headed households with children (33%), particularly if the children are younger than five (50.9%). Six percent of all households do not have telephone service, and 7 percent of households lack access to a vehicle for private use.

Analysis

South Carolina is a solidly Red state that went to McCain in 2008. Of the elected members of the U.S. Congress, there is only one Democrat in the South Carolina delegation, and in the State Legislature, Republicans control both houses. In 2009, South Carolina Rep. Joe Wilson shouted," You lie!" at President Obama during his healthcare speech to a joint session of Congress, and was easily re-elected by his constituents after that. Possible Republican presidential candidates like Sarah Palin and Newt Gingrich have made stops in South Carolina to campaign in what is called the "invisible primary" season, because the real South Carolina primary is considered one of the more important ones. It is early in the season and calls itself the "first in the South" primary.

Sanford had a promising future before the scandal broke, but after he was censured by the South Carolina House of Representatives and his star fell fast. No longer considered a possible presidential candidate, the voters of South Carolina now view him as simply an ex-governor, since they allowed him to remain in office until the end of his term. Mark Sanford has since left public office, but his last round of public events before he handed over the keys to the governor's mansion to Nikki Haley were indicative of his post-scandal posture: "We're going to end this administration the same way we began it—by going from one corner of the state to the other, touching base with people from all walks of life, connecting with friends old and new, and saying 'thank you' for the grace and support extended to me and my family over the years" (McClatchy 2011). Sanford has made no public statement as to his future plans.

South Carolina has a clearly restrictive political climate: Sanford's personal failure—as exemplified by his weepy press conference and pseudo-apology—was overshadowed by his professional failure, since he disappeared for almost a week, leaving his constituents completely baffled and (for the time) without a governor. Thus, although Sanford served out the remainder of his term, he was politically ruined. The combination of the political environment with the nature of his scandal was too much to overcome.

Conclusions

It is evident that place and demographics are important factors in the outcome of a political sex scandal. Of course, mitigating factors include the nature of the scandal and the conditions under which the scandal is revealed. However, there is something to be said about an elected official's constituency and their understanding, expectation, and devotion to their leader that also has much to do with the conclusion of the sensational events.

What is, perhaps, most evident is the discrepancy between the national narratives and the local accounts of these scandals. Because each constituency sees themselves as unique, they also view their elected official as uniquely theirs, and as a result they either take it upon themselves to throw the bum out or forgive his indignity. While it is obvious that sex scandals make a politician a national figure of contempt, ridicule, and scorn, they sometimes, too, can make a politician a sympathetic (or even heroic) figure to a constituency. This was clearly the case in the Craig and Vitter scandals, where the politicians were allowed to remain in office until the voters themselves got to make a choice. For Larry Craig, there was no re-election, and for David Vitter, the voters sent him back to Washington, tired of the prostitution tale. In Mark Foley's case, the scandal was so inappropriate and wrong that the voters did not even have the time to register their displeasure. In New York, Eliot Spitzer was excoriated in the press, resigned, and came back to life after the public said they did not care enough to hold a grudge. Mark Sanford was punished in public and let go, and John Ensign's fate was sealed with his political ruin.The political environment of a constituency plays a significant role in determining electoral outcome.

All decisions are eventually in the hands of the voting public—unless there are criminal charges filed that take a politician away against his will. But as Stephanie Jirard demonstrates later in this book—that is almost never the case. And so when Foley and Spitzer stepped down, they did so because they knew they had no other choice. The voters—either by popular vote or by representative censure—would have removed them if they had not removed themselves. Larry Craig must have known that Idahoans would have enough faith in him to remain in office, since he first announced his resignation and then reneged on this promise. Vitter, Ensign, and Sanford simply moved forward, assuming they could weather the storm. Ultimately, it is the constituents' decision and a politician must have a good enough sense of his constituents to gauge their feelings accurately enough to get elected in the first place. He must know how to behave in the face of adversity.

Hypocrisy (or irony) is a common theme among all political sex scandals. Gay scandals seem to attract more antagonistic consideration, especially when the scandalous is found in the Republican Party among the GOP's anti-gay rights politicians. Such was the case of Larry Craig, and the nature of this specific type of hypocrisy is fodder for national attention and local derision. Even with the heterosexual scandals, the more tantalizing were among conservatives who preached family values and then betrayed them, as in the cases of David Vitter and John Ensign. Hypocrisy was seen in Eliot Spitzer's case, since he was once valued as a do-good reformer who was then caught in illegal behavior. Mark Foley was in charge of a congressional caucus on exploiting children, even as he himself was exploiting them. Hypocrisy made each of our case studies tantalizing to examine and deconstruct—and yet this duplicity was sometimes not enough to drum the hypocrites out of office. What was different? The constituencies.

There is a saying in political science that Americans hate Congress but love their Congressman. What else could explain the ridiculously low approval ratings of Congress that run contrary to the high incumbency re-election rates? The literature shows that the reason for this discrepancy is the love of the local representative: They are ours. When a constituency goes out to vote on Election Day, the voters take ownership of the public official, feeling the man elected is "one of us." This elected official may be flawed, but sometimes voters give him a pass, arguing: "We are all flawed. Leave him alone. We will do what we want to with them, but let it be our choice." This was the precise trajectory of the Vitter scandal: When the senator was caught, there was condemnation, but that ran its course and the voters wholeheartedly agreed to ignore the past and give David Vitter another shot in office. Ensign stayed in office as long as he could before the authorities got to him – and not his voters..And if Spitzer and Sanford make political comebacks (because there is evidence that they are aiming to do just that), then this approach will work for them, as well.

Politicians can make such comebacks because the scandal becomes part of their larger narrative of experience. It becomes their story, their tale of triumph over adversity. In some ways, they are saying: "I am what I am. Love me for my mistakes and imperfections," and often times the voters will do exactly that. Case in point: President Clinton. But in the end, it is up to the constituents to decide how they will accept or reject their tarnished politician, and despite the nationalizing factors that help shape the story, in the end all politics is local.

Works Cited

Agnew, John. *Place and Politics: the geographical mediation of state and society.* 1987. Boston: Allen and Unwin.

Association of Statisticians of American Religious Bodies. Religious Congregations Membership Study 2000. Accessed December 1, 2010 (http://www.nytimes.com/2008/03/11/nyregion/11reax.html).

Bafumi, Joseph, and Robert Shapiro. "A New Partisan Voter." *The Journal of Politics*, 2009: 1–24.

Barron, James. "I Apologize to the Public, to Whom I Promised Better." *New York Times.* March 11, 2008. Accessed December 8, 2010 (http://blog.nola.com/times-picayune/2007/07/vitter_reemerges_and_again_ask/1324/comments-newest-2.html).

Bourg, Lynette. "Vitter's Not the Only One." *nola.com.* July 17, 2007. Accessed November 30, 2010.

Boyer, Peter. "Frat House for Jesus." *The New Yorker.* September 13, 2010. Accessed December 13, 2010 (www.newyorker.com/reporting/2010/09/13/100913fa_fact_boyer?printable=true).

Child and Adolescent Health Measurement Initiative. National Survey of Children's Health 2003. Accessed December 1, 2010 (www.nschdata.org/)

Collins, Gail. "The Love Party." *New York Times.* June 24, 2010. Accessed December 3, 2010 (www.nytimes.com/2009/06/25/opinion/25collins.html).

Cotliar, Sharon. "I Would Like to Move On." *People Magazine,* October 11, 2010: 111–114.

Craig, Larry. "Sen. Larry Craig's Statement." *CNN.com.* August 28, 2007. Accessed November 29, 2010 (http://articles.cnn.com/2007-08-28/politics/sen.craig.statement_1_idahoans-witch-hunt-minneapolis-airport?_s=PM:POLITICS).

———. "Sen. Larry Craig's statement from President Clinton's impeachment trial." *Idaho Statesman.* August 28, 2007. Accessed November 29, 2010 (www.idahostatesman.com/2007/08/28/145345/sen-larry-craigs-statement-from.html#ixzz16hQXoqr6).

Douthat, Ross. "Social Conservatism and Double Standards." *The Atlantic.* August 29, 2007. Accessed November 30, 2010 (http://rossdouthat.theatlantic.com/archives/2007/08/social_conservatism_and_double.php).

Dowd, Maureen. "Genius in the Bottle." *New York Times.* June 27, 2009. Accessed December 13, 2010 (www.nytimes.com/2009/06/28/opinion/28dowd.html).

Editors. "The Foley Matter." *New York Times.* October 3, 2006. Accessed November 30, 2010.

———. "Waiting for Mr. Spitzer." *New York Times.* March 12, 2008. Accessed December 8, 2010.

———. "Ensign Woes." *Las Vegas Review-Journal.* July 12, 2009. Accessed December 13, 2010 (www.lvrj.com/opinion/50575347.html).

"Ending Mystery, A Governor Says He Had an Affair." *The New York Times.* June 25, 2009.

Frias, Mariecar. "Sanford's Unorthodox Apology for Affair 'Will Sink Him.'" *ABC News.* June 25, 2009. Accessed December 3, 2010 (http://abcnews.go.com/GMA/Politics/story?id=7922704&page=1).

Fruhlinger, Josh. "Man-Whore Mark Sanford Takes Obama's Dirty Money, Like A Prostitute." *Wonkette.* August 11, 2010. Accessed December 13, 2010 (http://wonkette.com/417332/man-whore-mark-sanford-takes-obamas-dirty-money-like-a-prostitute).

Gill, James. "Vitter's Sins Are Yesterday's News." *nola.com.* October 4, 2009. Accessed November 29, 2010 (www.lexisnexis.com/hottopics/lnacademic/).

Gowler, Vicky. "*Statesman*Editor Responds to Claims That the Newspaper's Investigation Forced Craig to Plead Guilty." *Idahostatesman.com.* September 10, 2007. Accessed November 29, 2010 (www.idahostatesman.com/2007/09/10/154845/statesman-editor-responds-to-claims.html).

Hulse, Carl, and Raymond Hernandez, "Top G.O.P. Aides Knew In Late '05 of E-Mail to Page." *The New York Times,* October 1, 2006. Accessed November 8, 2010 (http://query.nytimes.com/gst/fullpage.html?res=9C03E6D61730F932A35753C1A9609C8B63).

Jijo Jacob, "Chronicle of John Ensign's rise and fall" International business Times, April 22, 2011, Accessed May 15, 2011 (www.ibtimes.com/articles/137218/20110422/john-ensign-nevada-resigned-resigns-republican-senator-affair-cynthia-hampton-extra-marital-ethics-c.htm).

Jones, Dale E., Sherri Doty, James E. Horsch, Richard Houseal, Mac Lynn, John P. Marcum, Kenneth M. Sanchagrin and Richard H. Taylor. 2002. *Religious Congregations and Membership in the United States 2000: An Enumeration by Region, State and County Based on Data Reported by 149 Religious Bodies.* Nashville, TN: Glenmary Research Center.

Jones, Jeffrey, "State of the States: Political Party Affiliation" Gallup Polling, January 28, 2009.

Knoke, David. "A Causal Synthesis of Sociological and Psychological Models of American Voting Behavior." *Social Forces,* 1974: 92–101, p. 2.

Layne, Ken. "GOV. ELIOT SPITZER IS A WHOREMONGER." *Wonkette*. March 10, 2008. Accessed December 8, 2010 (http://wonkette.com/365997/gov-eliot-spitzer-is-a-whoremonger).

Layne, Ken, "A Disgusted Nation Begs Wendy Vitter Not To Chop Off Diaperman's Dick." Wonkette, July 17, 2007. Accessed May 15, 2011 (http://wonkette.com/279525/a-disgusted-nation-begs-wendy-vitter-not-to-chop-off-diapermans-dick).

Manny, Bill. "*Statesman*Response to Craig Press Conference." *Idahostatesman.com*. August 28, 2007. Accessed November 29, 2010 (www.idahostatesman.com/2007/08/28/144418/statesman-response-to-craig-press.html#ixzz16hdl9yoF).

"Mark Foley Scandal" Bloggers Blog, Accessed December 5, 2010 (www.bloggersblog.com/foleyscandal/).

Marszalek, Keith. "Vitter Had Five Calls with D.C. Madam." *nola.com*. July 11, 2007. Accessed November 29, 2010 (http://blog.nola.com/updates/2007/07/vitter_had_five_calls_with_dc.html).

McNamara, Melissa, "Foley Scandal a 'Perfect Blogstorm.'" CBS Blogofile, October 4, 2006. Accessed December 5, 2010 (www.cbsnews.com/stories/2006/10/03/blogophile/main2057997.shtml).

Moran, Kate, Bill Walsh, and Brendan McCarthy. "Vitter Re-emerges and Asks Again for Forgiveness." *nola.com*. July 16, 2007. Accessed November 30, 2010 (http://blog.nola.com/times-picayune/2007/07/vitter_reemerges_and_again_ask.html).

Murphy, Patti. "Idaho Senator Says He Regrets Guilty Plea in Restroom Incident." August 29, 2007.

Newell, Jim. "Lame Ensign Scandal Getting Super-Funny in A Hurry." *Wonkette*. July 9, 2009. Accessed December 13, 2010 (http://wonkette.com/409766/lame-ensign-scandal-getting-super-funny-in-a-hurry).

Phuestis. "EXCLUSIVE: 'I Had Sex with Larry Craig!'" *Wonkette*. October 27, 2007. Accessed November 20, 2010 (http://wonkette.com/314897/exclusive-i-had-sex-with-larry-craig).

Raju, Manu. "Tom Coburn Gives Feds E-mails on John Ensign." *Politico*. Judly 23, 2010. Accessed January 2, 2011(www.politico.com/news/stories/0710/40163.html).

Rich, Frank. "I Did Have Sexual Relations With That Woman." *nytimes.com*. July 22, 2007. Accessed November 29, 2010.

Ross, Brian. "Foley Resigns Over Sexually Explicit Messages to Minors." *abcnews.com*. September 29, 2006. Accessed November 30, 2010 (http://blogs.abcnews.com/theblotter/2006/09/foley_resigns_o.html).

Rutenberg, Jim, "A Governor Goes Missing," *The New York Times*, June 23, 2009. Accessed May 11, 2011 (http://thecaucus.blogs.nytimes.com/2009/06/23/a-governor-goes-missing/).

"Sanford plans goodbye tour." *McClathcy Newspapers*, Sunday, January 02, 2011. Accessed May 16, 2011 (www.thesunnews.com/2011/01/02/1898283/sanford-plans-goodbye-tour.html).

"Senator, Arrested in an Airport Bathroom, Pleads Guilty." August 28, 2007. Accessed November 10, 2010 (http://query.nytimes.com/gst/fullpage.html?res=9502E1DE113CF93BA1575BC0A9619C8B63)

Social Explorer. Accessed December 1, 2010 (//www.socialexplorer.com/)

Spillman, Benjamin. "Watchdog Group Adds Ensign to List." *Law Vegas Review Journal*. September 16, 2009. Accessed December 13, 2010 (www.lvrj.com/news/Watchdog-group-adds-Ensign-to-list.html).

Wenger, Yvonne. "Senator: Sanford Drops SLED detail and Is MIA." *Postandcourier.com.* June 22, 2009. Accessed December 3, 2010 (www.postandcourier.com/news/2009/jun/22/ senator_sanford_drops_sled_detail_and_mia/).

U.S. Census Bureau. American Community Survey. Accessed December 1, 2010 (//www.census.gov/acs/www).

Yi Fu-Tuan. "Community and Place: A Skeptical View," in *Person, Place and Thing, in Geoscience and Man,* edited by S.T. Wong, Vol. 31,1992: 47–59.

CHAPTER 6

Men, Mistresses, and Media Framing: Examining Political Sex Scandals

Carrie Sipes

Politics, sex, and the sexual antics of politicians and government officials have always made news, often much to the chagrin of those involved. In the past, media coverage of such sexual dalliances often focused on the bizarre, such as Arkansas Representative Wilbur Mills's sexual affair in the 1970s with stripper, Fanne Foxe, dubbed the "Argentine Firecracker." Mills's affair with Foxe became a media sensation when police in Washington, DC, stopped Mills for speeding, and Foxe tried to escape by jumping into the Tidal Basin.

However, in the late 1980s, the parameters of media coverage of politicians' sexual lives seemed to evolve. Then presidential-hopeful Gary Hart challenged the media to catch him in an extramarital affair to prove rumors that Hart was unfaithful to his wife, and the media took up the challenge. They soon linked Hart to an extramarital affair with Donna Rice. A photograph of the two of them embracing on the deck of the luxury yacht, Monkey Business, hit all the major media outlets and provided weeks of comic fodder for late-night television shows. The media microscope peering into the personal lives of politicians and government officials has continued unabated since, exposing numerous extramarital affairs and sexual antics across the political spectrum.

As politicians find themselves engaging in extramarital affairs, often labeled as "scandals" in the media, they soon capture the attention of media actors. These actors choose how much to cover the extramarital affair, how to construct and relay messages about it, and which aspects of the affair to emphasize or downplay. This chapter compares and contrasts media coverage and framing among several recent political sex scandals in order to investigate differences in the way in which the media portray the story. In other words, do different types of media frame stories in different ways, do different types of media produce more or less content on the subject, do some scandals get treated differently than others? This chapter aims to find out.

Agenda Setting, Framing & Priming

"Sex sells and everybody's interested in sex, so when there's a sex scandal, it's go everything—you're talking about sex, you're talking about power and in a lot of cases, money is involved. You are talking about how the mighty have fallen," Sally Quinn, power-player and Washington journalist (Keck 2009). As Quinn rightfully points out, political sex scandals are never only about sex. While the sex scandal itself may provide lurid details and a frenzy of media coverage of the private lives of the politically powerful, it is the implications of the scandal that are ultimately important. Implications can range from being labeled a hypocrite, being seen as unethical, and being viewed as abusing power to more serious implications such as being found guilty of committing crimes.

June 2009 was a busy month. Two Republican hopefuls for the 2012 presidential nomination, Nevada's Senator John Ensign and South Carolina Governor Mark Sanford, admitted to extramarital affairs. In the case of Gov. Sanford, his alleged innocent hike on the Appalachian Trail turned into an international investigation, a tryst with a "dear, dear friend from Argentina," and intense media coverage. Likewise, Sen. Ensign attracted media attention after admitting to an affair with a married, family friend, an ex-campaign staffer. Ensign had been a vocal critic of former Sen. Larry Craig, who had been arrested in a 2007 sex sting, which added to the irony of the situation. The media have relayed hundreds of stories about politicians and sex scandals. Craig led the total number of stories over Eliot Spitzer, Sanford, John Edwards, and Kwame Kilpatrick. Craig's and Spitzer's scandals even attracted more media attention than did Tiger Woods's multiple affairs (Sartor and Page 2010).

While any political scandal may be considered newsworthy and may capture audiences' attention, political sex scandals tend to capture media attention more than others. A *Pew Project for Excellence in Journalism* study found that the coverage of the Spitzer and Craig scandals was more pervasive than non-sex-related political scandals. They received more coverage than the Lewis "Scooter" Libby scandal of outing CIA operative Valerie Plame, the Dick Cheney secret methods of operation scandal, the Paul Wolfowitz World Bank scandal, and the Ted Stevens gifts and services scandal ("Which Scandals Make Big News?" 2008).

It is difficult to argue that a politician's sexual activity with other consenting adults is more important than some of these other political scandals, but by sheer numbers of media stories, the media emphasize political sex scandals as important for audiences to recognize and think about. This is an example of the agenda-setting function of the media. In the first stage of agenda setting, the media draw attention to an issue through repeated coverage, which results in the public recognizing that this issue is important. McCombs and Shaw (1972) were the first to scientifically examine agenda-setting in their Chapel Hill study of undecided voters in the 1968 presidential election. The results showed a strong relationship between the media's emphasis on campaign issues and the perceptions of issue importance by voters.

However, the agenda-setting is not limited to issue importance. The second level of agenda-setting examines the attributes of an issue that the media has deemed important. For purposes here, the media may draw attention to certain sub-issues of political sex scandals. Sub-issues could include items such as infidelity, legality, honesty (or the lack thereof), ethics, or job performance. These items representing the second level of agenda setting can also be described as media frames.

One useful definition for the concept of news frames is "a central organizing idea for news content that supplies a context and suggests what the issue is through the use of selection, emphasis, exclusion, and elaboration." According to Entman (1993), frames have four functions, to "define problems, diagnose causes, make moral judgments, and suggest remedies." Quite simply, frames here are the media's version of reality. Goffman described frames as construction of reality as early as the 1970s. As is the case for any story the media report to their audiences, there is choice when it comes to covering scandals. The media may present the scandal as "sexual indiscretion," "legal wrongdoing" (Joslyn 2003), "private life," "just sex" (Joslyn 2003), "dramatic, prime-time style entertainment," "a political event" (Owen 2000), or many other frames, as other scholars have demonstrated. When the media define problems for its audiences in essence it is describing the issue and filling in how the issue fits with the norms and values of the society. In an effort to explain how the issue came to be, the media identify potential causes for the behavior—does the problem lie in someone's character, position of power, marriage satisfaction, or were they pursued and manipulated by their lover? Media frames are powerful because they have the ability to draw attention to specific aspects of a political scandal, define the causes, and judge the event. As Entman posits, the media frames do not stop there. Media frames give people possible solutions to the problem—the candidate, mayor, governor, senator should resign his position, the accused should be tried in the court of law, the accused should be punished, the accused will be a liability for his political party, which will create additional problems. McCombs and Estrada (1997) even go so far as to say that the media don't just tell us "what to think about, they also may tell us how and what to think about it, and even what to do about it" (247).

Although agenda-setting and framing are closely connected, as is the concept of priming, there are a couple of important differences. Kosicki (2002) explains the similarities and differences among these concepts well. Agenda-setting, much like priming, is much more concerned with the frequency of the coverage of news items than with its content (Kosicki 2002; Cappella and Jamieson 1997). Framing, on the other hand, is much more concerned with details of the content (Kosicki 2002). "Framing takes as a starting point the idea that language matters in the study of media" (Kosicki 2002 70; Pan and Kosicki 2003)

The following sections examine the frames employed during the first days of media coverage of three recent political sex scandals, John Edwards, Mark Sanford, and Larry Craig. These scandals took place between 2007 and 2009, and each led to intense media coverage. Scandals, affairs, and liaisons are considered newsworthy because they are full of intrigue, conflict, unusualness, and sometimes deviance. These kinds of stories not only provide information to the public, but also serve as dramatic entertainment in some cases. For example, when Mark Sanford held his press conference to address his affair with his Argentinian mistress, he cried nearly uncontrollably and provided details of his liaison, two things that most politicians do not exhibit or elaborate. Who can deny that e-mail messages such as Sanford writing, "You opened up a new chapter last week wherein I was happy and content just being," or his mistress writing (in broken English),"Last Friday I would had stayed embrassing and kissing you forever" (Rutenberg and Brown 2009), are not dramatic, attention grabbing, and unusual?

In examining the first days of sex scandal coverage, the chapter specifically looks at the headlines and content of stories from publications such as *New York Times*, the *Washington Post*, *ABC News*, CNN, *Fox News*, blogs, and talk radio. The purpose of this examination is to provide anecdotal evidence of framing across different kinds of media. In addition, the three scandals were chosen because they depict heterosexual scandals representing a Democrat and a Republican, and a scandal with a Republican alleged to have been involved seeking homosexual activity.

John Edwards

Although many now regard John Edwards as another lying politician, Edwards had a largely successful law career, which spanned 22 years, and won millions of dollars for his clients. He had four children with his wife of 33 years, Elizabeth, served as a one-term senator, was selected as Sen. John Kerry's running mate in the 2004 presidential election, and ran for the presidency himself in 2008 ("Milestones: John Edwards" 2007). Interestingly, Edwards also served as part of the defense team for President Clinton's impeachment trial in 1999. Unfortunately for the success of his political career, while he saw what could happen to a popular politician who engages in extramarital affairs and then lies about it, it appears he needed to learn the effects on his own. The John Edwards sex scandal with campaign videographer Rielle Hunter began in 2006 and was exposed by *The National Enquirer* in August 2008. Although the *Enquirer* had been following Edwards closely for two years, they were unable to get him to admit to the affair. Few other media outlets investigated the story during the years of the affair. However, all that changed on August 8, 2008.

Just how much coverage did John Edwards receive following his admission of an extramarital affair? During the week of August 8, 2008, the week the mainstream media began reporting the affair, the Edwards scandal consumed 81 percent of the cable news hole, 15.3 percent of the network television news hole ("How TV News Played the Edwards Scandal" 2008). The Edwards scandal broke on a relatively slow news day, which may have contributed to the intensity of its coverage. Other top stories in the news included coverage of the 2008 presidential campaign, Russia and its conflict with Georgia, and the Olympics ("How TV News Played the Edwards Scandal" 2008).

The *New York Times* headline read, "Edwards Admits to Affair in 2006" (Seelye 2008), the *Washington Post* headline read, "Edwards Admits He Had An Affair," (Kurtz and Romano 2008) and *USA Today's* headline was somewhat different, "Edwards' Political Future in Doubt after Admitting Affair" (Schouten and Jackson 2008). The *Times* and *Post* articles presented similar frames, frames included just the facts, lying, and cover-up. Both articles emphasized the boldness with which Edwards lied and how money had been funneled to one of his aides in an attempt to cover up the scandal. The *USA Today* article emphasized the consequences of the scandal on Edwards's political future. This story used sources that questioned Edwards's ability to come back from this scandal. For example, Kerry Haynie, a Duke University political scientist, said, "I think essentially his political career is over" (Schouten and Jackson 2008).

Edwards, in an attempt to frame the scandal message for himself, requested an interview with ABC's Bob Woodruff. The *ABC News* interview became a widely cited source of information for other media outlets. The frame that Edwards attempted to sell was the frame of personal/private indiscretion. When Woodruff asked Edwards to elaborate or provide more details about the affair, Edwards responded with statements like this one, "Well, here's the way I feel about this Bob, I think that my family is entitled to every detail. They've been told every detail. Elizabeth knows absolutely everything. I think beyond the basics, the fact that I made this mistake and I'm responsible for it and no one else. I think that's where it stops in terms of the public because I think everything else is within my family and those privacy boundaries ought to be respected" (Woodruff 2008).

Another *ABC News* story, "Democrats Move Quick to Lessen Damage of John Edwards Affair," framed the story in terms of the consequences of the scandal, personal characteristics, and private matter. The story emphasized the fallout such as what should happen at the Democratic National Convention, should Sen. Barack Obama distance himself from Edwards, and the call from prominent Democrats for Edwards to back away from any spotlight in the Democratic Party. This story also framed Edwards as having deep flaws, given the extended and excessive nature of the lying that took place. The authors write, "Even beyond the public denials, Edwards had vehemently denied the allegations privately to aides. . . . Many aides repeated his denials to reporters—not aware that they were being told a lie" (Klein and Parker 2008). The story also picked up on the frame of personal/private issue when it gave attention to Elizabeth Edwards's request to treat this as a "private matter." Beyond this, the story also gave attention to the way Democratic Party representatives wanted to address the scandal—it's not a Democratic Party problem, it's a "human condition" problem (Klein and Parker 2008).

CNN's story, "Edwards Admits to Extramarital Affair," framed the story first as one of personal responsibility. Quoting the ABC interview, the author quotes Edwards saying, "I am responsible for it. I alone am responsible for it," "I made a serious error in judgment," and "You cannot beat me up more than I have already beaten up myself." The story also addressed Edwards's political future and ended with a quote from Edwards's own website, "Before entering politics, winning a Senate seat from North Carolina in 1998, Edwards was a lawyer representing families 'being victimized by powerful interests' and gaining 'a national reputation as a forceful and tireless champion for regular, hard-working people'" ("Edwards Admits to Extramarital Affair" 2008).

The following day, CNN's story "Edwards Could Face Political Free Fall from Affair," focused entirely on the political future/fallout frame. CNN political analysts presented Edwards's future as bleak and potentially damaging to the Democratic Party. James Carville said, "Certainly, his political career is in shambles. It's not going to come back. I humanly feel sorry for Mrs. Edwards. I feel sorry for the Edwards's children. But I'm not shocked." While Gloria Borger offered, "Obviously, lying like this, brazenly, is going to put an end, probably, to his political career and could affect whether he gets any role if Barack Obama were to win the presidency." David Gergen was perhaps the most concerned with the effect of the scandal on the party when he said the situation has put the party in "jeopardy" ("Edwards Could Face Political Free Fall from Affair" 2008).

The frames that CNN employed, especially during the first day of coverage, seemed to be much more in line with Edwards's desired message—that he made a mistake, it was a private matter, and his family is dealing with the affair—than were those of *Fox News* or other news outlets. During its initial coverage, CNN also emphasized the potential ramifications for the Democratic Party much more than did the other news outlets.

The *Fox News* frames of the Edwards scandal were similar to CNN during the initial breaking news, although the words chosen for its headlines painted a more dramatic picture than did the CNN headlines. Headlines on foxnews.com for August 9, 2008, read, "John Edwards Admits to Affair, Denies He's Father of Lover's Child" and "Edwards Ex-Mistress Rules out Paternity Test; Strange Behavior Leaves Many Unanswered Questions in Edwards Affair." For example, the first article also began with John Edwards's own comments about his "error in judgment" and that he has beaten himself up over this more than the media can. The story also included the "political future" and "cover up" frames. The *Fox News* stories did emphasize the likely cover up of the affair and followed a trail of possible hush money leads. Although the frames used by *Fox News* were similar, the headlines are more sensational. Using phrases like "Lover's Child" and words like "Ex-Mistress" and "Strange" grab the attention of readers and connote different meanings from a title that reads "Edwards Admits to Affair."

The *Huffington Post* presented the story on August 8, 2008, as a just-the -acts frame ("John Edwards' Affair with Rielle Hunter: Admits Infidelity" 2008). However, the following week the coverage of the Edwards scandal turned toward the legality of Edwards's payments to his mistress.

So, what are the results of stories framed such as these? The sheer number of stories told regarding this scandal and the largely negative frames used to tell it, in conjunction with the Gallup data that showed that 92 percent of Americans say affairs between married people are morally wrong, suggests that this is an issue that would be salient to the audience (Gallup Polls 2009). Gallup public opinion polls conducted prior to Edwards's admission of his affair showed a 48 percent favorability rating (Gallup Polls 2008). Polls conducted after the affair paint a much different picture. After his admission and after the hundreds of stories relayed in the media, Edwards's favorability rating had dropped to 21 percent (Gallup Polls 2009). According to the Gallup pollsters, "Gallup has never before found as steep a decline in consecutive measurements of a prominent figure using the favorable/unfavorable format, which it began using in 1992" (Gallup Polls 2009). People's negative perceptions of Edwards appeared to be related to the negative media coverage of the scandal. When respondents were asked to choose the person who disappointed them most from a list of people who had been involved in scandals in 2009, 33 percent chose John Edwards (Hart and McInturff 2009). The respondents chose John Edwards more than Tiger Woods, Chris Brown (physically abused his girlfriend), and David Letterman, who had been involved in a sex scandal, too.

In a matter of ten months, John Edwards went from being a prominent figure in the Democratic Party with nearly a majority of people in the public feeling favorable about him to being a political liability with the majority of people in the public expressing unfavorable opinions about him. The media covered this story hundreds of times and if the initial days of coverage are any indication of how the story was framed in the subsequent investigations, it is no wonder that the public would adopt the media's negative framing of the scandal. As we now know, Edwards was not even truthful in his confessional with Bob Woodruff, as he in fact is the father of Rielle Hunter's baby. Edwards repeated public betrayal of trust certainly added to the negative frames used by those in the media. Perhaps the *New York Times* put it best, "Edwards overcame hardships both personal—childhood poverty, the death of a son, his wife's cancer—and political, including a failed 2004 vice presidential bid. But after his second attempt to win the Democratic presidential nomination ended in 2008, it was his admission to an affair that left his political future in doubt" ("Milestones: John Edwards" 2007).

Mark Sanford

The Sanford scandal has its similarities to the Edwards scandal. He was also married, the father of four children, and a prominent Southern politician. He is also one of four siblings, worked for Goldman Sachs, was elected to Congress with no prior political experience, served three terms, and served two terms as South Carolina governor (Sauer 2008).

South Carolina Gov. Mark Sanford presents another case of media framing of political sex scandals. Before discussing how the media framed Sanford's indiscretion, here is some context to consider. During the week of June 22–28, 2009, the week his scandal broke, other top news stories included Michael Jackson's death and protests in Iran. These other big news stories, especially Michael Jackson's passing, took a large portion (18%) of the news hole across different media, which left the Sanford scandal filling 11 percent of the news hole for the week and 13 percent of the stories on cable news channels (Rosenstiel, Hitlin, and Khan 2009; "Media Swing from Protests in Iran to the Passing of the King of Pop" 2009). However, these authors are quick to point out that "that time unit doesn't capture the feel of the week" (Rosenstiel et al. 2009). "By week's end, every other event struggled for attention amid the cascade of Jackson video clips and remembrances, panel discussions and interview segments" (Rosenstiel et al. 2009). Compared with John Edwards's scandal, which received 81 percent of the cable news hole during the first week of his scandal, Sanford received little attention initially (Jurkowitz 2009; "How TV News Played the Edwards Scandal" 2008).

When the Sanford scandal broke, there appeared to be a real crisis for the Republican Party. This scandal would be the second in two weeks to rock the party, as John Ensign's sex scandal had been revealed just a week earlier. Rather than the media focus all its efforts in discussing the scandal and framing it around Mark Sanford, the media began to frame this story as one about the Republican Party (Rosenstiel et al. 2009). Because some in the Republican Party promote the party as the party of "values voters," these scandals caused concerns among many party members (Rosenstiel et al. 2009). Their cause for concern was certainly legitimate, as 92 percent of married men and women in the United States cite extramarital affairs as morally wrong and as the most reproachful moral issue polled (Newport 2009). According to the *PEJ News Coverage Index*, the story was also framed as one of the "strength of political connections" (Rosenstiel et al. 2009).

Sanford's scandal was presented as one that affected the state of South Carolina, not one that affected his family or one of personal flaws or failings. For example, stories focused on how the governor left South Carolina in an irresponsible manner; no one knew of his whereabouts. Stories also focused on his mix of state business and personal pleasure. This is much different from how former President Bill Clinton's scandal with Monica Lewinsky was framed. Clinton's scandal could be said to have been framed as a sex scandal that was a personal indiscretion (Yioutas and Segvic 2003). In fact, a number of people in the public "viewed the situation more as a private matter having to do with Clinton's personal life" (Yioutas and Segvic 2003). In spite of the media coverage of Clinton's sex scandal, he continued to enjoy approval ratings of more than 60 percent (Holland 1998). Perhaps because of Clinton's high approval ratings and general popularity, he had much more political capital to spend compared to Mark Sanford, not a particularly popular member of the Republican Party. This was evidenced by calls from GOP representatives for his resignation only one day after his public admission. For example, Glenn McCall, South Carolina Republican national committeeman, and 14 out of 27 state Senate Republicans called for his immediate resignation (Rutenberg and Brown 2009; Berger 2009).

The *PEJ News Coverage Index* for June 22–28, 2009, ranked the Sanford scandal as the fifth-ranked story in newspapers and network television news, third in cable television news, second in online news, and first in radio talk shows.

The headline on *ABC News* for June 25, 2009, was "Sanford's Unorthodox Apology for Affair 'Will Sink Him'—While Most Philandering Politicians Keep Apologies Brief, Sanford Gave Details of Affair" (Frias, Netter, and Ibanga 2009). The frame for the story was clearly one regarding his political future. The story also emphasized his bizarre apology, describing his emotional, tearful admittance. The *New York Times* article, "Mysteries Remain after Governor Admits Affair" again used the frame of Sanford's political future. The article states, "his disappearance over Father's Day weekend . . . considerably dampen (ed) his prospects for a national political career." In addition to the political future frame, the *Times* emphasized the dishonesty of Sanford and his staff. A quote from state Senator John C. Land III demonstrates this well, "Never in my 32 years as a state senator have I witnessed a governor and his staff act in a more dishonest, secretive and bizarre manner" (Brown and Dewan 2009). Another *New York Times* article, "Governor Used State's Money to Visit Lover," emphasized the legal issues with the governor using taxpayer money to fund his travel to visit his lover, his political future, dramatic elements, and private life. South Carolina majority leader Harvey Peeler, Jr. said, "Leaving aside his personal life, when you use taxpayer dollars, that's what Republicans are all about—spending tax dollars wisely. This was not spending tax dollars wisely" (Rutenberg and Brown 2009). The article also included excerpts from e-mail messages exchanged by Sanford and his mistress. These exchanges provided an unusually intimate glimpse into the affair, which some have described as juvenile, and certainly gave the public a new way to look at the governor. Some people, such as Andy Brack, a syndicated columnist, argued that the governor should not have to resign, because "his job had nothing to do with his infidelity" (Rutenberg and Brown 2009).

CNN's headline read "South Carolina Gov. Sanford Admits Extramarital Affair." Although this headline is similar to ones used in the John Edwards scandal, the story details were much different. The facts in this instance were framed by their dramatic elements. It is not until the end of the article that readers find information regarding his political future, which appears to make that aspect of the story somehow less important. Using descriptors such as "his voice choking at times" and many quotes from Sanford and his wife presented an emotional story of betrayal, marital strain, romance, and sex. In e-mails published in a Columbian newspaper months prior to Sanford's apology, he allegedly wrote, "I could digress and say that you have the ability to give magnificent gentle kisses, or that I love your tan lines or that I love the curve of your hips, the erotic beauty of holding yourself (or two magnificent parts of yourself) in the faded glow of the night's light—but hey, that would be going into sexual details" ("South Carolina Gov. Sanford Admits Extramarital Affair" 2009).

Unlike CNN, the *Washington Post* story, "The Fix: S.C. Governor Mark Sanford Admits Affair" (Cillizza 2010) focused much more on the facts of the case and on his apology. The story did not relay the e-mail messages or present the information in a dramatic manner. The article also relayed the doubtfulness of his future political career. The author writes, "Sanford's 2012 candidacy (for the Republican nomination for the presidency) is almost certainly over."

Fox News had perhaps the most interesting coverage of the Sanford scandal. In its story, "Sanford Admits Affair after Secret Argentina Trip" ("Sanford Admits Affair after Secret Argentina Trip" 2009) facts were framed using dramatic elements, similar to the CNN story. *Fox News* also chose to include some of the sordid details of the affair through the e-mail messages. "My heart cries out for you, your voice, your body, the touch of your lips, the touch of your fingertips and an even deeper connection to your soul," Sanford writes to his lover in the summer of 2008. An interesting tidbit about the *Fox News* story is that in addition to burying the fact that Sanford was a Republican governor toward the end of the lengthy story, *Fox News*'s on-air coverage of the Sanford's press conference labeled him a Democrat ("Fox News Apologizes for Identifying Sanford as a Democrat" 2009). It is difficult to imagine that this was an innocent gaffe on the part of *Fox News*. Mark Sanford, while perhaps was not a well-known politician to people nationwide, was the leader of the Republican Governor's Association—something of which employees of any news service would be aware. Although *Fox News*'s subsequent coverage of the Sanford scandal properly identified his political party, the "damage" had already been done. The problem with corrections and retractions of facts is that once misinformation has been distributed, it is difficult to reach all those who heard the misinformation and it is difficult to have them remember new facts. The audience has already formed its initial impressions about the Sanford scandal and has already perceived something about the scandal based on the information provided.

Research from Media Matters found that in four hours of coverage of the scandal on *Fox News* during the day following his press conference, the news outlet only featured scandals committed by Democrats to try to explain what may happen with Sanford ("Fox News Omits Republican Scandals" 2009). The combination of the Democrat label and the examples of sex scandals committed by Democrats certainly appear to show *Fox News* attempting to frame the scandal as a "Democrat scandal" or as an issue more in line with the behavior of Democrats than Republicans. This is not to imply that *Fox News* never discussed Republican sex scandals in relation to the Sanford case, as later that same day there was discussion regarding the John Ensign scandal. However, this coverage appears to be an attempt in trying to prime audience members to associate the Mark Sanford scandal with being a Democrat.

Talk radio hosts such as Rush Limbaugh also had interesting theories about the Sanford scandal. The *Rush Limbaugh Show* on June 25, 2009, framed the scandal as an example of how hope has been lost in the United States. Limbaugh is correct that Sanford had recently lost his battle to refuse federal stimulus money, but it seems an extreme stretch that because Barack Obama was elected president, Sanford lost all hope in the United States, decided to engage in an extramarital affair with an Argentinian woman, had no desire to continue his political career, and took off because the "Country was going to hell in a handbasket . . . and I just want to enjoy life" (Linkins 2009). Limbaugh frames the story as one where the true responsibility for Sanford's actions lies with other people, Barack Obama, Democrats, the recession, the stimulus money, stress, and lack of hope for the future. In other words, circumstances resulted in Sanford's decisions that lead to his affair, not any personal or ethical flaws.

As has been mentioned, the overwhelming majority of Americans say that extramarital affairs are morally taboo (Newport 2009). So, stories that emphasize affairs are likely to negatively affect the public's perception of the offender. A CNN poll demonstrates this as it found that 54 percent of respondents thought Sanford should resign his position (Steinhauser 2009). Interestingly, there was no difference between Republicans and Democrats on this matter, despite the varied frames of news organizations and talk show hosts (Steinhauser 2009).

With regard to Limbaugh's discussions regarding the Edwards scandal, he frames the story as one of personal character flaws and a calculating political mind—both internal attributions as the cause of the Edwards affair. Quotes such as, "There's nothing genuine about John Edwards, he is a walking, talking political calculation," and "Political people are different than you and I, and, you know, most people when told a family member's been diagnosed with the kind of cancer Elizabeth Edwards has, they turn to God. The Edwards turned to the campaign. Their religion is politics and the quest for the White House, and it's not just with them. I mean that's part and parcel of political people" (Limbaugh 2008).

While Limbaugh gave Sanford a pass on his behavior because of the state of the country and other external causes, he did not use the same explanations for the Edwards scandal. The frames Limbaugh chose in these two scandals demonstrate a social psychological concept named the Ultimate Attribution Error (Hewstone 1990). The Ultimate Attribution Error occurs when negative behaviors of members from an in-group are attributed to external causes, and the same or similar behaviors of members of an out-group are attributed to internal causes. In other words, when members of an out-group commit behaviors as seen as undesirable, the behavior will be attributed to internal flaws and dispositional causes (Pettigrew 1979). On the other hand, if members of an out-group act in a desirable manner, behaviors will be perceived as an exception to the rule, luck, or the result of lots of effort (Pettigrew 1979).

Although relatively little empirical evidence has examined intergroup causal attribution, Pettigrew predicted that the ultimate attribution error would be more pronounced in situations where the groups have negative histories with one another. Although he was referring to racial and ethnic differences, this concept appears to work in the political realm, as well. There are perhaps few groups who attack one another as publicly and regularly as those who are staunchly conservative Republican and those who are staunchly liberal Democrats.

Limbaugh's framing of Sanford as a leader who was just trying to do right by the people of South Carolina by fighting the federal government, while calling Edwards a "fraud" and a "liar" for his actions presents an interesting case study of the framing of members of in groups versus members of out groups.

As for Sanford's political future, only time will tell if he can come back to political power. It appears that the media coverage of the Sanford scandal also influenced what people thought about him and his position as governor. A CNN poll conducted in June 2009 revealed that, "54 percent think Sanford should step down, with 44 percent saying he should continue to serve as South Carolina governor" (Steinhauser 2009). Interestingly, there was no difference among Republicans and Democrats polled on this matter. The poll results also indicated that six out of ten people do think that voters should know about politicians' sexual indiscretions, especially when the politician is married. Polls from *USA Today* also found that the majority, 63 percent, identified Sanford as a political "loser" for 2009 (Page 2009). A poll from *Rasmussen Reports* in May 2010 ("Election 2010" 2010) revealed a 72 percent disapproval rating, but only three months later his disapproval rating had fallen to 53 percent of South Carolina voters. Although he cannot seek another term as governor, it appears despite his sex scandal, he may still have a political future.

Larry Craig

Sen. Larry Craig, another Republican involved in a sex scandal, served as a member of Congress for 28 years ("Craig, Larry Edwin" 2010). He is a married and the father of three adopted children ("Larry Craig Biography" 2010). Craig had been a "vigorous fighter for conservative causes" and an outspoken critic of Bill Clinton during his affair with Monica Lewinsky, something that would come to haunt him in 2007 ("Larry Craig Biography" 2010).

The Larry Craig scandal also presents competing frames among liberal and conservative leaning media outlets. The *Pew Excellence in Journalism Talk Show Index* for September 2–7, 2007, listed the Craig scandal as comprising 16 percent of the news hole in talk shows (Jurkowitz 2007a). *Fox News* host Sean Hannity seemed unable to decide how to frame the Craig scandal. "Either he's the unluckiest guy in the world or he's leading a double life . . . I can't determine . . . I don't know," Hannity said. Bill O'Reilly took a pragmatic approach, Craig is a political liability, while liberal host Randi Rhodes emphasized the hypocritical nature of Republicans and called Craig a "front-runner phony" (Jukowitz 2007b). Host Ed Schultz, a liberal/centrist host framed the issue as one of secrecy. Schultz quips, "The thing that bothers me the most about the Craig thing is that something happened with law enforcement and it went unreported to the Ethics Committee or Republican leadership. (Craig) shouldn't have the liberty . . . to be able to hide an arrest."

The Craig scandal received more coverage from radio than from any other media outlet. The *News Coverage Index* for September 2–7, 2007, reveals that 3 percent of newspaper stories, 4 percent of online news sources, 5 percent of network television news, 10 percent of cable news, and 16 percent of radio stories were devoted to the Craig scandal (Jurkowitz 2007a). Radio talk shows continued to discuss this story for the next several weeks, even when other media outlets had moved on to other issues.

Although these story ratings are much smaller than Edwards had during the initial coverage of his scandal, Craig's scandal produced the most stories over time than any of these scandals or other political sex scandals such as the Eliot Spitzer, John Ensign, and Kwame Kilpatrick scandals, and even more stories than the Tiger Woods sex scandal. There may be many possible explanations for the differences in media coverage, but one that must be considered is that this scandal involved homosexuality, an arrest essentially for lewd behavior, and Craig's history of rumors regarding his sexuality.

In the early 1980s, he had allegedly been involved with a congressional page, although the House Ethics Committee's investigation failed to find evidence to support the claim ("Larry Craig Biography" 2010). The rumors regarding his sexual activities ran counter to Craig's long list of votes that could be considered anti-gay. For example, he voted "No" to adding sexual orientation to the definition of hate crimes in 2002, "No" to prohibit job discrimination based on sexual orientation in 1996, and "Yes" to a constitutional ban of same-sex marriage in 2006 ("Larry Craig on Civil Rights" 2010).

How did media other than talk shows frame the scandal? The *Washington Post* article, "Idaho Senator Asserts: I Never Have Been Gay," framed the story as a legal and ethical issue (Kane 2007). Similarly, *the New York Times* story, "Senator, Arrested at Airport, Pleads Guilty," framed the story as a legal issue as it relayed facts from the arrest ("Senator, Arrest at Airport, Pleads Guilty" 2007). The *Times* article also used the political future frame as it described the upcoming election year.

Fox News also framed the story as a legal and political issue. The Fox story was titled "Idaho Senator Larry Craig Resigns" (Garrett 2007).The story did not discuss the details of the arrest or the fact that he was arrested for allegedly attempting to engage in sex with another man in the Minnesota airport. It is not until the very last sentence that the story includes any reference to Craig's denial of homosexuality. On the other hand, CNN's story on August 28, 2007, "Craig: I Did Nothing 'Inappropriate' in Airport Bathroom," was framed as a story first of denial, then dramatic elements, and the ethics investigation. The story began with a quote from Craig that reads, "[I] overreacted and made a poor decision." It continues with Craig's denial of homosexuality, "Let me be clear: I am not gay and never have been," his perception that he is a victim of a "witch hunt" investigated by the *Idaho Statesman* newspaper, and his remorse at pleading guilty to the lewd conduct charges: "In pleading guilty, I overreacted in Minneapolis, because of the stress of the Idaho Statesman's investigation and the rumors it has fueled around Idaho" ("Craig: I Did Nothing 'Inappropriate'" 2007). Unlike the *Fox News* story, the CNN article detailed Craig's arrest using dramatic details from the arrest report such as "Craig's blue eyes were clearly visible through the crack in the door" and "Craig would look down at his hands, fidget with his fingers, and then look through the crack into my stall again" ("Craig: I Did Nothing 'Inappropriate'" 2007). *ABC News*'s story, "Craig Resigns after Sex Scandal" (Cook 2007) frames the story as one of political fallout and an ethical issue. "The news of Craig's arrest and plea elicited a swift response from scandal-weary Republicans"

(*Craig Resigns* 2007). Similar to the Sanford case, Craig's colleagues in the Senate were quick to abandon him and several Republicans, including John McCain, Norm Coleman, and Peter Hoekstra, called for his resignation (Stout 2007). Additional party leaders such as Mitch McConnell, Trent Lott, and Jon Kyl issued a statement relaying that Craig had "agreed to comply" with their request to step down from his leadership positions until the Ethics Committee resolved the situation (Stout 2007). Although Craig did comply with Republican Party leaders' requests to step down from leadership roles in the committees on which he served, he did not resign his seat. Despite the lack of support by his party, Craig finished his term and did not seek re-election.

The big question that needs to be examined is how did the public respond to these stories in the media? It appears that the result of the media blitz, the largely negatively framed messages, and perhaps even the calls for Craig's resignation by his own party leaders made this a salient story among members of the public. Similar to the other scandals discussed here, the majority of those polled, 67 percent, said Craig should resign his Senate seat ("Majority Says Craig Should Stick with Resignation" 2007). Also, similar to the Sanford scandal, this CNN poll found, "Solid majorities of both Republicans and Democrats said that the embattled Idaho senator should go" ("Majority Says Craig Should Stick with Resignation" 2007).

Analysis

Given the hundreds of stories relayed through the media regarding each of these political sex scandals, it appears the media is performing an agenda-setting function, it is telling people what to think about. In the scandals discussed here, it also seems that the media were successful in telling people how to think about the scandals and what to do about it. The polling data for each scandal shows an overwhelmingly negative perception of each politician and, in fact, reveals that, based on information presented in the media, many people polled were in favor of removing the politician from office.

Among these three scandals, two frames are present in each one: the lying/denial frame and the political future frame. However, examining the headlines during the first days of a political sex scandal shows that different media do tend to frame the stories differently. The *New York Times* and the *Washington Post* tended to frame the scandals as a more factual accounting of the events that happened, when compared to cable news channels. Cable news channels, on the other hand, tended to emphasize the dramatic elements of the scandal, especially in the cases of Mark Sanford and Larry Craig, where details were available from the source, as in the case of Sanford, or from police reports in Craig's case. The headlines presented here also show differences in cable news scandal coverage based on ideology.

Thompson (2000) examined three elements that tend to be featured in political sex scandals: hypocrisy, conflicts of interest, and "second-order transgressions" (125). Although political sex scandals rarely produce much surprise among citizens today, given their regularity, scandal coverage certainly produces backlash among voters. Some, like Thompson, argue that it is the hypocrisy of the "Do as I say, not as I do" mentality of politicians caught in sex scandals that is so damaging.

As the Mark Sanford scandal demonstrates, "A politician whose private life is seen to diverge significantly from his or her publicly stated policies (or those of his or her party or government) may find that his or her position becomes untenable" (Thompson 2000, 126). Sanford's decisions to engage in an extramarital affair, to double state-funded business trips as trysts, and to leave his responsibilities as governor unquestionably put him at odds with the Republican Party. The Larry Craig scandal also demonstrates a private life that is at odds with his stated policies. The hypocrisy of his voting record and alleged activities as well as his membership in the conservative Republican Party resulted in immediate calls for his resignation.

Perhaps the most damning element of political sex scandals is lying. All three of the scandals presented in this chapter included the ramifications of misleading the public. John Edwards, who denied his affair for nearly two years, finally owned up to his actions when mounting evidence against him could no longer be denied; Mark Sanford admitted his affair after he was found to be out of the country and not hiking the Appalachian Trail as he had reported; Larry Craig hid his arrest from his party and his colleagues and continues to deny what police report to have had happened in that fateful airport men's room. Of these scandals, it is Edwards who has likely lost the most politically and he appears to be the politician who lied the most. Edwards's lying and the media's coverage of the scandal have, to this point in time, abbreviated his potentially long-lasting, high-profile political career. His lying has also invited investigations into his campaign finances and as recently as October 2010, subpoenas have been served as part of the ongoing investigation. The investigation stems from his purported attempts to cover up his affair. "To me, John Edwards is despicable, he broke the trust of everyone who believed in him, and worse. I would not vote for him for dog catcher" (Skipling 2010). If this sentiment is in any way shared by others, it is clear that nearly two years after his actions and lying, this is what people remember about John Edwards.

Works Cited

Berger, Judson. "What Is He Thinking? Sanford Violates All Rules of Sex Scandal Management." *Fox News*, July 1, 2009. Accessed October 22, 2010 (http://www.foxnews.com/politics/2009/07/01/thinking-sanford-violates-rules-sex-scandal-management/).

Brown, Robbie, and Shaila Dewan. "Mysteries Remain after Governor Admits an Affair." *New York Times*, June 24, 2009. Accessed September 2, 2010 (www.nytimes.com/2009/06/25/us/25sanford.html?ref=mark_sanford).

Cappella, Joseph, and Kathleen Hall Jamieson. *Spiral of Cynicism: The Press and the Public Good*. Oxford: Oxford University Press, 1997.

Cillizza, Chris. "The Fix: S.C. Governor Mark Sanford Admits Affair." *Washington Post*, June 24, 2009. Accessed September 2, 2010(www.washingtonpost.com/wp-dyn/content/article/2009/06/24/AR2009062402504.html).

Cook, Theresa. "Craig Resigns After Sex Scandal." *ABC News*, September 1, 2007. Accessed September 22, 2010(http://abcnews.go.com/Politics/story?id=3546350&page=1).

"Craig: I Did Nothing 'Inappropriate' in Airport Bathroom." *CNN*, August 28, 2007. Accessed September 20, 2010 (http://articles.cnn.com/2007-08-28/politics/craig.arrest_1_idaho-republican-senator-craig-airport-bathroom?_s=PM:POLITICS).

"Craig, Larry Edwin." *Biographical Directory of the United States Congress*. Accessed October 12, 2010 (http://bioguide.congress.gov/scripts/biodisplay.pl?index=c000858).

"Edwards Admits to Extramarital Affair," *CNN*, August 8, 2008. Accessed August 15,2010 (http://articles.cnn.com/2008-08-08/politics/edwards.affair_1_edwards-campaign-aide-john-edwards-rielle-hunter?_s=PM:POLITICS).

"Edwards Could Face Political Free Fall from Affair." *CNN*, August 9, 2008. Accessed August 15, 2010 (http://articles.cnn.com/2008-08-09/politics/edwards.affair_1_elizabeth-edwards-john-edwards-political-career?_s=PM:POLITICS).

"Edwards Ex-Mistress Rules Out Paternity Test; Strange Behavior Leaves Many Unanswered Questions in Edwards Affair." *FOX News*, August 9, 2008. Accessed August 1, 2010 (www.foxnews.com/story/0,2933,400962,00.html).

"Election 2010: South Carolina Democratic Primary for Governor." Rasmussen Reports. May 21, 2010. Accessed October 9, 2010 (www.rasmussenreports.com/public_content/politics/elections/election_2010/election_2010_governor_elections/south_carolina/election_2010_south_carolina_democratic_primary_for_governor).

Entman, Robert. "Framing: Toward Clarification of a Fractured Paradigm." *Journal of Communication*, 1993; 43: 51–58.

"Fox News 'Apologizes' for Identifying Sanford as a Democrat, Saying, He Is, Of Course, a Republican." *Media Matters*, June 25, 2009. Accessed October 1,2010 (http://mediamatters.org/mmtv/200906250030).

"Fox News Omits Republican Scandals in Assessment of Sanford Prospects." *Media Matters*, June 25, 2009. Accessed October 1, 2010 (http://mediamatters.org/research/200906250041).

Frias, Mariecar, Sarah Netter, and Imaeyen Ibanga. "Sanford's Unorthodox Apology for Affair 'Will Sink Him'—While Most Philandering Politicians Keep Apologies Brief, Sanford Gave Details of Affair." *ABC News,* June 25, 2009. Accessed September 2, 2010 (http://abcnews.go.com/GMA/Politics/story?id=7922704&page=1).

Gallup Polls. 2008. "Favorability: People in the News." Accessed July 25, 2010. (www.gallup.com/poll/1618/Favorability-People-News.aspx#3).

Gallup Polls. 2009. "John Edwards, Sarah Palin Both See Favorable Ratings Slide." Accessed July 25, 2010(www.gallup.com/poll/123698/John-Edwards-Sarah-Palin-Favorable-Ratings-Slide.aspx).

Garrett, Major. 2007. "Idaho Senator Larry Craig Resigns." *FOX News,* September 3. Accessed September 20, 2010 (www.foxnews.com/story/0,2933,295457,00.html).

Goffman, Erving. 1974. *Frame Analysis*. New York: Harper & Row.

Hart, Peter, and Bill McInturff. 2009. *NBC/WSJ Poll*. Accessed November 20, 2010 (www.pollingreport.com/people.html).

Hewstone, Miles. "The 'Ultimate Attribution Error'? A Review of the Literature on Intergroup Causal Attribution." *European Journal of Social Psychology* 20 (1990): 311–335.

Holland, Keating. 1998. "Clinton's Approval Rating Hits New High," *CNN*, February 1. Accessed October 1, 2010 (http://articles.cnn.com/1998-02-01/politics/clinton.poll_1_approval-rating-timecnn-poll-latest-poll?_s=PM:ALLPOLITICS).

"How TV News Played the Edwards Scandal." *Pew Research Center's Project For Excellence in Journalism*. 2008. Accessed October 9, 2010 (www.journalism.org/node/12358).

"John Edwards Admits to Affair, Denies He's Father of Lover's Child." *FOX News*, August 9, 2008. Accessed August 1, 2010 (www.foxnews.com/story/0,2933,400481,00.html).

"John Edwards' Affair with Rielle Hunter: Admits Infidelity." *The Huffington Post*, August 8, 2008. Accessed August 5, 2010 (www.huffingtonpost.com/2008/08/08/edwards-admits-sexual-aff_n_117780.html).

Joslyn, Mark R. "Framing the Lewinsky Affair: Third-Person Judgments by Scandal Frame." *Political Psychology*, 2003; 24: 829–844.

Jurkowitz, Mark. "A Message From Osama Puts Terror in the News." *Pew Research Center's Project for Excellence in Journalism*, News Coverage Index, September 2–7, 2007a. Accessed August 17, 2010 (www.journalism.org/node/7469).

——. "Talk Hosts Sound Off On Craig and Thompson," *Pew Research Center's Project for Excellence in Journalism*, 2007b. Accessed August 17, 2010 (www.journalism.org/node/7522).

——. "As the Plot Thickens, The Jackson Saga Dominates." *Pew Research Center's Project for Excellence in Journalism*, 2009. Accessed July 29, 2010 (www.journalism.org/index_report/pej_news_coverage_index_june_29_july_52009).

Kane, Paul. "Idaho Senator Asserts: I Never Have Been Gay." *Washington Post*, August 29, 2007. Accessed September 20, 2010 (www.washingtonpost.com/wpdyn/content/article/2007/08/28/AR2007082801196.html).

Keck, Kristi. "Political Sex Scandals a Nonpartisan Affair." *CNN*, July 14, 2009. Accessed July 25, 2010 (www.cnn.com/2009/POLITICS/07/14/political.sex.scandals.index.html?iref=allsearch).

Klein, Rick, and Jennifer Parker. "Democrats Move Quick to Lessen Damage of John Edwards Affair." *ABC News*, August 8, 2008. Accessed August 15, 2010 (http://abcnews.go.com/Politics/Vote2008/story?id=5544983).

Kosicki, Gerald. "The Media Priming Effect," in *The Persuasion Handbook: Developments in Theory and Practice*, edited by James Price Dillard and Michael Pfau. Thousand Oaks, CA: Sage Publications, 2002: 63–81.

Kurtz, Howard, and Lois Romano. "Edwards Admits He Had An Affair." *Washington Post*, August 9, 2008. Accessed August 15, 2010 (www.washingtonpost.com/wp-dyn/content/article/2008/08/08/AR2008080802371.html).

"Larry Craig Biography." *Biography*. Accessed October 12, 2010(www.biography.com/articles/Larry-Craig-588884)

"Larry Craig on Civil Rights." *On the Issues*. Accessed October 13, 2010(www.ontheissues.org/senate/Larry_Craig.htm).

Limbaugh. 2008. "Edwards Has Always Been A Fraud." Accessed October 9, 2010 (www.rush-limbaugh.com/home/daily/site_081208/content/01125114.guest.html).

Linkins, Jason. "Limbaugh Blames Sanford's Affair On Obama, Because Why Not?" *The Huffington Post*, June 25, 2009. Accessed October 9, 2010(www.huffingtonpost.com/2009/06/25/limbaugh-blames-sanfords_n_220993.html).

"Majority Says Craig Should Stick with Resignation." *CNN*, September 10, 2007. Accessed November 20, 2010 (http://politicalticker.blogs.cnn.com/2007/09/10/majority-says-craig-should-stick-with-resignation/)

McCombs, Maxwell, and George Estrada. "The News Media and the Pictures in Our Heads," in *Do the Media Govern? Politicians, Voters, and Reporters in America*, edited by Shanto Iyengar and Richard Reeves. Thousand Oaks, CA: Sage, 1997: 237–247.

McCombs, Maxwell, and Donald Shaw. "The Agenda Setting Function of Mass Media." *Public Opinion Quarterly*, 1972;36: 176–187.

"Milestones: John Edwards." *New York Times*, November 20, 2007. Accessed October 3, 2010 (www.nytimes.com/interactive/2007/11/20/us/politics/20071120_EDWARDS_TIMELINE.html?ref=john_edwards).

Newport, Frank. "Extramarital Affairs, Like Sanford's, Morally Taboo." *Gallup Polls*, June 25, 2009. Accessed July 25, 2010 (www.gallup.com/poll/121253/Extramarital-Affairs-Sanford-Morally-Taboo.aspx).

Owen, Diana. "Popular Politics and the Clinton/Lewinsky Affair: The Implications for Leadership." *Political* Psychology, 2000; 21: 161–177.

Page, Susan. "The Biggest Political Winners and Losers of 2009." *USA Today*, December 31,2009. Accessed November 20, 2010 (www.usatoday.com/news/washington/political-inners-losers-2009.htm).

Pan, Zhongdang, and Gerald Kosicki. "Framing as Strategic Action in Public Deliberation," in *Framing Public Life: Perspectives on Media and Our Understanding of the Social World*, edited by Stephen Reese, Oscar Gandy and August Grant. Mahwah, NJ: Lawrence Erlbaum, 2003; 35–65.

Pettigrew, Thomas P. "The Ultimate Attribution Error: Extending Allport's Cognitive Analysis of Prejudice." *Personality and Social Psychology Bulletin*, 1979; 5: 462–477.

Rosenstiel, Tom, Paul Hitlin, and Mahvish Shahid Khan. "Media Swing from Protests in Iran to the Passing of the King of Pop," *Pew Research Center's Project for Excellence in Journalism*. 2009. Accessed July 29, 2010 (www.journalism.org/index_report/pej_news_coverage_ index_june_22_28_2009).

Rutenberg, Jim, and Robbie Brown. 2009. "Governor Used State's Money to Visit Lover." *New York Times*, June 25. Accessed September 2, 2010(www.nytimes.com/2009/06/26/us/26sanford.html?scp=4&sq=mark%20sanford%20june%202009&st=cse).

"Sanford Admits Affair after Secret Argentina Trip." *FOX News*, June 24, 2009. Accessed September 2, 2010 (www.foxnews.com/politics/2009/06/24/sanford-admits-affair-secret-argentina-trip/).

Sartor, Tricia, and Dana Page. "When Infidelity Makes Headlines." *Pew Research Center's Project for Excellence in Journalism*, February 24, 2010. Accessed July 25, 2010 (www.journalism.org/numbers_report/when_infidelity_make_headlines).

Sauer, Bobbie Kyle. "10 Things You Didn't Know About Mark Sanford." *US News and World Report*, May 22, 2008. Accessed October 6, 2010 (http://politics.usnews.com/news/campaign-2008/articles/2008/05/22/10-things-you-didnt-know-about-mark-sanford.html).

Schouten, Fredreka, and David Jackson. "Edwards' Political Future in Doubt After Admitting Affair." *USA Today*, August 8, 2008. Accessed August 15, 2010(www.usatoday.com/news/politics/election2008/2008-08-08-edwards_N.htm).

Seelye, Katharine Q. "Edwards Admits to Affair in 2006." *New York Times*, August 9, 2008. Accessed September 7, 2010(www.nytimes.com/2008/08/09/us/politics/09edwards.html?pagewanted=1&_r=1).

"Senator, Arrested at Airport, Pleads Guilty." *New York Times*, August 28, 2007. Accessed September 20, 2010 (www.nytimes.com/2007/08/28/washington/28craig.html?_r=2&ref=larry_e_craig).

Skipling. "John Edwards Case Subpoenas Issued." *The Huffington Post*, October 7, 2010. Accessed October 10, 2010 (www.huffingtonpost.com/2010/10/06/john-edwards-case-subpoenas-issued_n_753511.html).

"South Carolina Gov. Sanford Admits Extramarital Affair." *CNN*, June 24, 2009. Accessed September 2, 2010 (http://articles.cnn.com/2009-06-24/politics/south.carolina. governor_1_jenny-sanford-south-carolina-gov-buenos-aires?_s=PM:POLITICS).

Steinhauser, Paul. 2009. *CNN Poll: Americans Think Sanford Should Resign*. June 30. Accessed October 20, 2010 (http://politicalticker.blogs.cnn.com/2009/06/30/cnn-poll-americans-think-sanford-should-resign/).

Stout, David. *Idaho Senator's Colleagues Say He Should Resign*. August 30, 2007. Accessed November 20, 2010 (www.nytimes.com/2007/08/30/washington/30craig.html).

Thompson, John B. *Political Scandal: Power and Visibility in the Media Age*. Oxford: Polity Press, 2000.

"Which Scandals Make Big News?" *Pew Research Center's Project for Excellence in Journalism*, August 6, 2008. Accessed August 1, 2010. (www.journalism.org/node/12243)..

Woodruff, Bob. "John Edwards Interview." *ABC News*, August 8, 2008. Accessed August 15, 2010 (http://abcnews.go.com/Politics/story?id=5544981).

Yioutas, Julie, and Ivana, Segvic. "Revisiting the Clinton/Lewinsky Scandal: The Covergence of Agenda Setting and Framing." *Journalism & Mass Communication Quarterly*, 2003;80: 567–582.

Yost, Pete, and David Scott. 2008. "Edwards Ally Defends Payment to Mistress from PAC." *The Huffington Post*, August 15. Accessed August 5, 2010(www.huffingtonpost. com/2008/08/15/edwards-ally-defends-paym_n_119114.html).

CHAPTER 7

Love Means Sometimes Having to Say You're Sorry

Richard Knight

"I don't think there is a fancy way to say that I have sinned."
—*Bill Clinton, September 11, 1998*

The American public is often criticized for its lack of political knowledge, voter apathy, and ignorance of important political issues. As sociologist Michael Schudson asks, "[H]ow can the United States claim to be a model democracy if its citizens know so little about political life" (Schudson 2000, 16)? He then answers his own question, stating that, "one reason Americans have so much difficulty grasping the political facts of life is that their political system is the world's most complex" (Schudson 2000, 17). Ilya Somin further argues that low levels of political knowledge in the United States are "in large part a result of 'rational ignorance' caused by the insignificance of any one vote to electoral outcomes" (Somin 2003, 4). But while an alarmingly large number of Americans may not grasp the system or be able to tell you who their representatives are, it is a safe bet that most can tell you who Eliot Spitzer, Larry Craig, and Mark Sanford are, and what they are best known for: political scandals.

Political scientists and communication specialists agree that the media are more interested in scandals than more complex political issues, as they are a way of humanizing politicians (Brenton 2007). Additionally, the power distance between the constituency and their representatives is certainly reduced when ignominy befalls the powerful. And while it likely titillates the mentality of the public to hear about their elected officials being caught with their pants down, they also demand explanations, details, and an apology or defense every time it happens. Whether the motivation is found to be love, lust, or the devil himself, sex scandals have shown us how important it is for our public figures to learn how to correctly apologize for their misdeeds. In fact, it is an art form that has been practiced since antiquity (likely around as long as the oldest profession in the world).

The study and practice of *apologia*, or the speech of self-defense, was prescribed as far back as Aristotle and is still analyzed today, particularly in the context of instant media promulgation. *Apologia* and political rhetoric are interwoven any time an elected official responds to an accusation against his or her character, and public response is often judged according to the message's perceived sincerity and accuracy. By analyzing the responses of various politicians who have found themselves entangled in scandals of a sexual nature, we begin to better understand the character of political discourse and rhetorical self-defense. Thus, it is imperative to explore *apologia* as a rhetorical genre, the apologies for inappropriate behavior involving politicians' sex scandals as a subject for rhetorical investigation, and to devise a way to compare and contrast the messages to better recognize the nature of contemporary responses by fallen politicians.

Traditionally, *apologia* is defined as a speech of self-defense. A feature common to *apologia* is that those accused of an offense will be expected to face their accusers and speak in defense of themselves (Vartabedian 1985). *Apologia* includes responses to personal affronts, such as "the questioning of a man's moral nature, motives, or reputation" (Ware and Linkugel 1973, 274). Accordingly, the questioning of one's policies would not typically occasion an apologetic response. The speech of self-defense is also a vehicle for repairing a person's damaged *ethos,* or credibility (see Butler 1972; Kruse 1981). The more we learn about the prescribed speech that is typical of this genre, the more we begin to see that the English word "apology" derives chiefly from a strategy of response (and maybe not actually meaning we are sorry, despite the way our parents explained it to us). Indeed, we may also view *apologia* as a "symbolic strategy" as well as a responsive one (Downey 1993, 60), particularly in cases where any type of immediate response is deemed necessary. In these cases, the strategies chosen are crucial to a politician's image.

Apologia has been the subject of substantial research both ancient and contemporary. A lasting feature has been the use of self-defense rhetoric to exonerate oneself. Self-defense rhetoric in this form will typically "manifest a variety of styles including appeals to traditional cultural values, invective, references to a greater divinity, reliance upon legitimate bases of power, factual accounts of an issue, and inductively reasoned organization" (Downey, 1993, 42–43). Indeed, the recurring theme of an accusation followed by the accused person's response permeates the history of public address.

Contemporary *apologia* is typically divided into periods prior to and following 1960, when political responses became regular television fare. After the sixties, the development of mass media, and thus the heightened need for political defense, gave rise to a period of self-serving apologetic responses. Afterward, with the proliferation of the media and political exigencies, the responses provided by public figures reflected the deliberative roots of this type of speech. Politicians typically used the occasions as vehicles of explanation, but would often usually shift the blame for their wrongdoing to others. Avoidance of a defense altogether in the face of inexplicable circumstances was another strategy often employed (e.g., Richard Nixon during the Watergate scandal, and Bill Clinton for a long period during 1998 after the Monica Lewinsky scandal came to light).

Formulas for apologies have traditional threads, but different theories have emerged to describe what types of responses are the best or at least the most typical. Since ancient times, it has been rightfully argued that one should analyze two variables in any given apologetic situation: (1) the actual defense in light of, (2) the specific attack. By doing so, we can better understand those issues most relevant to the act of self-defense as "the critic cannot have a complete understanding of accusation or apology without treating them both" (Ryan 1982, 254). Expanding upon these two variables, rhetorical scholar George Alexander Kennedy explains that the four fundamental tasks of the contemporary apologist are also still much the same as those practiced by the classical rhetorician:

> (1) a statement of the accusations, (2) a refutation of the charges, as well as a counter-attack or redirection of blame, (3) an explanation of the self-defense, and (4) the summation which reasserts the moral integrity of the apologist. (Kennedy 1963, 151)

In what is now regarded as a classic study on self-defense rhetoric entitled, "They Spoke in Defense of Themselves: On the Generic Criticism of *Apologia*," B. L. Ware and Wil Linkugel devised an approach to *apologia* that advanced our understanding of modern apologies significantly (Ware and Linkugel 1973). Previously, scholars would often explore the apologetic tradition from a historical or Aristotelian perspective, but Ware and Linkugel devised a critical framework to "discover those factors which characterize the apologetic form" and "to discover the subgenres or the types of discourses within the genre" (Ware and Linkugel 1973, 274). The authors postulated that there are four "factors" that invariably appear in self-defense rhetoric: Denial, Bolstering, Differentiation, and Transcendence. The Denial strategy is a renunciation by a speaker of any participation in, relationship to, or positive sentiment toward that which has repelled the audience ("I didn't do it!"). Bolstering amounts to the apologist's attempt to be identified with that perceived as commendatory by an audience ("Remember all the good I have done for the people since I have been in office!"). Differentiation strategies have an apologist particularize the charges at hand that moves the audience toward a new and less abstract perspective ("This has nothing to do with my job as a politician!"). Finally, Transcendence steers an audience away from an accusation's circumstances and toward a more abstract and general view of the accused person's character ("What is more important here— that we learn about some possible personal transgressions or that I do what I was elected to do and that is continue to serve my constituency and make their lives better?").

The formula for a speech of apology can provide a solid blueprint for observers and apologists alike, but each situation dictates a comprehension of its unique circumstances. For example, while those engaging in public self-defense usually attempt to appear sincerely contrite for misconduct, we can surmise that a repair of their reputation is probably the general motive for their discourse. This objective, in turn, determines the manner in which apologists focus upon the "presentations of their characters as they wish their audiences to perceive them . . . occurring when one's character is attacked or is perceived to have been attacked" (Kruse 1981, 290). Therefore, *apologia* has also been conceptualized as "public discourse produced whenever a prominent person attempts to repair his character if it has been directly or indirectly damaged by overt charges, or rumors and allegations, which negatively value his behavior and/or his judgment" (Kruse 1977, 13). A significant study that elucidates this further in the case of political scoundrels is "Political Apologia: The Ritual of Self-Defense" by Ellen Reid Gold, who states that any attack casting suspicion upon a public leader's moral character may hinder his or her ability to function as a public leader, and that "aspiring presidents can literally be made or broken on their ability to practice the ritual of self-defense" (Gold 1977, 316).

Political Sex Scandal and Public Apology

Arguably the most notorious political sex scandal in recent American history was the one that was instrumental in leading to the imbroglio of Bill Clinton's second term as president. In January 1998, accusations that president Clinton committed perjury, suborned perjury, and obstructed justice to cover up the Monica Lewinsky affair were taken seriously. Underlying the matter were moral implications of adultery and lying while under oath. This scandal resulted in a congressional inquiry and impeachment. Special Counsel Kenneth Starr was granted permission from Attorney General Janet Reno in January 1998 to expand his Whitewater investigation to include a possible sexual relationship with former White House intern Monica Lewinsky. He believed Clinton had lied to Paula Jones's attorneys about that relationship in a legal deposition. Legal authorities debated whether Clinton's testimony constituted perjury, but there were additional charges, as well.

Starr found that Clinton had possibly suborned perjury by promising Lewinsky employment in a Fortune 500 company if she would lie about the affair under oath. Starr also claimed that Clinton obstructed justice by asking Lewinsky to return gifts allegedly given to her (Abse and Crites 1998). If Clinton had had a sexual relationship with Monica Lewinsky and persuaded her to make false denials under oath, then Clinton would be in jeopardy of possible impeachment, criminal prosecution, or both. These circumstances detail two main accusations levied against Clinton. In January 1998, he was accused of (1) committing adultery, and (2) suborning of perjury.

Particularly interesting about Clinton's case is the revelation of a sex scandal in the process of investigation of other matters. This appears to be one common theme among politicians who have had their extramarital scandals revealed. Gaining a better understanding of the modern phenomenon of having to say you are sorry for getting caught in the act often involves exploring the surrounding context. Often, the sex scandal is unearthed while digging for a different kind of dirt. The statements that politicians create providing responses to the accusations surrounding sexual scandals are usually analyzed for their own qualities, but it should also be noted that many other factors surrounding the scandal are often utilized by politicians during their remarks. For example, by focusing primarily on aspects of their job, many of these individuals attempt to obfuscate the issue that their accusers have brought to the nation's attention. For the purpose of better understanding contemporary responses to sex scandals, we will explore the Clinton case further, but consider several other cases, as well.

In August 2004, Jim McGreevey announced that he would resign as governor of New Jersey after it was revealed that he had carried on an extramarital affair with Golan Cipel, the homeland security advisor whom McGreevey had appointed in 2002. McGreevey had endured severe criticism for the appointment, as Cipel could not gain federal clearances (as he was not a United States citizen) and public suspicions arose when the governor had confirmed a close friendship with Cipel, with whom he also traveled often. After being asked to step down from his appointed position, Cipel later threatened McGreevey with a sexual harassment lawsuit, which prompted the governor's resignation speech and his now-famous proclamation with his wife at his side: "I am a gay American" ("McGreevey" 2004).

Not everyone who is accused of having a homosexual affair is so forthcoming, especially when it is viewed as an inconsistent lifestyle choice for one's character. That was the case for Idaho Senator Larry Craig, who was arrested on June 11, 2007, and accused of soliciting an undercover police officer for sexual activity in an airport bathroom in Minneapolis-St. Paul. Craig initially insisted that he was innocent, but later pleaded guilty and paid a fine for a charge of disorderly conduct. Craig would later claim that the guilty plea was a mistake, and that he was just trying to handle the matter quickly to avoid publicity. The senator continually denied the incident and questions about his sexual orientation arose that he also denied, but he publicly announced that he would resign his office in September 2007, due to the shame he had brought to his state and the office he held. He later changed his position and served out his Senate term, leaving office on January 3, 2009, without seeking reelection.

The personal lives of politicians are public fare, especially when laws are broken in the process of personal transgression. As already addressed, in March 2008, *The New York Times* reported that New York Governor Eliot Spitzer was a client of an exclusive prostitution ring, and cited in particular that he had met with a $1,000-an-hour call girl named Ashley Rae Maika DiPietro. It was quickly revealed that Spitzer was a regular client with women from the agency over several years and investigators documented that he paid up to $80,000 for prostitutes in that time. Two days after the initial revelation, Spitzer delivered his resignation speech on March 12, 2008, avoiding impending impeachment proceedings.

The New York Times isn't the only newspaper that receives credit for breaking stories of sexual scandal in the political world. In addition to its earlier exposé of the Clinton–Jones entanglement, *The National Enquirer* reported in October 2007 that John Edwards had been involved in an extramarital affair with former campaign worker and videographer Rielle Hunter. Over the next year, it was also reported by several outlets that he had fathered a child with Hunter, which he initially denied but to which he later admitted. In the August 18, 2008, issue of *Newsweek*, Edwards achieved the dubious distinction of being the first person to ever score "100" in their 1 to 100 scale known as the "dignity index" of dubious behavior ("Dignity Index" 2008, 8). This was undoubtedly chiefly due to the fact that the affair occurred while his wife suffered from terminal cancer.

In more groundbreaking coverage of illicit activity, in January 2008, the *Detroit Free Press* reported that Detroit Mayor Kwame Kilpatrick had lied under oath, as proven by text messages recovered during an investigation of misconduct involving illegal firings of city police. The smoking gun in this case centered on text messages shared with Kilpatrick's chief of staff, Christine Beatty. Both Kilpatrick and Beatty had denied under oath that they had been involved in an extramarital sexual relationship, but the records revealed them to actually be "engaged in romantic banter as well as planning and recounting sexual liaisons" (Schaefer and Elrick 2008, 1A). While many other controversies plagued Kilpatrick's term of office, his response to these allegations in particular shaped the rhetorical tone of his defense in his resignation speech.

South Carolina Governor Mark Sanford, as mentioned, disappeared for six days in June 2009, and was out of contact with his family as well as his security detail and staff. While he had told staffers that he was going to be hiking the Appalachian Trail, in fact Sanford had flown to Argentina to spend time with his mistress and "soul mate," María Belén Chapur. The incident sparked nationwide attention, and within a week after his return, Sanford issued a "confession" speech on national television, wherein he apologized to a list of individuals and his constituency for his disappearance as well as for the affair. While afterward Sanford's wife left him and filed for divorce, he continued to serve as governor, even after several impeachment proceedings were introduced in the South Carolina House of Representatives (which ultimately failed).

There are several common themes to be considered among these cases. Obviously, each is an account of a high-profile politician involved in a sex scandal. While there are other very interesting figures in modern politics that were embroiled in sex scandals as well, not all were included here. For example, Representative Mark Foley gained national attention when it was revealed that he was sending sexual text messages to a teenage page, but his *apologia* consisted of a three-sentence letter of resignation rather than a televised speech. For consistency's sake, the format of the *apologia* in all cases explored here will be similar. These examples typify some other considerations, including the fact that each individual spoke in defense of himself using national media to cover the response to the accusations at hand. While this action has become an expectation, and perhaps in many cases a necessity, it is imperative to analyze each discourse and compare and contrast the rhetoric utilized by each politician to determine the successes and failures afforded by similar as well as divergent strategies.

Analog Criticism and Apologia

Lawrence Rosenfield posits a theory of criticism in which "the generic resemblance" of speeches "invites what may be called analog criticism" (Rosenfield 1968, 435). Basically, the parts of a speech that are distinctly associated with a response to attacks on one's character are compared and contrasted so that the observer engages in a representative analysis of the motivations as well as comparative artistic merit of the speaker's statements. Rosenfield's model serves as a helpful framework for understanding the remarks of public officials offering self-defense strategies in a very public format.

In his influential work, Rosenfield developed a criticism that examined Richard M. Nixon's "Checkers" speech from September 23, 1952, and Harry S. Truman's November 16, 1953, refutation of claims that he knowingly "allowed a Communist agent, Harry Dexter White, to hold high government office" (Rosenfield 1968, 435). The similarity of approach, if not specific content, of Nixon and Truman to the officials that respond publically to accusations about sex scandals is notable. While Rosenfield's original subjects were not being scrutinized for sexual misconduct, like Nixon and Truman, the politicians examined here today sought direct access to the American public via mass media broadcast to bring their messages of self-defense. Also, while the mass media apology was a new and untested rhetorical option in Nixon and Truman's time, it is a firmly implemented expectation in modern political life. Application of such an analog criticism framework to the discourse of our modern respondents will help to clarify the strategies employed by various politicians facing similar situations.

According to Rosenfield, similar communicative acts may be compared "in such ways that each address serves as a reference standard for the other" (Rosenfield 1968, 435). There are two reasons for this. First, one may compare and contrast the speeches in order to examine the basic fundamental elements of the address. Secondly, this method allows the observer to review the comparative artistic merit of each speech when compared with the others. This method of comparing and contrasting dates back to the most classic method of criticism—Aristotle's *topoi,* or topics discerned by their value in effecting persuasion (Foss 1989).

The advantages of examining several speeches by such comparative methods involve (1) objectivity, (2) analysis of similarities, (3) distinct awareness of differences, and (4) opportunity to judge the artistic merit of the speaker. Objectivity is particularly important to truly understanding the nature of political discourse, and one must remember that in any venture of social criticism, "the nature of the critic's subjectivity has the potential to distort his or her judgment" (Andrews 1983, 12). Therefore, analog criticism should help us to control this distortion, especially in cases where it is easy to judge someone's character before we even explore their comments in-depth. Rosenfield's critical method is an effective, appropriate approach for comparing the apologetic exploits of the political figures discussed above. However, an exploratory attempt to adapt our analysis to several apologetic messages and speakers may also be better served by utilizing techniques specific to the elements within speeches of self-defense. Also, additional methods should supplement rather than replace current approaches, and any exploratory approach should prompt comparisons (Hart 1990, 53). William L. Benoit's Theory of Image Restoration, an established method for such speeches satisfies these requirements.

Benoit's method combines previously developed theories (such as Ware and Linkugel, Ryan, and Burke), and is thus considered an encompassing methodology for analyzing *apologia*. Benoit's theory has been utilized in myriad contexts, principally by its author, including political, corporate, and popular culture contexts (Benoit 1995). Describing image restoration as the goal of an apologist, Benoit developed his theory of image restoration based upon two key assumptions of *apologia*: (1) communication should be conceptualized as a goal-directed activity, and (2) the maintenance of one's positive reputation is a central goal of communication. Benoit's taxonomy consists of five major categories and fourteen different strategies (see Table 7.1).

Benoit notes that communication and rhetoric are goal-driven, even though a communicator may have incompatible, multiple goals. In general, behavior that functions to further one goal may leave other goals unmet or hinder the attainment of other desired goals. However, Benoit claims that "people try to achieve the goals that seem most important to them at the time they act, or to achieve the best mix

Table 7.1 Image Restoration Strategies

Strategy Key Characteristic
Denial
Simple denial accused did not perform act
Shifting the blame someone else performed act
Evading of Responsibility
Provocation responded to an act of another
Defeasability lack of information or ability
Accident it happened due to a mishap
Good Intentions rhetor meant well in doing it
Reducing Offensiveness
Bolstering rhetor stresses own good traits
Minimization the act is not that serious
Differentiation the act is not as bad as others
Transcendence other issues are more important
Attack accuser reduce accuser's ethos
Compensation reimburse victim
Corrective Action plan to solve/prevent recurrence
Mortification apologize/express remorse

Note: Adapted from "Accounts, Excuses, and Apologies: A Theory of Image Restoration Strategies," (Benoit 1995, 95).

of the goals that appears possible" (Benoit 1995, 65). When people have goals or desires, they present messages that facilitate their attainment. One such goal is the maintenance of one's reputation. Thus, when reputation is threatened, one is "compelled to offer explanations, defenses, justifications, rationalizations, apologies, or excuses" (Benoit 1995, 70). Because everyone wants to "save face," a need to absolve one's reputation impacts everyone's life, so based upon these assumptions (as well as apologetic literature), Benoit devised a list of strategies to form a theory of image restoration. The five types of strategies are: Denial, Evading Responsibility, Reducing Offensiveness, Corrective Action, and Mortification.

Denial occurs when a person disputes performing a wrongful act, or simply denies any undesirable action. Benoit states that Denial may also be reinforced through explanations of damaging facts, or by an accuser's lack of evidence. Denial may be supplemented with alibis (providing evidence that the accused did not commit the crime) or with blame-shifting (providing a target for the audience while supporting the claim that the accused is not guilty). These strategies are more effective than Denial because they target others, thereby causing an audience to hesitate in ascribing blame to the accused.

Evading Responsibility involves four variants: Provocation, Defeasability, Accident, and Good Intentions. Provocation occurs when the accused claims that the act or statements in question were performed as a response or as a retort to another wrongful act. The aim is for the audience to then shift blame. Defeasability claims that the accused lacked significant information or control over a situation, thus reducing responsibility. Accident pertains to situations where a mishap has occurred, and thus the accused should not be held responsible. Good Intentions occur when a wrongful act was committed in an attempt to do something good, and it is hoped that the audience will thus exonerate the accused.

Reducing Offensiveness of an event involves six variants: Bolstering, Minimization, Differentiation, Transcendence, Attacking One's Accuser, and Compensation. Bolstering is similar to Ware and Linkugel's explanation of the same term. Those accused of doing wrong exhibit past attributes or actions in order to improve their reputation. Minimization reduces the significance of the accused individual's offense. Differentiation distinguishes a wrongful act from actions even less desirable, thus making the present act look less offensive. Transcendence places the offending act in a different context so to describe the act favorably. For example, attacking one's accusers may reduce their credibility, thus counterbalancing accusations. Finally, Compensation occurs when a person offers to recompense victims in order to atone for wrongful actions. Benoit points out that "none of these six strategies of decreasing offensiveness denies that the actor committed the objectionable act or attempts to diminish the actor's responsibility for that act" (Benoit 1995, 78). Rather, they attempt to diminish ill feelings toward the apologist by increasing audience esteem and decreasing any negative feelings.

Corrective Action amends problems incurred, and may take two forms: restoring the situation and/or promising to "mend one's ways." Rather than simply counterbalancing any injury (Compensation), Corrective Action applies to the source of the injury. Mortification is the admission of negligence on the part of the accused, and is followed by a plea for forgiveness. If an audience believes that the apology is sincere, they will hopefully choose to forgive the accused person's careless, wrongful, or neglectful action.

Benoit claims that the procedure adopted in applying his method to each artifact he has analyzed is similar:

> First, texts of the defensive utterances were collected and closely analyzed. Consideration of the backgrounds of these incidents provided insights into which issues or topics would probably become important. The categories listed (in Table 7.1) were used to identify instances of image restoration strategies in the defensive discourse. Then the strategies employed were evaluated in terms of their appropriateness considering the attack and the apparent audience. (Benoit 1995, 94)

For the purposes of understanding the politician's motivations and strategies in saying sorry for their love affairs, the texts of the self-defense rhetoric contained in speeches delivered to the media with a key component of responding to the accusations regarding sexual scandal need to be considered. In four of the cases, the politicians gave speeches of resignation from their elected offices, in three cases they continued to serve, and in the case of John Edwards, he dropped out of the presidential race of 2008. Benoit's typology was consulted to identify the strategies used by each office holder. After determining the strategies they used (or did not use), an evaluation in relation to accusers and the audience are also considered.

Clinton's *Apologia*

In response to the accusations surrounding the Monica Lewinsky scandal, Bill Clinton chose to provide a traditional and internationally televised *apologia* on August 17, 1998. He delivered a very brief speech, considering the fact that the scandal had been daily news for more than seven months: 543 words in a four-minute time span ("Numbers" 1998, 22). Clinton addressed the nation at 10:02 p.m. from the Map Room of the White House, the same location where he had given testimony earlier that day. Though brief, the presentation was rife with myriad approaches to self-defense, where he used the following strategies (placed in order of their frequency): Attack Accuser, Corrective Action, Transcendence, Mortification, Bolstering and Differentiation, Denial, Good Intentions, and Provocation.

Clinton spent most of his time on national television attacking the Independent Counsel and Kenneth Starr. He stated, "I had real and serious concerns about an Independent Counsel investigation that began with private business dealings 20 years ago," and "The Independent Counsel investigation moved on to my staff and friends, then into my private life. And now the investigation itself is under investigation. This has gone on too long, cost too much, and hurt too many innocent people"

(Office of Federal Register 1998, 1638). He also blamed the investigation by stating, "It is time to stop the pursuit of personal destruction and the prying into private lives. . . . Our country has been distracted by this matter for too long." While it was placed under the guise of a Corrective Action, Clinton also attacked the investigators in a plea to the public: "And so, tonight I ask you to turn away from the spectacle of the past 7 months . . . " The statement clearly implies that the "spectacle" was caused and perpetuated by the Independent Counsel.

There is some clear Mortification in this address: "I must take complete responsibility for all of my actions, both public and private." Additionally, there is some apparent Mortification or contrition regarding a relationship with Miss Lewinsky that was "not appropriate," "wrong," "a critical lapse in judgment," and a "personal failure"(Vartabedian and Vartabedian 2003, 36).

More careful scrutiny of this address reveals that a combination of Evading Responsibility and Reducing Offensiveness dominate this *apologia*. More than two-thirds of this brief address focuses on the investigation conducted by the independent counsel (Kenneth Starr) and the need to move on to the more pressing needs of the country. In sum, Clinton's attempts at Mortification serve as an apparent smoke-screen for his strong subtext of Evading Responsibility and Reducing Offensiveness due to the overzealousness of the independent counsel.

McGreevey's *Apologia*

Jim McGreevey held a televised news conference to announce his resignation, and to respond to the media reports about his extramarital affair. His wife, Dina, stood beside him. While McGreevey's six-minute speech consisted chiefly of Mortification and Corrective Action strategies, there was also brief Bolstering, as well. Most of the speech featured a contrite and deliberate tone whereby McGreevey accepted blame and asked forgiveness: "shamefully, I engaged in an adult consensual affair with another man, which violates my bonds of matrimony. It was wrong. It was foolish. It was inexcusable. And for this, I ask the forgiveness and the grace of my wife" ("McGreevey" 2004). He transitions from Mortification to Corrective Action when he states, "I accept total and full responsibility for my actions. However, I'm required to do now, to do what is right to correct the consequences of my actions. . . . I have decided the right course of action is to resign." In finishing his statement, McGreevey briefly uses Bolstering when he states, "I'm very proud of the things we have accomplished during my administration."

While the three strategies utilized by McGreevey are fairly common in political *apologia* in lieu of a Denial strategy, it is interesting to note that there is actually a two-tiered approach to the message that involves a clear shifting of blame. For the first half of the speech, McGreevey discusses how his situation evolved: "By virtue of my traditions, and my community, I worked hard to ensure that I was accepted as part of the traditional family of America." He moves on to discuss that despite his recognition early on that he was gay, that he "forced what I thought was an acceptable reality onto myself, a reality which is layered and layered with all the, quote, 'good things,' and all the, quote, 'right things' of typical adolescent and adult behavior." McGreevey does not overtly state that society's norms are to blame for the problems he has caused, but the implications are clear. He does not deny wrongdoing, but he does provide a rationale, which involves sharing blame with the culture that he felt forced him to live a life that was a lie.

Craig's *Apologia*

Senator Larry Craig addressed reporters in Boise, Idaho, in a televised speech responding to two significant accusations: (1) the activities at the airport and his questionable sexual orientation, especially in light of his voting record against gay-friendly legislation, and; (2) the guilty plea itself, which seemed to confirm Craig's guilt in regard to the first accusations. For the actions at the airport, Craig issued unequivocal Denial statements in the form of simple denial: "I did nothing wrong at the Minneapolis airport" ("Transcript: Sen. Larry Craig" 2007). He also shifts blame when he says,"[L]et me apologize to my family, friends and staff and fellow Idahoans for the cloud placed over Idaho." Craig implies from the start that someone else placed the cloud over his home state, and he extends on this idea further later in the speech. Craig also states, "Let me be clear: I am not gay. I never have been gay."

While the bathroom activity he was accused of caused emphatic Denial statements, Craig changes course about halfway through the speech, where he employs the Evading Responsibility tactic of provocation when he states, "Still, without a shred of truth or evidence to the contrary, the *Statesman* has engaged in this witch hunt. In pleading guilty, I overreacted in Minneapolis because of the stress the *Idaho Statesman* investigation and the rumors it has fueled all around Idaho." In building upon this strategy, he declares that the plea was an accident, as he claims that in response to the pressure from the media, "that overreaction was a mistake and I apologize for my judgment." After sharing one more time that he is not gay, Craig briefly employs the popular Bolstering approach by reminding listeners, "Over the years I have accomplished a lot for Idaho, and I hope Idahoans will allow me to continue to do that." Mortification comes in the form of apologies for his part in exacerbating the problems stemming from the media, but is very much a tertiary part of Craig's address. By the end of the speech, he accepts blame for the stormy metaphor that he opened with: "It is clear, though, through my action, I have brought a cloud over Idaho. And for that, I seek and ask the people of Idaho to forgive me."

Spitzer's *Apologia*

On March 12, 2008, Eliot Spitzer gave his resignation speech at his Manhattan office with his wife Silda at his side. Spitzer's statement was brief, direct, and employed three clear strategies: Mortification, Reducing Offensiveness through Bolstering, and Corrective Action. The Mortification statements were clear: "I am deeply sorry that I did not live up to what was expected of me" ("Full Text of Spitzer Resignation" 2008). He further states, "I have insisted, I believe correctly, that people, regardless of their position or power, take responsibility for their conduct. I can and will ask no less of myself." He briefly Bolsters his image when he says, "as a public servant I, and the remarkable people with whom I worked, have accomplished a great deal." The speech then focuses chiefly on the Corrective Action strategy. Spitzer declares that resigning is the best course of action because, "There is much more to be done, and I cannot allow my private failings to disrupt the people's work." He then expands on the decision:

> I go forward with the belief, as others have said, that as human beings, our greatest glory consists not in never falling, but in rising every time we fall. As I leave public life, I will first do what I need to do to help and heal myself and my family. Then I will try once again, outside of politics, to serve the common good and to move toward the ideals and solutions which I believe can build a future of hope and opportunity for us and for our children. ("Full Text of Spitzer Resignation" 2008)

While the three strategies utilized by Spitzer are fairly common in situations where guilt is accepted, the course of his resignation as a corrective action expands beyond the office. While Spitzer speaks of life "outside of politics," it is clear that his political career is over in his own eyes, but what is not clear is whether the "us" and "children" he speaks of are in reference to his immediate family or a part of the larger collective.

Edwards's *Apologia*

The chosen format of John Edwards's *apologia* was an August 8, 2008, "questions and answer" segment of *ABC News* "Nightline" with interviewer Bob Woodruff. At the beginning of the segment, Woodruff clearly states that Edwards asked "me to come here" to talk about reports related to Edwards's "personal life" ("Transcript: John Edwards interview" 2008). Forty questions and answers follow Woodruff's opening statement. It becomes readily apparent that Edwards's main response is to use the Mortification strategy.

When asked if he had an affair with Ms. Hunter, he stated: "I made a serious mistake . . . none of them [his family] are responsible for it. I alone am responsible for it." As to motives for his mistake, Edwards blames "a self-focus, an egotism, a narcissism that leads you to do whatever you want." As Woodruff probed further into whether Edwards thought he would be caught, he admitted: "I didn't think anyone would ever know about it." Finally, invoking Biblical purification, Edwards states. "she [Elizabeth] understands what I understand which is that I am imperfect."

The other dominant image restoration response of this segment appears to be that of Reducing Offensiveness. This position subsequently received a lot of coverage in the press. When asked by Woodruff how he "could have done this" to his ailing spouse,

Edwards responded, "it happened during a period after she was in remission from cancer." Obviously, such a rationalization did not endear Edwards with the public—particularly after it was used as a sound bite over and over again. Similarly, Edwards's comment about guilt did not serve him well to reduce offensiveness: "anybody watching this broadcast . . . can't possibly beat me up more than I have already beaten myself up." While Edwards did not deny involvement with Hunter, he does deny (1) that her baby was his (he finally admitted that the baby was his in January 2010), (2) he was in love with her; and, (3) he paid anyone to cover-up this scandal. In sum, Edwards used a non-traditional question and answer format for his *apologia*. His primary strategy appeared to be that of Mortification. However, his secondary and seemingly ineffective strategy of Reducing Offensiveness appeared to overshadow other aspects of his message—particularly given the repeated focus of the press. Finally, he did provide some direct Denial of questions, some of which may prove verifiable with the passage of time, and others which have already been disproven.

Kilpatrick's *Apologia*

Kwame Kilpatrick gave a considerably longer resignation speech than did his fellow sufferers of sex scandals. In a speech that clocked in at more than 20 minutes, Kilpatrick appeared to enjoy the theatre of his televised address, and took the opportunity to utilize similar strategies to others who have admitted guilt, but in much different proportions. The speech consisted chiefly of Reducing Offensiveness.

Kilpatrick used three different aspects of Reducing Offensiveness during his speech. He regularly bolstered his image with statements like, "Detroit has become an example of progress and resilience. I am proud of the fact that we as a community have been able to accomplish so much at a time when most people around the country and around the world thought it was impossible" ("Excerpts" 2008). He also continued in this vein when he referred to turning the mayor's office over to Kenneth Cockrel Jr., saying, "I know that he inherits a city that is in much better shape than the city that I inherited seven years ago. We have made profound structural changes in our basic operation of city government and have brought our budget back into control." Kilpatrick also attacked his primary accuser to reduce her ethos (and bolstered himself again, implying that he was still wishing her good tidings), stating, "The new spirit of this city . . . has been tangled up in what I believe is the pursuit of many people's own political ambitions, even our governor, Jennifer Granholm, who I wish well." He then moves to attack his accuser while moving on to transcendence, where he makes clear that there were many other issues that were far more important than the scandal that she used to plague him:

> Rather than focusing on finding solutions to the huge issues that are facing our state, from record home foreclosures to the lack of affordable health care, a record unemployment in our state, Kwame Kilpatrick was at the top of her list. ("Excerpts" 2008)

While the bulk of Kilpatrick's speech focused on Reducing Offensiveness strategies, he utilized Corrective Action showing his intentions for the future: "I'll turn my attention to the healing that I need to do in my family. We can turn our attention as a city to the healing that we must do in our city." He also utilized the Mortification strategy, though sparingly, but in an instant, skillfully turned to Denial through blame shifting: "I want to emphasize tonight that I take full responsibility for my own actions and for the poor judgment that they reflected. I wish with all my heart that we could turn back the hands of time and tell that young man to make better choices, but I can't." Kilpatrick starts his statement with contrition, and finishes it by absolving his present self by shifting blame to a "young man" that he now wants to help. While it was not a response to a specific accusation, Kilpatrick closed his speech with more bolstering, showing that he had been forgiven already by his wife Carlita ("someone who took a wretch like me and said that, 'I am standing by you through thick and through thin'") and the city as well ("I want to tell you, Detroit, that you done set me up for a comeback"). From his statements, we can ascertain that Kilpatrick was clearly envisioning the creation of an impervious response to his accusers.

Sanford's *Apologia*

Governor Mark Sanford gave a televised speech on June 24, 2009, in which he informally utilized bolstering to open when he recounted conversations that he had with a reporter earlier in the day, recounting his hard work as a congressman and a governor, and in particular his lack of political ambition. The informal stories quickly turned to a speech of confession in which Mortification was used extensively throughout an 18-minute press conference. He first apologized to his family:

> In so doing, let me first of all apologize to my wife Jenny and our four great boys, Marshall, Landon, Bolton, and Blake, for letting them down. One of the primary roles, well before being a governor, is being a father to those four boys, who are absolute jewels and blessings, that I've let down in a profound way. And I apologize to them. ("Full text of Gov. Mark Sanford's" 2009)

He then continued in a similar fashion, apologizing to his staff, several friends, his in-laws, the "people of faith" across South Carolina and the nation, and then he explicated more about what he actually did wrong to extend the Mortification strategy:

> And so the bottom line is this: I have been unfaithful to my wife. I developed a relationship with a—what started out as a dear, dear friend from Argentina. It began very innocently, as I suspect many of these things do, in just a casual e-mail back and forth, in advice on one's life there and advice here. But here recently over this last year, it developed into something much more than that. And as a consequence, I hurt her. I hurt you all. I hurt my wife. I hurt my boys. I hurt friends like

Tom Davis. I hurt a lot of different folks. And all I can say is that I apologize. ("Full text of Gov. Mark Sanford's," 2009)

Sanford also used Corrective Action to finish the speech, citing that his resignation as the chair of the Republican Governor's Association was "the appropriate thing to do," and he closed by saying that he was going to work with his family and South Carolina: "And so that means me going one by one and town by town to talk to a lot of old friends across this state in—in what I've done and, indeed, asking for their forgiveness."

From Bill Clinton to Mark Sanford, each politician employed a series of apologetic strategies in response to attacks regarding the allegations of inappropriate behavior resulting in sexual scandal. The televised speech or news conference was the most popular method of delivery, with the exception of John Edwards, who chose to be interviewed on television, instead. Interestingly, Edwards's statements, while undoubtedly rehearsed, did not significantly deviate in form from his fellow apologists. Allegations questioning the credibility of accusers undoubtedly shaped some of the apologetic strategies, whereas a focus on expediency shaped others. The types of apologetic strategies that each man employed in each rhetorical situation were revealing in terms of the type of response they wanted to create. Image restoration was clearly the goal for each address. In accordance with Rosenfield's analog, the rhetorical similarities and differences in these apologetic situations should be considered, as well as the relative merits and problems encountered in these discourses.

Apologetic Implications

There were many similarities and some significant contrasts between the apologetic discourses examined in this chapter. Some of the parallels are obvious, and one could argue, beneficial in creating a consistent essay that makes accurate comparisons. Each politician who was involved in a sexual scandal was a married man at the time of the allegations; meaning adultery was an issue in each case. As mentioned previously, each man spoke in a televised medium, and while some broadcasts were aired nationally on network television (Clinton and Edwards), all were available to the nation via cable news (and shall live immortally on the internet). Each case was profiled in the national news media and this was likely the reason that each chose such a public forum for the *apologia*. While there were many similarities, the choices made by each politician did differ if not in apologetic strategy, at least in the ways that they were enacted.

The strategies that were used most often by all of the men in their speeches are Mortification, Reducing Offensiveness, and Corrective Action. While every speaker used them to some extent, the style and manner in which they were used did vary greatly. For example, Sanford was the undisputed heavyweight in his statements of contrition, whereas for Craig, his attempts at Mortification were far less damning in regard to himself than they were vehicles for blaming others. Kilpatrick also used the Mortification strategy to actually set up blame shifting, a key characteristic in building effective Denial.

Reducing Offensiveness comprises six key characteristics, but clearly, bolstering is the one that is used in every speech of self defense observed here. In each situation, it is obvious that whether or not the accused party admits or denies guilt, and no matter how they proportion the strategies of their message, at some point they are going to stress their own positive traits. In the case of each politician, the attribute they highlight involves the work they have done for the public during their time in office. One could even argue that there is an implied tactic of transcendence in the speeches, underpinning the fact that if the public official did their job well than that was really more important than the innuendo and accusations that befell them.

Corrective Action is employed by each speaker, as well, but the approach to what should be done to fix the problem varies from general to specific, and from functional to outright confusing. In each case where an official stated that they were going to resign, they associated the act itself with corrective action as being "the right thing to do." In cases where they were to stay in office, the corrective action was going back to work for the constituency. In each case of admitted guilt, there was a stated intention to rectify the wrong that was done to the spouse and family. The more perplexing corrective actions involved Craig's repeating that he hired counsel for advice, Spitzer's vague idealistic vision, and Sanford's declaration to go "one by one and town by town."

As revealed in the analysis of each speech, the weight of each strategy used by the various speakers differed greatly. This undoubtedly also worked as a function of the level of contrition that each man displayed. While six of the seven admitted some level of guilt for the accusations involving illicit sexual activity, it can be argued that Mortification was the key strategy for four of them (Edwards, McGreevey, Sanford, and Spitzer), while clearly Reducing Offensiveness, and in particular, attacking their accusers, was much more key for Clinton and Kilpatrick. Notably, Clinton was also the only one of the seven speakers who clearly utilized all five of Benoit's strategies for image restoration, and did so in the shortest address. Unlike many of his contemporaries, Clinton's style "involves a distinct evolution and reflects several strategic shifts designed to shape public perceptions" (Knight 2000, 38).

The time expended on the *apologia* varied for the politicians using speeches, as well, from four minutes for Clinton to more than 20 minutes for Kilpatrick. Sanford timed in at 18 minutes and the rest were well under ten. While each speaker undoubtedly had prepared what they were going to say, it is obvious that some of the addresses involve reading from a teleprompter or script, whereas others seem much more extemporaneous. The two longest speeches appear to include much more ad-libbing than do the short, read statements.

Another variable that unquestionably shaped the *apologia* of each speaker was the controversy that surrounded each individual's political career, whether it was in connection to the accusations of adulterous behavior or not. In each case, the sexual allegations weighed heavily in the necessitated self-defense, but the issues facing each politician varied greatly. Clinton was faced with the threat of a charge of perjury, and ultimately was impeached and disbarred for related activities. Spitzer was already unpopular as a governor and involved in questionable activities involving the use of the state police force for surveillance. McGreevey's scandal emerged due to an investigation into his appointment of Golan Cipel, and Sanford's disappearance was under investigation not only for the affair he was having, but also for the question of who was paying for his travel. Craig's entire scandal emerged from him being charged by police for soliciting sex, and Kilpatrick at the time of this writing is still in prison on charges stemming from perjury and interrelated with multiple investigations of mayoral misconduct ranging from allegations of money funneling to the murder of an exotic dancer. While each man similarly shaped his messages with strategies to address the charges involving sexual misconduct, the unique cases of each individual, and how heavily they weighed in the need for a public self-defense, certainly had a large impact, as well.

Elements of the speeches that also showed a contrast involved traditional party themes emerging, particularly for the more conservative individuals. A major part of Craig's speech was using the Denial strategy and he stated three different times that he was not gay. While this may have been an attempt to reconcile his voting record with his actions, the vehemence and repetition seemed to send a deeper message about his opinion of homosexuality. Sanford's references to the "people of faith," of which he still counted himself as one, also played a major part in his speech. Other than McGreevey's openness about his own homosexuality and his comments regarding the importance of civil rights in the United States, the more liberal politicians did not actively pursue imagery or stylistic devices that would allude to political persuasion.

Each *apologia* certainly had a rhetorical impact, but the outcomes for each speaker cannot be traced solely to their political self-defense. Of the six office-holders, three utilized the speech occasion to announce their resignations, and the other three remained in office. John Edwards suspended his presidential campaign. However, Clinton suffered the embarrassment of impeachment, a fate that Sanford narrowly escaped. After initially indicating that he was going to resign, Craig finished the final few months of his term without seeking reelection. In general, while sex scandals certainly have a negative impact upon a political career, whether guilty or not, calling it quits, or attempting to proceed, if a political figure finds themselves involved in one, an *apologia* is a required course of action, and it appears that there is a definite formula of strategies that is used as a core for this type of message.

Conclusion

Applying Benoit's theory of image restoration and Rosenfield's analog framework to selected self-defense discourses by several prominent political figures resulted in an analysis of each man's unique approach to *apologia*. It also revealed some common forms the discourse appears to characterize. The remarks were analyzed for rhetorical appropriateness and coherence, and subsequently, the relationship of the discourse surrounding sex scandal and accusations brought against a public official were identified more clearly. Also, looking at an individual's response compared to other contemporary apologists in the political forum provides valuable insights into the persuasive nature of politics in times of self-imposed crises.

Some potential limitations impact this inquiry: the concise nature of the politicians' *apologia* in some cases, the text-only nature of the method, and the timeframe of the speeches in relation to the study. The outcomes of this investigation are significant, but the following discussion may guide or benefit future scholars investigating self-defense strategies. The terse nature of the *apologia* prepared for the television audience does not always lend itself well to the examination of a particular speaker. For example, Clinton's speech, although packed with strategic awareness, was short and very concise. The average length of Clinton's speeches to the nation when he was president was 50 minutes ("Numbers" 1998, 22). Thus, the concise nature in itself is unique. Longer texts, obviously, are potentially more revealing if one wants to learn more about the rhetorical nature of the speaker as opposed to focusing mainly on the types of messages that are being shared.

Benoit's method prescribes using speech texts in order to discern the nature of the apologist. While this has enabled a satisfactory examination of political rhetoric, emotional and contextual factors are often lost in such an examination. For example, as noted in this essay, Kilpatrick's tone during his apologetic address was one of joy, and the wives of some of the apologists stood at their side while they spoke (Craig, Spitzer, and oddly, McGreevey). It is obvious that one would have to watch the video to make such an observation. While Benoit does not prohibit using other formats specifically, the emotional context for the speech has no bearing on or application to Benoit's method, and this is an additional critical observation that may be considered less objective. This is not a debilitating limitation, but it has the potential for allowing misuse of the method, as well as causing the critic to ignore certain important factors about the speeches being analyzed.

A final limitation is the inquiry's timeframe. Temporally, it was conducted very close to the time that many of the events occurred. Critically, two flaws may have emerged. First, the critic is involved in much more than just the texts and the rhetoric in question. Indeed, as a concerned citizen and scholar, he or she has a stake in national issues, especially those involving elected officials. Therefore, the "current events" nature of the writing has the potential to cloud the researcher's objectivity. Second, the lasting implications of *apologia* in response to sex scandals cannot be discussed in great detail, as they have yet to unfold.

The degree of political survival after a sex scandal will potentially change the manner in which future politicians "defend their character," including non-traditional methods of character defense. Studies could also compare *apologia* in response to attacks on character versus those attacking policies. From the research focus here, it is obvious that the role of the apologist changes in diverse situations, yet similarities in approach abound. This examination could be extended to other political figures to assess the gap between such areas as apologizing or responding for the personal and for the state.

It is apparent that the speeches delivered in response to a sex scandal serve as prototypes for future *apologia*. As critics, we often study only moments of rhetorical greatness or failure. The ephemeral nature of such labels creates a compelling locus of analysis. Communication scholars still have much to learn from discourse that evolves temporally. Also, it is important to remember that ordinary rhetorical moments that adequately respond to accusations often carry more theoretical weight than memorable, stylized speeches.

From Socrates to Martin Luther to Susan B. Anthony, history has witnessed the apologetic form and those who spoke in defense of themselves. The reactions and speeches of the individuals here may appear common sense to the uninitiated, but it is significant that each speaker typically used a standard set of strategies ameliorated with specific characteristics determined by the individual's situation. The *apologia* and image restoration strategies were successful, at least in the short term, for some of those charged with allegations of sexual misconduct. Others determined their fate when they initiated the content of the speech, and apparently were attempting to restore their image more than anything else. The persuasive strategies used by political officials ranged from denying to attacking to expressing regret and pleading for forgiveness. The circumstances of each situation demanded different responses, and in most cases, the speakers provided them. Clearly, lies or half-truths should be denounced as unethical. For example, when John Edwards lied about his paternity matter and later had to recant, he obviously elected to place his welfare before the considerations of the constituency. The controversial political career of each apologist presented here is reflected in a unique use of *apologia*. How these apologies will impact future assessments of politicians, their speech acts, and our political system in general will be the greatest measure of their self-defense.

Works Cited

Abse, Nathan, and Alice Crites. "Presidency in Crisis." *Washington Post*, January 25, 1998: A19.

Andrews, James. *The Practice of Rhetorical Criticism.* New York: Macmillan Publishing Co, Inc., 1983.

Benoit, William. *Accounts, Excuses, and Apologies: A Theory of Image Restoration Strategies.* Albany, NY: SUNY Press, 1995.

Brenton, Scott. "Political Scandals: When the Personal Becomes Political," paper presented at the annual meeting of the International Society of Political Psychology, Portland, OR: July 4–7, 2007.

Butler, Sherry Deveraux. "The Apologia, 1971 Genre," *Southern Communication Journal*, 1972; 37: 280–291.

"Dignity Index," *Newsweek*, August 25, 2008: 8.

Downey, Sharon. "The Evolution of the Rhetorical Genre of Apologia," *Western Journal of Communication*, 1993; 57: 42–64.

"Excerpts from Detroit Mayor Kilpatrick's Address," *MLive*, September 5, 2008. Accessed November 18, 2010 (http://blog.mlive.com/news_impact/print.html?entry=/2008/09/excerpts_from_detroit_ mayor_ki.html).

Foss, Sonja. *Rhetorical Criticism: Exploration and Practice.* Prospect Heights, IL: Waveland Press, 1989.

"Full Text of Governor Mark Sanford's Affair Confession Today," *Los Angeles Times*, June 24, 2009. Accessed November 18, 2010 (http://latimesblogs.latimes.com/washington/2009/06/mark-sanford-transcript.html).

"Full Text of Spitzer Resignation," *New York Times*, March 12, 2008. Accessed November 18, 2010 (http://cityroom.blogs.nytimes.com/2008/03/12/full-text-of-spitzer-resignation/).

Gold, Ellen Reid. "Political Apologia: The Ritual of Self-Defense," *Communication Monographs*, 1977 45, 306–316.

Hart, Roderick. *Modern Rhetorical Criticism*. New York: Harper Collins, 1990.

Kennedy, George. *The Art of Persuasion in Greece*. Princeton, NJ: Princeton University Press, 1963.

Knight, Richard. "Evolution and Strategy Shift in Presidential Apologia: Bill Clinton's Self-Defense Rhetoric." PhD diss., University of Southern Mississippi, 2000.

Kruse, Noreen. "Motivational Factors in Non-denial Apologia," *Central States Speech Journal*, 1977; 28: 13–23.

———. "The Scope of Apologetic Discourse," *Southern Communication Journal*, 1981; 46: 278–291.

"McGreevey: 'I Am a Gay American,'" *CNN.com*, August 13, 2004. Accessed November 18, 2010 (www.cnn.com/2004/ALLPOLITICS/08/12/mcgreevey.transcript/).

"Numbers," *Time*, August 31, 1998, 22.

Office of the Federal Register, National Archives and Records Administration. *Weekly Compilation of Presidential Documents, August 24, 1998*. Washington, DC: Government Printing Office, 1998.

Rosenfield, Lawrence. "A Case Study in Speech Criticism: The Nixon-Truman Analog," *Speech Monographs* 1968; 35: 435–450.

Ryan, Halford Ross. "Kategoria and Apologia: On their Rhetorical Criticism as a Speech Set," *Quarterly Journal of Speech* 1982; 68: 254–261.

Schaefer, Jim, and M. L. Elrick. "Kilpatrick, Chief of Staff Lied Under Oath, Text Messages Show," *Detroit Free Press*, January 24, 2008: 1–A.

Schudson, Michael. "America's Ignorant Voters," *Wilson Quarterly*, 2000; 24: 16–23.

Somin, Ilya. "Political Ignorance and the Counter majoritarian Difficulty: A New Perspective on the 'Central Obsession' of Constitutional Theory." *George Mason University Law Review On-line*. Accessed July 16, 2010 (www.law.gmu.edu/assets/files/publications/working_papers/03-47.pdf).

Thompson, John. "Scandal and Social Theory," in *Media Scandals: Morality and Desire in the Popular Culture Marketplace*, edited by James Lull and Stephen Hinerman. Cambridge: Polity Press, 1997.

"Transcript: John Edwards Interview." *ABCNews.com*, August 8, 2008. Accessed July 21, 2010 (http://abcnews.com/print?id=5544981).

"Transcript: Sen. Larry Craig." *FOXnews.com*, August 28, 2007. Accessed July 16, 2010 (www.foxnews.com/story/0,2933,294961,00.html).

Vartabedian, Robert. "Nixon's Vietnam Rhetoric: A Case Study of Apologia as Generic Paradox," *Southern Communication Journal*, 1985; 50: 366–381.

Vartabedian, Robert, and Laurel Vartabedian. "Clinton's Address to the Nation: A Case Study of Apologetic Goals," *Speaker and Gavel*, 2003; 40: 28–46.

Ware, B. L., and Wil Linkugel, "They Spoke in Defense of Themselves: On Generic Criticism of Apologia," *Quarterly Journal of Speech*, 1973; 59: 273–283.

"Weekly Compilation of Presidential Documents," *Office of the Federal Register, National Archives and Records Administration*. (Washington, DC: Government Printing Office, August 24, 1998).

CHAPTER 8

It May Be Wrong, But It Is Not a Crime: The Negligible Legal Consequences for the Amoral Sexual Activity of Men in Public Office

Stephanie Jirard

In February 2008, New York Governor Eliot Spitzer, a married father of three daughters, paid to have sexual intercourse with a woman not his wife. Known as "Client #9" of the $1,000 an hour call-girl ring, Emperor's Club V.I.P., Spitzer was in Washington, DC, to address Congress on behalf of his constituents when he caused prostitute "Kristen" (really Ashley Dupré), to travel from New York City to satisfy his sexual needs. Spitzer could have been prosecuted for violating the *Mann Act* that makes it a federal crime to have individuals cross state lines for sex for hire, but he suffered no legal consequences. A year later, United States Senator John Ensign of Nevada, a married father of two sons and one daughter, revealed that he had had a sexual affair with Cynthia Hampton, a married employee. When she stopped working for Ensign, Hampton received a $25,000 severance and a "gift" of $96,000 from the Ensign's wealthy parents. Because Ensign conducted the affair on the job, he could have been charged with violating Nevada's Revised Statute Annotated §613.330, the Unlawful Employment Practices statute, that forbids differential treatment of employees based on sex, but Ensign suffered no legal consequences. One week after Ensign's disclosure, South Carolina Governor Mark Sanford in June 2009 exposed his secret that instead of hiking on the Appalachian Trail for five days—which would explain why his staff could not reach him—he was really in Argentina crying in the arms of his lover, Mariá Chapur, with whom he wanted to spend his life. When Sanford, a married father of four sons, declared Chapur his "soul mate" (hence, the tears), he could have been charged with the crime of adultery in his home state under South Carolina's Code §16-15-60 that punishes adultery by imprisonment for not less than six months, but Sanford suffered no legal consequences.

This chapter examines the government's choice not to prosecute for the sexual escapades of the men who hold public office. The acts of Spitzer, Ensign, and Sanford were immoral and seemingly criminal, yet none were considered "crimes."

Nor, too, was the behavior of United States Senator David Vitter from Louisiana whose phone number was one of thousands in the book of the woman known as the "D.C. Madame," or John Edwards, former United States Senator from North Carolina who had an affair with a videographer on his campaign trail, or Mark Foley former Representative from Florida who sent inappropriate text messages to teenage boys working as Congressional Pages, or James McGreevey former Governor of New Jersey who placed his male lover in a government job the lover was unqualified for, or United States Senator Larry Craig from Idaho who pled guilty to disorderly conduct after making sexual overtures in a men's room at the Minneapolis airport, or former President Bill Clinton impeached for lying about his sexual contact with a White House intern. Only if the official's extracurricular sexual activities metastasized into other abuses of power, as the case of Kwame Kilpatrick former mayor of Detroit who used the City's coffers as his personal automatic teller machine and the power as Mayor to execute vendettas on public servants, does both the public and government prosecutors clamor for a legal consequence of significance. But as the case studies in this chapter show, despite their protestations to be family men of virtue, many broke the law, but few held accountable.

Crimes Against Morality

> His Far More Egregious Offenses were Committed Against God, the Institution of Marriage and Family, Our Boys and Me.—Jenny Sanford, the governor's wife, commenting on his adultery

Deborah Palfrey, the woman known as the D.C. Madame, said she would never return to prison. She had been there once and was traumatized. From her home in California, Palfrey managed a stable of prostitutes who served the Beltway, the region immediately surrounding the nation's capital saturated with government workers and elected officials. When she was under investigation for the federal crimes associated with living off the earnings of prostitutes, for example, money laundering, tax evasion, pimping, one client in the list of thousands was Louisiana Senator David Vitter. As reported by Adam Zagorian of *Time Magazine* on May 1, 2008, when confronted by *Hustler* magazine in 2007, Vitter acknowledged in a written statement his connection to Palfrey and said:

> This was a very serious sin in my past for which I am, of course completely responsible. Several years ago, I asked for and received forgiveness from God and my wife in confession and marriage counseling. Out of respect for my family, I will keep my discussion of the matter there—with God and them. But I certainly offer my deep and sincere apologies to all I have disappointed in any way. (Murray 2007)

Vitter's confession without acknowledging specific wrongdoing came to fit the standard *apologia* for the sexual wildcat during the decade: Admit God's probably not too happy with you, but will forgive you anyway, mention your benevolent significant other who you know will still love you even though you trashed your vows of fidelity, and then say sorry to all those who might be offended by your selfish acts. Chapter 4 addresses other types of apologies in great depth, but religious apology is important here. God and religious atonement rate highly in the apology for infidelity because, traditionally, moral offenses were punished by the church and the church was the primary institution to control man's behavior, especially his sexual behavior (Karras 1996). The combination of law and social pressure on people to conform to a particular expectation of sexual behavior was a way to guarantee community survival, "Society may use the law to preserve morality in the same way it uses it to safeguard anything else if it is essential to its existence" (Devlin 1965, 11). One way to guarantee that people act morally is to punish them when they fail to conform appropriately.

As church law became the basis for secular law, crimes became defined by the wrong the act created rather than the harm it caused (Murphy and Hampton 1988). Criminal law is designed to make the offender pay society for his crimes. Leading legal philosopher H. L. A. Hart writes that the definition of an act as "criminal" tells society "that these actions are not to be done and to secure that fewer of them are done."(1968, 6). Society condemns the offender by punishment and is justified in treating the criminal poorly by the infamy of the crime (Feinberg 1970). The problem occurs when crimes against morality hurt "society" in general but no one in particular: What shall the punishment be? Social justice requires the disgraced politician be publicly shamed for sexual amorality, but there is no similar call for legal punishment. The shame that was often the province of the church is captured in Nathaniel Hawthorne's *The Scarlet Letter* (1850) in the scene where adulteress Hester Prynne is on the scaffold in the town square as penance for her illicit love, Hawthorne writes of the power of public humiliation:

> . . . a portion of a penal machine, which now, for two or three generations past, has been merely historical and traditionary among us, but was held, in the old time, to be as effectual an agent, in the promotion of good citizenship, as ever was the guillotine among the terrorists of France. (Hawthorne, 1850 and 2003, p. 68)

The town's collective rebuke has equal power to a machine dedicated to decapitation, and the power of the church continues to play a major role in fashioning the rules and regulation of sexual conduct. When the U.S. Congress was in session in the early part of this decade, Governor Sanford and Senator Ensign used to take Bible study classes at the aforementioned row house located on C Street near the Capitol. The townhouse was dedicated to infuse Christian lawmakers with the "teachings of Christ" and applying those teachings to the business of making laws. Although the C Street townhouse was ineffective in influencing Sanford and Ensign to not commit adultery, the Christian fellowship did provide religious cover when their affairs were exposed: They begged for forgiveness from the divine, be it from God or their humiliated wives.

Historically, religious teachings and public condemnation were sufficient to coerce the public to comply with moral constraints, but it was not until the Progressive Era that laws were enacted to enforce a common morality. From the late 1890s to 1920s, American social structure changed with the influx of immigrants and better-educated Americans took it upon themselves to eliminate the poverty and squalor of the inner city through education, both formal and moral (Timberlake 1970). By the time Prohibition became law in 1919 and liquor-related offenses became federal crimes, criminal courts took a more active role in enforcing public morality. As Hofstra Law Professor Joanna Grossman (2009) examined in her December 16, 2003, column at *Find Law Legal News*, the prosecution of crimes against morality most frequently charged in 1922 Dane County, Wisconsin, were those against chastity, morality, and decency such as fornication, spousal abandonment, and lewd conduct. Today, the lack of prosecutions for adultery indicates society is no longer interested in enforcing a code of common morality. Therefore, let the punishment fit the crime.

Sex Outside of Marriage

> Adultery is not about sex or romance. Ultimately, it is about how little we mean to one another.—Leonard Michaels, writer

Elizabeth Edwards knew as far back as 2006 that her husband, Senator John Edwards, was having an affair. Rielle Hunter was hired by the Edwards campaign to make videos to help Edwards win the 2008 presidential election. Edwards had been Democratic presidential nominee John Kerry's vice-presidential pick in Kerry's losing effort to win the White House in 2004. When the *National Enquirer* broke the story that Edwards might have a fathered Hunter's infant daughter in addition to his four children with his wife Elizabeth, Edwards made a public declaration that "in 2006, I made a serious error in judgment and conducted myself in a way that was disloyal to my family and to my core beliefs. I recognized my mistake and I told my wife that I had a liaison with another woman, and I asked for her forgiveness." In her book *Resilience* (2009), Mrs. Edwards claims she wanted to keep her husband's affair a private family matter, but researchers suggest a woman keeps an unfaithful husband because of a fear of losing a man's protection and support. Mrs. Edwards was willing to minimize her husband's moral failings. When she endorsed him as the best candidate to lead the country and campaigned for him wholeheartedly, she tacitly endorsed the notion that adultery is not a disqualifying factor to hold high office.

Marriage creates a set of responsibilities and embraces the moral ideals of faithfulness. Pledging to be with just one partner imposes a psychic restraint and sexual prison that makes sexual liaisons outside of marriage an attractive escape (McMurty 1984). Historically, laws regulating the sexual acts of married couples had, at their base, the concept that a man could treat his wife and children as property. Adultery is the act of sexual intercourse with one to whom you are not married. Making extramarital sex, bigamy, and polygamy crimes reflected not only the state's interest in maintaining monogamous unions, but ensured marital benefits bestowed only upon one lawful wife and heirs who could inherit their father's estate. Given the contractual nature of marriage, redress for adultery was for a husband to sue the "other man" in civil court for interfering with the husband's relationship with his wife. William Blackstone, the scholar credited with codifying common law in England, declares the legal basis of awarding the aggrieved husband monetary damages from the man who has intercourse with his wife, as:

> Adultery, or criminal conversation with a man's wife, though it is, as a public crime, left by our laws to the coercion of the spiritual courts; yet, considered as a civil injury (and surely there can be no greater,) the law gives a satisfaction to the husband for it by action of trespass vi et armis [with force, arms] against the adulterer, wherein the damages recovered are usually very large and exemplary. (Blackstone, 1765)

Blackstone acknowledged the adultery was on parity with a trespass action in property law, and the compensation for the husband could be substantial. Adultery remains a crime in 24 states, conviction of which can lead from a fine to jail time (Haggard 1999). To assign legal consequences for the crime of adultery, the law must determine the identity of the aggrieved party—is it the victim spouse or the state? In some states, the aggrieved spouse must initiate the criminal complaint; the state will not intervene (Sherwin 1949, 58–59). In some states, the dumped lover can become the complainant, as when attorney John R. Bushey Jr. was prosecuted in 2004 for adultery in Luray, Virginia, on a complaint brought by his ex-mistress, Nellie Mae Hensley.

A review of the state codes of the officials in this chapter reveal that Spitzer of New York; Kilpatrick of Detroit, Michigan; Edwards of North Carolina; and Sanford of South Carolina could have all been prosecuted for adultery in their home states. In New York under Criminal Law Statute §255.17, it is a class B misdemeanor (minor offense) to "engage in sexual intercourse with another person at a time when he has a living spouse." John Edwards under North Carolina General Statute §14–184 could have faced misdemeanor charges for having sexual intercourse with Rielle Hunter while "not being married to each other" and associating together "lewdly and lasciviously." Under Michigan law, Kilpatrick could have been convicted of a felony for sexual relations with Christine Beatty, and Sanford could have faced at least six months in jail under South Carolina law for the crime of adultery for his affair with Maria Chapur. A review of cases in the respective jurisdictions for the officials above from 2006–2008 revealed adultery was an issue in paternity, custody, and rape cases, and as a defense to a charge of killing a spouse or lover, but not as a crime charged alone. The one forum where adultery as a singular charge remains common is the military. Under the general principle that deceit is conduct unbecoming a member of the armed forces, the Uniform Code of Military Justice defines both adultery and attempted adultery as felonies. In 2005, the Army relieved four-star general Kevin

P. Byrnes of his command at Fort Monroe for having sexual relations with a woman not his wife, but chose not to criminally prosecute him. In general, society views adultery as a private affair between a husband and wife and not a crime for which the adulterer should pay back society for the "harm" caused to the community.

Sex for Hire

How could I?—Former Governor Eliot Spitzer of New York

What name was he going to use? Spitzer was registered at the Mayflower Hotel in Washington on February 13, 2008, but had to rent a room for "Kristen" and him. He rented the room for sexual relations under the name of a good friend and political contributor, George Fox, a real-life hedge fund investor. Spitzer had made the arrangements for Kristen in secret and, when she arrived at the hotel, had to find some way to sneak into her room. He snuck past his security detail acting as a 16-year-old going to a forbidden party. To pay for this illegal love, Spitzer moved large sums of cash from his personal account into the front business for the prostitution ring. Personally, Spitzer is worth millions, but when he tried to structure the prostitute's financial transaction to evade bank reporting requirements, the tough prosecutor with the nickname "Mr. Clean" got caught and immediately resigned. Asked later to explain his actions, wrote Jonathan Darman in an April 2009 *Newsweek* article, Spitzer could not, but offered "there's got to be some element to its being a result of tension and release. And that builds up." (*New York Times*, March 10, 2008) Later investigation revealed that Spitzer had hired many prostitutes and spent thousands of dollars over an 18-month period doing business with the Emperor's Club.

Often called "the world's oldest profession," prostitution is classified as the crime of exchanging sexual services for something of value, money, drugs, something to eat, a place to sleep. Prostitutes call men who buy their sex "johns" because they are indistinguishable from one another (MacNamara and Sagarin 1977). According to researchers who have spent time interviewing sex workers, prostitution is not a "victimless" crime, because the two parties have bartered an agreement to engage in consensual sex acts: Prostitution is illegal because prostitutes are a vulnerable population (Balos and Fellows 1999).

Nineteenth-century feminists wanted to decriminalize prostitution in an effort to remove the stigma and shame associated with the sex trade, but their efforts backfired. Prostitution remained a crime, the women became social outcasts, and turned to pimps for police protection and emotional support (Tong 1984). In 1988, sex workers were interviewed in San Francisco, California, to gauge the level of violence in their lives; out of the 130 respondents, 82 percent reported having been assaulted, 68 percent reported being raped, and 48 percent reported being raped more than five times (Farley and Barkan 1998). Many female prostitutes reported a history of childhood physical and sexual abuse, many were recruited into the illegal sex trade before the age of 15, and many had suffered the ills of homelessness and drug addiction (Vanwesenbeeck 1994). Spitzer's call girl "Kristen" fit the prototype of a young prostitute: She reported on her MySpace page that she left "a broken family" at age 17, was abused, had used drugs, and had "been broke and homeless."

Long-time statistics indicate that customers outnumber available prostitutes but data show that, when arrests are made, "the prostitutes seem to bear virtually the entire weight of legal reprisals" (James 1982, 293). A study to examine whether a change in New York's prostitution laws designed to reduce the disparity of pandering arrests to include more patrons showed that prostitution arrests in Buffalo from 1977–1980 continued to exclusively focus on arresting females as prostitutes, rather than on male customers. Thus, while the law appeared to be gender-neutral, on its face allowing for the arrest of any party involved in prostitution, the study concluded that police routinely declined to arrest the men (Bernat 1985). Because prostitution is viewed mainly as a public nuisance that introduces a lower standard of living where the sex trade thrives, most people arrested spend little to no time in jail or, if convicted, usually receive light sentences (Franklin 2007). Feminists argue that the inherent inequality of the sexes plays a role in shaping societal view on appropriate punishment for sex acts (Okin 1981). The disparity in meting out punishment allowed David Vitter to suffer no legal consequence for his infidelity and use of prostitutes, for his apology was sufficient public justice, while the D.C. Madame kept true to her vow to stay out of prison. Before she being sent back to jail, Palfrey committed suicide by hanging herself in the shed attached to her mother's trailer.

All types of men hire prostitutes for sex. As reported by the *Kansas City Star* on June 19, 2003, in the article "Police tout success of prostitution ring that led to 100 arrests" a priest, a high-school track coach, a Baptist college executive and a sheriff's deputy were caught soliciting prostitutes; they suffered minimal legal consequences. Says feminist scholar Jennifer James:

> Customers of prostitutes are, of course, acting outside the law, but where the law and the accepted male sex role come into conflict, the norms of sexual role playing overshadow the power of the law to label deviance. Men are expected to have a wide variety of sexual needs and to actively seek fulfillment of those needs. As part of that search, men are allowed to illegally purchase the sexual services of women with relative impunity, as arrest statistics demonstrate (1982, 296).

During the Progressive Era, legislators enacted 18 U.S.C. §2422 the White Slave Traffic Act of 1910, known as the Mann Act, that provides, "Whoever knowingly persuades, entices, any individual to travel in interstate commerce to engage in prostitution, shall be fined or imprisoned not more than 20 years." Federal jurisdiction to prosecute in federal courts those who forced women into prostitution is largely premised on crossing state lines and, although the law was aimed at those who promoted prostitution as a criminal enterprise, the Mann Act was used to prosecute men who took females across state lines simply to engage in sexual activity or adulterous liaisons (Langum 1994). Eliot Spitzer could have been prosecuted for a Mann Act violation for making call girls travel from New York to meet him in three different states. A review of criminal sentences awarded from cases that began on or about the time Spitzer had his tryst with "Kristen" in February 2008 until federal prosecutors decided not to charge Spitzer in November 2008, revealed that no "john" was prosecuted under the Mann Act. For instance, on August 7, 2009, retired New York State Supreme Court Judge Ronald Tills was sentenced to 18 months in prison after pleading guilty to violating the Mann Act. In his capacity as director of the Buffalo Chapter of the Royal Order of Jesters, an all-male division of the Freemasons, Tillis had brought Asian women illegally into the country to have sex for money at the Jesters's social gatherings. Tillis, as the ringleader of interstate prostitution, received the harshest sentence, while the Jesters patrons who paid the women to have sex, another judge and a police captain, received probation. Similarly on July 25, 2009, Evangelist Tony Alamo was found guilty of violating the Mann Act for taking minors across state lines to have sex. Alamo claimed his activity was legal because church doctrine dictates that when young girls reach puberty, they must marry. The jury rejected Alamo's defense.

Similarly, the punishment suffered for the actors in Spitzer's case follows the prosecutorial trend. Spitzer, the john, was charged with no crime. Temeka Lewis, a University of Virginia graduate with a bachelor's degree in literature who became known as the "hooker booker" because she arranged for "Kristen"—Ashley Dupré—to meet with Spitzer in Washington, DC, pled guilty to promoting prostitution and received one year probation, as did Tanya Hollander, a nutritionist from Rhineback, New York, who plead guilty to conspiracy charges arising for managing Emperor V.I.P. The ringleader, Mark Brener, received 30 months in prison and his young lover and executive assistant, Cecil Suwal, received six months in prison. The decision not to prosecute Spitzer for any prostitution-related offense is not unusual, as the majority of men arrested as johns are caught on the streets in the direct act of solicitation.

Same-Sex Liaisons

He reiterates unequivocally that he has never had sexual contact with a minor.—David Roth, Mark Foley's attorney

Mark Foley was a sloppy drunk. A long-time closeted gay man, Foley at 54, loved to be around teenage boys and wanted to be their friend. He especially liked the teenage boys who were part of the Congressional Page program, which brought teens from around the country to Capitol Hill to live and work during high school. The teens lived in a special dormitory and attended school there, as well. On October 4, 2006, a fellow Representative, Deborah Pryce (D-OH), asked the House Clerk to investigate the rumor that one summer night in 2000 or 2003 Foley had showed up drunk at the page dormitory, asking to see a special friend and was turned away by Capitol Police. What had led Pryce to ask for the investigation was a revelation that one page had been contacted by Foley repeatedly and was distinctly uncomfortable about the congressman's attention. In one 2003, in e-mail exchange reported by *ABC*

News, Foley, identified as Maf54 is asking the underage page to measure his penis for Foley's enjoyment:

Maf54 (8:08:31 PM): get a ruler and measure it for me
Xxxxxxxxx (8:08:38 PM): ive already told you that
Maf54 (8:08:47 PM): tell me again
Xxxxxxxxx (8:08:49 PM): 7and1/2
Maf54 (8:09:04 PM): ummmmmmmmmmmmmmmmmm
Maf54 (8:09:08 PM): beautiful
Xxxxxxxxx (8:09:38 PM): lol
Maf54 (8:09:44 PM): thats a great size
Xxxxxxxxx (8:10:00 PM): thankyou
Maf54 (8:10:22 PM): still stiff
Xxxxxxxxx (8:10:28 PM): ya
Maf54 (8:10:40 PM): take it out
Xxxxxxxxx (8:10:54 PM): brb . . . my mom is yelling
Maf54 (8:11:06 PM): ok Top of Form

Bottom of Form

When the text messages came to light, Foley resigned overnight on September 29, 2006. The Federal Bureau of Investigation (FBI) initiated an investigation and the House Ethics Committee lead an inquiry into whether the Republican leadership had ignored prior complaints about Foley's predatory behavior. Investigation by authorities determined that no crime had been committed, but Foley could have been charged with violating the Federal Communications Decency Act of 1996, 42 U.S.C. §223(f)(2), which states that anyone who "knowingly uses an interactive computer service [including phone lines] to send a specific person under 18 years of age any patently offensive comment or request shall be fined not more than $100,000 or imprisoned for more than 2 years." The problem with prosecuting Foley was determining the time frame of both the offensive messages and the applicable law. The minimum age of consent in many jurisdictions, including the District of Columbia, is 16 years old, the same minimum age to become a Congressional Page. The United States Supreme Court has held most laws passed to regulate and monitor sexually explicit material transmitted through the internet and cell phone communication to be illegal suppression of free speech. The problem with filtering certain communication to protect minors is that it blocks scores of information that adults can legally access. With the exception of child pornography and other obscene material, the government cannot tell adults what or what not to look at or enjoy. Notwithstanding Foley's graphic requests of the teenager to describe his genitals and Foley responding with his own state of sexual arousal, the government concluded sending the messages was not a crime. Once in a rehabilitation facility for alcoholism after he resigned from Congress, Foley admitted he had been sexually abused by a priest as a youth, took responsibility for his acts, and apologized for the harm he had caused.

Public perception of obscenity and acceptable moral behavior changed with the rise of sexual liberty in the 1960s and women's increasing financial, emotional, and professional independence. The United States Supreme Court (the High Court or Court) set the pace for social change. By incorporating to the states the freedoms in the Bill of Rights (Second Amendment: to bear arms, Fourth Amendment: to be free from unreasonable search and seizure), and their protection from government abuse of power (First Amendment: Congress shall make no law abridging the freedom of religion . . .), the Court guaranteed for people certain freedoms. In 1965 when the Court overturned a Connecticut law that made it a crime to use contraception, in *Griswold v. Connecticut*, 381 U.S. 479 (1965), they began to expand rights for Americans. In 1967, the Court decided the case of Mr. and Mrs. Loving, a white man married to an African-American woman who had to leave their native Virginia or risk being arrested under the state law criminalizing interracial marriage. In the decision *Loving v. Virginia*, 388 U.S. 1 (1967), the Court declared anti-miscegenation laws unconstitutional because the Fourteenth Amendment guarantees due process that the law treat everyone equally; laws preventing "race mixing" were illegal. The Court expanded the concept of fundamental due process preserving for Americans the right to choose without government interference who to marry, whom to live with, and how many children to have in the exercise of life, liberty, and the pursuit of happiness.

In 1964, the High Court decided *Jacobellis v. Ohio* 378 U.S. 184 (1964), concerning the French movie *The Lovers*, which Ohio tried to suppress as obscene. Noting that hard-core pornography defied definition, Justice Potter Stewart famously claimed, "I know it when I see it." Finding additional support for a judicial right to privacy in the home, the Court decided it was legal to possess obscene material in one's home in *Stanley v. Georgia*, 394 U.S. 557 (1969), and by the time the Court legalized abortion in *Roe v. Wade*, 410 U.S. 113 (1973), the Court had confirmed that government shall have a limited role, if any, in the sexual affairs of adults. But not all adults were free to have consensual relations with one another; states could criminally prosecute adults for consensual acts of homosexual sodomy. It took until the decision in *Lawrence v. Texas*, 539 U.S. 558 (2003), where the High Court recognized homosexual relations as a protected liberty interest under the Fourteenth Amendment. All of this said: Soliciting sex in public, even from a consenting adult, remains illegal.

The senator from Idaho, Larry Craig, an adoptive father of two sons and one daughter, insisted during the interrogation that he opens his legs wide when he has his pants pulled down while sitting on a public toilet, and this "wide stance" coupled with his picking up a piece of paper, is what the undercover police officer mistook for a proposition for a sexual encounter that June 11, 2007, in a public restroom at the Minneapolis-St. Paul International Airport. Sergeant Dave Karsnia was conducting an undercover sting in the restroom, due to increasing complaints about sexual activity within, when Craig was caught tapping his foot and waving his hand under the stall. As Rochelle Olson of the *Minneapolis Star Tribune* reported on January 8, 2009, about 50 men were arrested that summer. Karsnia's official complaint against Craig was that as he was undercover and in a bathroom stall, Karsnia witnessed Craig lingering outside of Karsnia's stall, peeked in the cracks between Karsnia's stall door and adjoining wall, and, from the next stall over with palm open and facing upward, Craig swiped his hand along the bottom of the stall divider, all in an effort to get Sergeant Karsnia to engage in sexual activity with Craig. Craig pleaded guilty to disorderly conduct, the lesser charge of solicitation. When the Congressional news the *Roll Call* reported his arrest on August 27, 2007, Craig tried, in vain, to withdraw his guilty plea, but to no avail. The legal standard to withdraw one's guilty plea is excessively high. The defendant must prove that they were unaware of the consequences of their plea or were somehow tricked or bamboozled into pleading guilty against their best interests. The judge denying Craig's appeal noted that Craig is "a career politician with a college education" and "knew what he was saying, reading and signing." A review of convictions for solicitation for the time frame of Craig's case indicates universally the charges are brought against those trying to seduce prostitutes for money. Disorderly conduct cases are misdemeanors and would not necessarily be reported in the state's criminal case law reporter.

While rumors of clandestine homosexuality had dogged Craig from his first days on Capitol Hill in 1982 as reported in August 2007 by Dan Popkey of the *Idaho Statesman*, so, too, did gay rumors hound Governor James McGreevey of New Jersey when he first took office in January 2002. McGreevy was married and had two daughters when he learned in 2003 that his male lover, Golan Cipel, was demanding $5million to settle a sexual harassment lawsuit. Cipel alleged that McGreevey had abused his position of power over Cipel to coerce sexual relations. In order to forestall the inevitable disclosure and embarrassment, on August 14, 2003, McGreevey held a press conference and declared with his wife Dina standing by his side, "My truth is that I am a gay American." Adultery with another male is not a crime in New Jersey, but appointing Cipel as head of homeland security for the State of New Jersey as a favor for a lover is illegal conduct—it's called using state money for purely personal gain. As a foreign national from Israel, Cipel could not acquire the requisite security clearance that would allow federal homeland security officials to discuss with him national security issues. Facing criticism from constituents for paying a six-figure salary to a man uniquely unqualified for the job and the swirling rumor mill about his sexual orientation, McGreevy asked Cipel to step down from his post in August 2000. McGreevey could have been prosecuted for federal mail and wire fraud for stealing Cipel's salary from New Jersey's coffers. Mail and wire fraud share the same elements to commit acts to defraud the public, one by mail the other using wires (telephones, wire transfers). Most politicians charged with public corruption offenses are charged with federal felonies because their crimes cross state lines and local law enforcement is ill-equipped to investigate and prosecute complex, interstate criminal activity. On the other hand, sentencing at the federal level for public corruption cases has been notoriously light. While it seems incongruous to use mail and wire fraud as the vehicle to prosecute public corruption, the statute at 18 U.S.C. §§1341, 1346 states:

"Whoever having devised a scheme or artifice to defraud [to deprive another of the intangible right of honest services] shall be fined or imprisoned for not more than 20 years, or both." Thus, all public officials have the obligation to give the public the value of the official's "honest services" and violation of that fiduciary duty by using public assets, to which the official has unique access, for personal enrichment is a crime: It's "stealing" the public's right to honest government. In 2004, Connecticut Governor John Rowland pleaded guilty to mail fraud when he accepted lucrative gifts from vendors who were then awarded profitable state contracts. By using his public office to get great deals on remodeling his vacation cottage, investing with businesses that received state contracts, selling personal real estate at great profit as a result of his position as governor, Rowland deprived his constituents of his "honest services." The question of the duty to be fair and just in an elected official's dealings with the public, specifically as it related to personal sexual gratification, dominated public discourse for two years as then-President Clinton was exposed for having an extramarital affair with a young White House intern from 1995–1996. President Clinton lied under oath when asked about the relationship with the intern, Monica Lewinsky, and in debating whether Clinton's lie was sufficient grounds to remove him from office, United States Senator from West Virginia Robert Byrd asked about Clinton's lie:

> has the President not committed an offense in violation of the public trust? Does not this misconduct constitute an injury to the society and its political character? Does not such injury to the institutions of Government constitute an impeachable offense, a political high crime or misdemeanor against the state? (Cooper 1999, 644)

McGreevey's act of placing his boyfriend on the public payroll constituted an "injury" to society, for which he suffered no criminal prosecution. President Clinton was prosecuted in the Senate for his "violation of the public trust," but was acquitted in large measure because Clinton's perjury was exclusively related to his sexual shenanigans in the Oval Office with a woman not his wife.

Sexual Harassment

> I did not have sexual relations with that woman, Miss Lewinsky.—President Bill Clinton

The government was shut down on January 7, 1996, and President Clinton was bored. He was taking the high ground in the budget impasse with Congress and rather than compromise, Clinton was betting that public sentiment was with him and would blame the Newt Gingrich-led movement for government operations grinding to a halt. While on the telephone with leaders on Capitol Hill, he was chomping on a cigar and according to Monica Lewinsky's August 26, 2998, testimony under oath, the president "was chewing on a cigar. And then he had the cigar in his hand and he was kind of looking at the cigar in . . . sort of a naughty way. And so . . . I looked at the cigar and I looked at him and I said, we can do that, too, some time." As the public learned in the Independent Counsel's report to Congress about Clinton and Lewinsky's oral sex, anal and oral contact and, at least on one memorable occasion, Clinton depositing a DNA sample on the intern's party dress, Adut (2008) observed that discussing the president's sex acts in public had become so unexceptional, for at one time:

> David Brinkley of NBC was prohibited from saying "venereal disease" on the air in 1962. It was too embarrassing for Americans. Compare this with the coverage of the Clinton scandals where the public was treated routinely to reports about the "distinguishing marks on the President's penis" and the semen-stained dress. (198)

The societal factors that lead to decreased sexual inhibition was but one factor that lead to the phenomena of the political sex scandal. A qualitative review of the social factors contributing to the rise of sex scandals by Thomson (2000) found four developments that created the social milieu where society would be privy to the private sex lives of political actors: (1) The changing culture of journalism after the Watergate scandal eroded the traditional bounds of respect for private acts; (2) The enactment of administrative regulations to guide the ethical behavior of government employees and associated emphasis on character; (3) The growing influence of the women's movement and the accompanying changing social perception of rape and sex crimes; and(4) The enactment of laws regulating political life, such as the rise of sexual harassment laws and implementation of procedures to prosecute sexual misconduct in the work place.

The opportunity for Clinton's impeachment was the United States Supreme Court's decision that a sitting president was not immune from civil lawsuits. Clinton had already appointed a special prosecutor to investigate his land deals made while he was governor of Arkansas, a decision he later lamented as "the worst" of his presidency when he was eventually investigated for committing perjury in connection with his lies about relations with Lewinsky. While perjury, lying under oath in an official proceeding, is a felony, it is rarely prosecuted in relation to civil cases and the Equal Employment Opportunity Commission (EEOC), the federal agency that ensures equality through the enforcement of anti-discrimination laws such as those prohibiting sexual harassment in the workplace, routinely receives annually approximately 25,000 complaints about sexual harassment. Clinton was being sued in civil court by a former Arkansas state employee, Paula Jones, who alleged Clinton had sexually harassed her.

In *Clinton v. Jones*, 520 U.S. 681 (1997), the High Court unanimously decided that the president was not immune from civil liability for torts (injuries) committed before he assumed high office. Jones sued Clinton for, among other indignities, violating her constitutionally protected right to be free from Clinton's "abhorrent sexual advances" under the federal civil rights statute 42 U.S.C. §1983 (1983 claim). The 1983 claim is not the traditional route to pursue a sexual harassment claim; it is typically the basis for civil claims against police for using excessive force or in race discrimination cases against government officials. The traditional route to file a sexual harassment claim is under Title VII of the Civil Rights Act, which prohibits workplace discrimination based on sex and the law also created the EEOC. The EEOC defines sexual harassment as any conduct that violates Title VII, which may include requests for sexual favors, unwanted sexual advances, and other types of verbal or physical behavior that creates an intimidating or hostile work environment for any male or female victim. In 1991, the Senate Judiciary hearings to recommend to the full Senate Clarence Thomas for confirmation as an Associate Justice to the United States Supreme Court riveted the nation when Oklahoma Law Professor Anita Hill claimed that when she had worked for Thomas when he was in charge of the EEOC, he spoke openly about pornography films, pubic hair, and various sex acts. In 1995, United States Senator from Oregon Bob Packwood resigned after a 31-month Senate ethics probe exposed Packwood's compulsive and unwanted sexual comments and acts with female staffers. Thus, while against the law, it is rare to be prosecuted for sexual harassment.

Clinton became the first sitting president to testify in depositions as a defendant in a civil case (Adut 2008). Jones's lawyers learned about Monica Lewinsky and asked Clinton under oath whether or not he had sexual relations with Lewinsky, and Clinton said no. Jones's cases was dismissed, but Clinton's perjury was exposed by Lewinsky. Clinton suffered a contempt charge from the federal judge in April 1999, a suspended Arkansas law license in 2001, and voluntary removal from the United States Supreme Court rolls (Toobin 1999). Clinton was the first president in 131 years to be impeached by the House of Representatives and tried in the Senate, where he was acquitted in February 1999. Although perjury is a federal crime for which Clinton could have been prosecuted, the social construction of his perjury in the context of lying to cover-up an extramarital affair was a byproduct of his adultery. Clinton's perjury was *mala prohibita*, something which you should not do, such as speed for example, because society collectively condemns such behavior. Again, Senator Byrd said it best about Clinton's deceit on the Senate floor:

> When the President of the United States, who was sworn to protect and defend the Constitution of the United States, and to see to it that the laws be faithfully executed, breaks the law himself by lying under oath, he undermines the system of justice and law on which this Republic—not this "democracy"—this Republic has its foundation. (Cooper 1999, 644)

Though Byrd concluded Clinton had committed a criminal act, he cited the public's opposition to removing the president simply for a lie to save face with his wife. Even if the public is willing to forgive sexual conduct that has no bearing on job performance, sometimes the sex acts overlap with a larger case of public corruption, as happened with Kwame Kilpatrick.

Abuse of Power

You are chosenMay 13, 2003, text message from U.S. Representative Carolyn Kilpatrick to her son, Detroit Mayor Kwame Kilpatrick

Was he really going to marry her? Christine Beatty, chief of staff for Mayor Kwame Kilpatrick of Detroit, had received from the mayor declarations of love via text message. Beatty and Kilpatrick had consummated their love on business trips taken on behalf of, and financed by, the City of Detroit. "You told me that you would be my boyfriend every day until I was your wife," Beatty texted the mayor on April 8, 2003. Kilpatrick replied and assured Beatty that he had every intention of becoming a stepdad to her daughters once their love could become public. The public finally did learn of their relationship when 14,000 published text messages sent on city-owned pagers not only revealed the graphic nature of their sexual practices with one another, but exposed their conspiracy to use the mayor's office as a source of personal enrichment for themselves, their friends, and their families.

The definition of public corruption encompasses tax collection, granting of contracts or other benefits with a public entity, fraud, bribery and, in general, "the breaking of the rules, be they written laws or implicit codes of conduct, which we expect public officials and politicians to observe in the conduct of public affairs" (Neild 2002, 5). Kwame Kilpatrick, the youngest person elected mayor of Detroit at the age of 31, was a walking abuse of power, reflected by his mother's sentiment that he was "chosen" for higher office.

Kilpatrick's downfall began with an investigation into whether or not strippers had attended a party at the mayor's mansion in 2003, and whether the drive-by killing of one of those strippers, Tamara Greene, was related to the after-hours activities of the mayor and his security staff. Detroit police officers Gary Brown and Harold Nelthorpe investigated the party, the strippers, and the murder, and then were unceremoniously fired. Brown and Nelthorpe then turned around and sued the mayor for unlawful termination—they claimed protection as whistleblowers of Kilpatrick's criminal behavior. Brown and Nelthorpe also knew Kilpatrick and Beatty were having sexual relations and when both were asked under oath in a court of law about the extent of their relationship, both Kilpatrick and Beatty lied and said they were just professional associates. To prevent the truth from coming out, Kilpatrick persuaded the Detroit City Council to award Brown and Nelthorpe $8.4 million dollars in exchange for settling their whistleblower lawsuit. A provision of that settlement was to keep the text messages between Kilpatrick and Beatty secret. When the *Detroit Free Press* won the right to publish the contents of the text messages, the public learned not only that Kilpatrick and Beatty had committed perjury about their relationship, but also that the two had conspired to wrongfully terminate Brown, conspired to award their friends lucrative contracts for Detroit business, and conspired to purchase personal items for themselves and bill those purchases to the city. Kilpatrick was charged with eight felony counts of conspiracy, perjury, misconduct in office, and obstruction of justice, and two felony assault charges stemming from an altercation where Kilpatrick had hit a police officer who tried to serve a subpoena on one of the mayor's friends. On September 5, 2008, Kilpatrick pleaded guilty to obstruction of justice, so, too, Beatty. Both were sentenced to four months in jail and after serving a portion of their sentence, went their separate ways to serve the rest of their sentence on probation. In 2009, Kilpatrick moved to Dallas, Texas, and Beatty stayed with her husband and daughters in Detroit.

Conclusion

> It's a bad boy, Bill Clinton. You're a naughty boy. The American people already know that Bill Clinton is a bad boy, a naughty boy. I'm going to speak out for the citizens of my state who in the majority think that Bill Clinton is probably even a nasty, bad, naughty boy.—Senator Larry Craig speaking on January 24, 1999, about Clinton's affair with Lewinsky

Oh the hypocrisy! It was bad enough that men elected to public office took action to break their marital vows, make their wives cry, embarrass their children, engage in high-risk behavior, misuse state property and money, and time; telegraph the message that the sacrifice and work relationships require are just no fun, but many officials profiled here had held themselves up as paradigms of moral virtue. To preserve the "sanctity of marriage," Larry Craig co-sponsored with David Vitter a federal constitutional amendment defining marriage as between one man and one woman. John Ensign and Mark Sanford both proclaim to be emblems of "family values" candidates. Mark Foley was chairman of a House Caucus on missing and exploited children, where he sponsored many bills to protect children, in part, from sexual predators. But the public makes the distinction between private moral failings and the criminal acts that may accompany such trysts. In 2001, Gallup published the results of a poll asking what the public should know about candidates for elective office. The majority of people polled, 83 percent, said the public should know whether a candidate handled money well or had an alcohol problem, while a mere 33 percent said voters should know whether a candidate was unfaithful to their spouse.

While the Gallup results indicate people care more about an official's fidelity to public office rather than to one's spouse, a politician's sexual indiscretions may indicate a proclivity for unethical behavior once in office. The lack of legal prosecution for crimes associated with sex scandals of political figures reinforces the public perception that breaching a marital vow. When the state chooses not to prosecute public officials for their sexual amorality, leaders may be inclined to risk the consequences of unethical behavior. And why not? Suffering no legal consequences may mean a public rebirth.

Mark Sanford remained governor of South Carolina until his term expired in January 2011. Immediately after November 19, 2010, when the Federal Election Commission dismissed an ethics complaint lodged against him for the alleged illegal $96,000 payment to his mistress and her husband, Senator John Ensign announced his intention to run for another six-year term in 2012, although the FBI investigation still looms. Eliot Spitzer is a co-host with Kathleen Parker on their cable network talk show "Parker Spitzer" where Spitzer cross-examines sitting politicians on current events. Mark Foley, too, is on the airwaves as host of a radio show for WSVU 960 AM in Palm Beach and, according to Andrew Abramson of the *Palm Beach Post*, announced on November 29, 2010, that he was contemplating returning to public service by running for mayor of West Palm Beach. John Edwards admitted in January 2010 that he had fathered a daughter with his mistress Rielle Hunter, but remains under investigation for misuse of campaign funds to pay Hunter her videography fees allegedly earned on the 2008 Edwards campaign. Edwards's wife, Eilzabeth, died of cancer in late 2010, with an outpouring of great national grief. And Kwame Kilpatrick is back in jail. In May 2010, Kilpatrick was sent to prison for a minimum 18 months and a maximum five years for violating his probation when he told his sentencing judge that he only had $6 to pay toward his million-dollar restitution when, in fact, Kilpatrick had hundreds of thousands of dollars at his disposal. Perhaps Kilpatrick will be the only one who will not make a public or political comeback because he, unlike the others, committed far more serious crimes surrounding his infidelity and is now paying a far more serious consequence. But if he does return to public service, he would not be alone. Because in America, a sex scandal is only enough to set up a political comeback. And, apparently, illegal behavior is not enough to stop that second act in American politics.

Works Cited

Adut, Ari. *On Scandal: Moral Disturbance in Society, Politics and Art.* London: Cambridge University, 2008.

Balos, Beverly, and Mary Louise Fellows. "A Matter of Prostitution: Becoming Respectable." *New York University Law Review*, 1999; 74: 1220–1303.

Bernat, Frances P. "New York State's Prostitution Statute: Case Study of the Discriminatory Application of a Gender Neutral Law." *Women and Politics*, 1985; 4(3): 103–120.

Blackstone, William, 1765. *Commentaries on the Laws of England.* New York: Garland, 1978.

Cooper, Charles. "A Perjurer in the White House?: The Constitutional Case for Perjury and Obstruction of Justice as High Crimes and Misdemeanors." *Harvard Journal of Law and Public Policy*, 1999; 22: 619–646.

Devlin, Lord Patrick. *The Enforcement of Morals.* New York: Oxford University Press, 1965.

Edwards, Elizabeth. *Resilience: Reflections on the Burdens and Gifts of Facing Life's Adversities.* New York: Broadway, 2009.

Farley, Melissa, and Howard Barkan ."Violence and Posttraumatic Stress Disorder." *Women & Health*, 1998; 27(3): 37–42.

Feinberg, Joel. *Doing and Deserving.* Princeton, NJ: Princeton University, 1970.

Franklin, Daniel J. "Eighth Annual Review of Gender and Sexuality Law: Prostitution and Sex Workers." *The Georgetown Journal of Gender and the Law*, 2007; 8: 355–370.

Grossman, J. *Punishing adultery in Virginia: A cheating husband's guilty plea is a reminder of the continued relevance of adultery statutes*. Accessed August 11, 2009 (http://writ,news.findlaw.com/grossman/20031216.html).

Haggard, Melissa. "Adultery: A Comparison of Military Law and State Law and the Controversy this Causes under Our Constitution and Criminal Justice System." *Brandeis Law Journal*, 1999; 37: 469–483.

Hart, H. L. A. *Punishment and Responsibility: Essays in the Philosophy of Law*. New York: Oxford University Press, 1968.

Hawthorne, N. *The Scarlet Letter*, 1st edn 1850. London: CRW, 2003, 68.

James, Jennifer. "The Prostitute as Victim," in *The Criminal Justice System and Women: Women Offenders, Victims, Workers*, edited by Barbara Raffel Price and Natalie J. Sokoloff. New York: Clark Boardman Company, 1982.

Karras, Ruth Mazo. *Common Women: Prostitution and Sexuality in Medieval England*. New York: Oxford University, 1996.

Langum, David J. *Crossing Over the Line: Legislating Morality and the Mann Act*. Chicago: University of Chicago, 1994.

MacNamara, Donal E., and Edward Sagarin. *Sex, Crime, and the Law*. New York: The Free Press, 1977.

McMurty, John. "Monogamy: A Critique," in *Philosophy and Sex*, edited by R. Baker and F. Elliston. Buffalo, NY: Prometheus, 1984.

Murphy, Jeffrie G., and Jean Hampton. *Forgiveness and Mercy*. Cambridge: Cambridge University Press, 1988.

Murray, S. "Senator's Number on 'Madam' Phone List", Washington Post online, July 10, 2007. Accessed May 13, 2011 (www.washingtonpost.com/wp-dyn/content/article/2007/07/09/AR2007070902030.html).

Neild, Robert. *Public Corruption: The Dark Side of Social Evolution*. London: Anthem Press, 2002.

The New York Times. "Spitzer is linked to Prostitution Ring." March 10, 2008. Accessed July 26, 2011 (http://www.nytimes.com/2008/03/10/nyregion/10cnd-spitzer.html?sq=eliot%20spitzer%20george%20fox&st=cse&adxnnl=1&scp=2&adxnnlx=1311614805-flhofmrkEpKokx4aUiWRsw)

Okin, Susan Moller .*Justice, Gender and the Family*. New York: Basic Books, 1981.

Sherwin, Robert Veit. *Sex and the Statutory Law (in all 48 states)*. New York: Oceana Publications, 1949.

Thompson, John B. *Political Scandal: Power and Visibility in the Media Age*. Cambridge: Polity, 2000.

Timberlake, James H. *Prohibition and the Progressive Movement, 1900–1920*. New York: Macmillan Publishing Company, 1970.

Tong, Rosemarie. *Women, Sex and the Law*. Totowa, New Jersey: Rowman & Allanheld, 1984.

Toobin, Jeffrey. *A Vast Conspiracy: The Real Story of the Sex Scandal that Nearly Brought Down a President*. New York: Random House, 1999.

Vanwesenbeeck, I. *Prostitutes' Well-Being and Risk*. Amsterdam: VU Uitguerij, 1994.

CHAPTER 9

Hedging the Bet: Constitutional Qualifications for National Public Office

Cynthia Botteron

Q: What do Gary Hart and the Boston Celtics have in common?
A: If they had played at home, they would have won.

—*'Playboy'* (1988)

Introduction

Sex scandals tear at the bond of public trust as few other scandal types can, because it is about sex. Sex is private. Sex demands discretion. Sex is not supposed to be politics. When a sex-scandal breaks in the press, the full scope of harm caused to the general welfare may never be revealed. Where there are scandals and secrets, there is little room for trust and even less room for democracy.

Yet, there are those rarest of times when the full scope of harm to the public's interest is revealed. Even during these times, however, citizens cannot be assured that the elected representative will in fact be found guilty, must less punished in a manner befitting the harm caused, because it is about sex. Where there is little justice, there is very little legitimacy.

Rather than risk damage to state legitimacy because of a terminally salacious representative; some legislators, and reformers across the world have placed into their constitutions qualifications that attempt to keep scoundrels out of office in the first instance. One might say it is a pre-emptive strike to favor the virtuous in order to save the state.

Is this an effective mechanism? It is unclear because it is very difficult to know for certain whether these types of qualifications keep out the troublesome candidate. However, one thing is certain, without these qualifications in place, there is no formal mechanism afforded to citizens or the ennobled official to ban an obviously flawed individual from gaining public office.

Before rushing in to reform a constitution, one should question whether these types of qualifications for public office, which are subjective by nature, could be abused by a political opponent. Truth be told, it is very likely they have been and will continue to be. What must be weighed, then, is whether the harm caused to an aspiring candidate by a wrongly applied rule is worse than the harm caused by a lascivious representative who trades the public interest for private pleasure. As will be argued, the harm caused by sex scandals to representative democracy, to public policy, and to the legitimacy of government can be so great and grievous that instituting even a flawed mechanism to prohibit a potentially damaging candidate from running for office may be worth the risk.

Representative Government: Delegates and Trustees

In spite of the fact that the democratic experiment has been ongoing for hundreds of years, the more subtle and complex structures that define "democracy" are still a point of contention among scholars. What scholars agree upon is that democracy is, at its core, a form of government that provides adults with equal access to the vote, opportunities for effective participation, enlightened understanding, and the ability to exercise final control over the agenda (Dahl 1998, 38). How is "effective participation" and "ability to exercise final control over the agenda" extended to citizens of modern, large democracies? On this question, John Stewart Mill asserted that "in a community exceeding a single small town," personal participation "in any but some very minor portions of the public business" is impossible; thus, "it follows that the ideal type of a perfect government must be representative" (Mill 1861, 55).

Under representative democracy, citizens choose from among a slate of contenders a winner whose sole purpose is to "stand in" for them and conduct the public's business. Candidates for office generally base their campaign on one of two strategies: the first promises to carry out a range of policies or programs should they be elected; the second promises to remain true to a set of values and principles when considering legislation. These appeals give rise to two very basic representation types respectively known as the "Delegate" and the "Trustee." Because each representation-type forges a particular contract with his or her constituency, each is subject to a range of unique charges when revelations about behavior of a rather lascivious nature are made. It is to an exploration of how each representation-type is undone by sex scandals we now turn.

The Delegate and Sex Scandals: The Making of "The Panderer"

Elaborating upon the nature of the contract between the citizen and their Delegate-type representative, one finds the Anti-Federalists:

> It must then have been intended that those who are placed instead of the people, should possess their sentiments and feelings, and be governed by their interests,

or in other words, should bear the strongest resemblance of those in whose room they are substituted. (Manin 1997, 110)

When speaking of the delegate-type representative, the assumption is that he or she is a megaphone that broadcasts accurately to the legislative body their constituents' interests and preferences. When the Delegate-type representative deviates from this role, the electoral contract is broken.

Sex scandals shred this contract when the delegate violates the most common-sense understanding of the public's interest; for example, when taxpayer revenue is used to solicit services of an illicit nature or to pay hush money to a blackmailer. The contract is also torn asunder when the Delegate-representative is bribed with sex to cast a vote that favors a particular interest rather than the general interest. The contract is also rendered null and void when the Delegate is consumed by the pursuit of carnal indulgences to the extent that few other pursuits are possible. When the Delegate has fallen prey to these temptations, he or she is no longer "Representative," but is now "The Panderer."

In July 2009, Piero Marrazzo, television journalist and governor of the Lazio region in Italy, "was allegedly filmed with a transsexual prostitute in a Rome apartment. The film also shows a line of cocaine on a table" (Eggleton 2009). Four police officers were also alleged to have gotten the film and extorted approximately $80,000 from Marrazzo, which he denied paying, although he did admit to "sporadic cocaine use and to other encounters with transsexual prostitutes" (Eggleton 2009). Potentially problematic for any representative, it did not rise to the level of shredding the contract between the Delegate and his constituency until it was revealed that Marrazzo was also under investigation for possibly using public funds to pay for the prostitutes and to pay off the blackmailers. Up to October 2009, he maintained he was innocent of the theft of public funds.

Consistent with the plea of innocence, Marrazzo continued his quest to seek the leadership position of the Democratic Party and governorship when "rumors surfaced about the existence of another, more damaging video" (Eggleton 2009). It was then that Marrazzo resigned from his post as governor and gave up his leadership position in the party, citing poor health (Eggleton 2009). All commentators agreed that Marrazzo was "politically finished" (Eggleton 2009). It is instructive that Marrazzo did not view admitted cocaine use, solicitation, and the public screening of both as politically damaging in and of itself, which demonstrates the nature of the Delegate-elector contract. The mind reels when trying to imagine what might have been on the "more damaging video" that persuaded Marrazzo to spend more time tending to his health and allowing someone else to tend to the public's interest.

In that same year, 2009, South Korea's largest cable-channel system operator, T-Broad Hanvit Broadcasting Company Ltd., was seeking permission from the government to merge with Orix Broadcasting, a regional cable channel. The Korea Communications Committee was scheduled to make the final decision on March 31, 2009 (*Korea Times* 2009). However, a "ranking official of cable TV network T-Broad treated two presidential aides . . . and a Korea Communications Commission official, at a restaurant," from which these same government officials were seen leaving with several women (Hyun-kyung 2009). Shortly before the final merger decision was to be made, the Communications Committee suspended consideration of the request "leading critics to raise suspicions that T-Broad might have arranged the drinking session and bought sex . . . as part of lobbying efforts for approval"(*Korea Times* 2009).

According to press reports, the first reaction by President Lee Myung-bak's administration was to "downplay the seriousness of the scandal by treating the aide's illegal behavior as a personal mistake" (*Korea Times* 2009). Chaffing at this explanation, a *Korean Times* news writer complained that government and the police were complicit in the effort first to suppress the event, but when that proved impossible, to down play it (*Korea Times* 2009). Pointing fingers at the highest level of government, the writer accused staff within President Lee Myung-bak's administration of not only succumbing to bribery of a tantalizing sort, but evading legitimate public oversight altogether (*Korea Times* 2009). Outraged, the ruling party urged President Lee Myung-bak to adopt a "zero-tolerance policy when dealing with the alleged sex-for-favors case involving the two presidential aides" (Hyun-kyung 2009). The presidential aide of primary interest was fired.

Sex in exchange for a policy vote is a clear violation of the unique contract struck between the delegate and his or her constituency. The virtue of President Lee Myung-bak's administration could have remained intact had he come forward and condemned the actions of his aids, demanded an open investigation, and acknowledged the violation of that sacred trust between representative and citizen. That was not, apparently, the tact taken.

Initially, the South Korean legislature itself was in disarray over how to frame the incident. The Liberty Forward Party (LFP) spokeswoman Park Sun-young called the incident a mere "sex scandal," whereas women lawmakers of the Grand National Party (GNP) and the Democratic Party (DP), among others, believed that the scandal "was not a matter of personal ethics of public servants in question but a shameful practice of using sex for lobbying in politics" (Hyun-kyung 2009). Representative Park Soon-ja of the GNP stated, "[President] Lee should take appropriate, stern measures to make sure that a similar incident does not recur during his term" (Hyun-kyung 2009). A full investigation was launched by the legislature; saving the South Korean government from lending the impression to its citizens that its agenda and policies could be purchased for a song, a drink, and a hooker or two.

When citizens are asked to pay the costs of governance, part of the contract is an implicit understanding that funds will be spent on enforcing the law, implementing policy, and paying the salaries and benefits of the elected and the properly vetted. When it is revealed that precious tax dollars have been spent to impress prostitutes, to solicit their favors, and keep them in a style few citizens can afford, fury and calls for impeachment seem quite appropriate.

Philippine citizens, in 2004, were likely stunned to learn during a talk show segment that was promoting actress-sometimes-prostitute Keanna Reeves's upcoming film, *Shut Up,* that several congressmen, a governor, and mayor were all regular clients of hers. Undoubtedly wishing that she would have followed the advice of her film title, she went on to explain that "her bread and butter came from working as an escort" rather than from acting (Robles 2004). One might be tempted to say, good for the working gal, but Reeves continued and told the audience that one lawmaker needed to schedule their tryst rather late because "he needed time to steal from his office funds" (Robles 2004).

Once Reeves pulled back the curtain, other actresses-sometimes-prostitutes also went on record to praise the generosity of Philippines's elected officials, "They will offer you a house, a car, money, anything to make you go all the way" (Robles 2004). Apparently, the official rate for "going all the way," was from a low of 10,000 pesos (HK$1,400) up to 100,000 (HK$14,000) "depending on the escort's reputation and popularity," according to Reeves's pimp (Robles 2004). Another prostitute came forward and praised Philippines's politicians, finding them to be rather "gallant clients" (Robles 2004); undoubtedly, not one of the sturdier planks of a party's platform.

What may have facilitated the illicit generosity of these politicians was the "pork barrel" account, amounting to several billion pesos a year. This account was divided up among the congressmen to invest back into their districts with very little oversight into how the funds were actually spent (Robles 2004). There had been widespread suspicion that "some of it end[ed] up as personal pocket money" (Robles 2004) and, apparently, G-string tinsel. "Aware that the issue could give the public the wrong impression that lawmakers [were] squandering public funds to pay for sexual services," Speaker of the House Jose de Venecia ordered an investigation into the allegations made by Reeves and others (Robles 2004). What made this a rather inconvenient truth was that at the time the scandal came to full light, President Gloria Macapagal-Arroyo was making a case to citizens for the need to raise taxes in order to avoid a looming budget crisis.

These few cases are a stark illustration of the damage done to public policy, the efficacy of political activity, and if carried to the extreme, the very legitimacy of government when The Panderer holds office. Although it is the responsibility of citizens to keep an eye on their representatives, the rules of the game favor those in power. Scandal can be swept under the carpet where it evades oversight and justice. The Panderer can appeal to colleagues in government for leniency should they get caught. When government fails to police itself, the job falls even harder on the citizen.

Yet, citizens are distracted and busy with their own affairs and do not or cannot provide sustained and focused attention on reigning in the ruttish behavior of a few elected officials. James Fearon in "Electoral Accountability and the Control of Politicians: Selecting Good types versus Sanctioning Poor Performance" (1999), argued that citizens are keenly aware of the fact that they cannot perform the type of oversight required for a full functioning republic. Rather than use their vote to approve or disapprove of the policies and programs pursued by a Delegate-type representative, citizens vote to place into government a *good type* representative who can be trusted, rather than tracked (Fearon 1999, 68). The *good type* candidate shares with the Delegate-type similar policy preferences of the voter, but goes beyond by also being honest, principled, and skilled enough to carry out what is in the public's interest (Fearon 1999, 68). It is here we find the alternative to the delegate: the "Trustee."

The Trustee and Sex Scandals: The Discovery of the "The Flawed"

Much as the Anti-Federalists promoted an ideal-type representative, so, too did the Federalists. The most eloquent portrayal of this representative type is found in the writing of James Madison. Madison argued that a "representative system" should not reflect citizens' immediate interests, rather, it should refine and enlarge citizens' perspectives "by filtering them through a wise, responsible elite, better able to discern the true interests of their country" (Pitkin 2004, 338–339). The representative is not the delegate of the citizen, he or she is their "Trustee."

When the "Trustee-type" candidate runs for office, he or she promises the electors to be a person of character, a *good type* as it were (Fearon 1999). Citizens cast their vote for the Trustee-type candidate believing that he or she will not waver from commitments made to a set of principles and values that define the "wise and responsible elite." The Trustee-type representative wins their bid to public office by successfully appealing to the better nature of citizens; thus, striking a contract whose foundation is based upon actualized or aspirational virtue.

When the Trustee representative is caught in a sex scandal, the betrayal is deeply personal because the contract was deeply personal, "Trust who I am and together we will transcend the mundane and venal!" Citizens rightfully wonder if they were duped in that their Trustee's true character was both deeply flawed and well concealed. Even more problematic than the failure of the Trustee is what the failure signifies. A Trustee represents the public's virtue and as such, is the agent that transfers the public's virtue to political office. When the transitive agent shows him or herself to be flawed, the integrity and dignity of the office itself is called into question.

Malawi's Second Deputy Speaker, Bester Majoni was caught in an affair with the wife of a junior colleague, Member of Parliament Jaji Banda. Majoni's affair with Rose (nee Kawale) ruined both marriages and disrupted the lives of the 12 children they had between them (*Malawi Standard* 2003). Malawi's Parliament moved to impeach Majoni "for bringing the office of his position into disrepute" by his misdeed of moral turpitude (*Malawi Standard* 2003).

Hong Kong, facing scandalous behavior by two of its provisional regional councilors, also framed this transgression as a problem of loss of dignity and damage to the image of government. The councilors were found guilty of "consorting with prostitutes at a Panyu karaoke bar" during a trip to play football (Kwai-Yan 1999a). Councilor Ann Chiang Lai-wan reminded them that, "Councilors are councilors all the time. They cannot say they are only councilors from eight to six and not after work" (Kwai-Yan 1999b)."If a member misbehaved to the extent that the council's image was damaged, the chairman, with members' support, should have the power to disqualify the member involved," concluded Vice Chairman Tony Kan Chung-nin (Kwai-Yan 1999b).

One might be tempted to conclude that the reaction by Councillor Anne Chiang Lai-wan was too demanding and unrealistic; that elected officials should have "time off" for bad behavior. However, this is precisely the burden a Trustee-type representative voluntarily bears. They appeal to voters not on the promise to "play" the part of the good type, but in "being" the good type. Being the Trustee-type representative means never having to take a vacation from one's self then needing to apologize later. Because the Trustee-type representative becomes the physical manifestation of their constituency's virtue, he or she shoulders the requirement of living and leading by example.

Caught having sex with women who were not their wives, two Indonesian legislators faced the fury of their Muslim constituency because their tryst occurred only 50 meters from the hotel where "local Muslims . . . were staging a Koran recital contest (MTQ)" (Sarosa 2002). Activists were calling for the PDI Perjuanga Party to recall the legislators, as their behavior "had tarnished the legislative council's image" and that the legislators had failed to set "a good example for the people they represent" (Sarosa 2002).

In 2008, South Africa conducted its "National HIV Survey," in which 15,000 homes representing a statistically valid cross-section of households were interviewed. Fieldworkers found that 10.9 percent of all South Africans over the age of 2 were living with HIV. Breaking this down by age, nearly 17 percent of those from the ages of 15–49 were (South Africa Human Sciences Research Council 2008). In another survey conducted by the South African Department of Health, of the 1,415 antenatal clinics located throughout the country, 28 percent of pregnant women were living with HIV in 2007, a thankful decline from the 2005 survey high of 30.2 percent, but still alarmingly high (South Africa Department of Health 2007). South Africa has struggled mightily to bring down these rates through well-funded and targeted safe sex campaigns.

Stepping into this public health crisis is President Jacob Zuma, who in February 2010, "allegedly fathered a child with the daughter of one of his friends." In South Africa this has not been framed as an issue of infidelity as the president now has five wives, but as "undermining his own government's safe sex campaign, designed to limit the spread of HIV and AIDS" (Guyson 2010). This is in the context where, in 2006, President Zuma was also charged with, then acquitted of, the rape of a family friend who was HIV positive. He claimed that he had "protected himself from the virus by having a shower after sex" (Guyson 2010). "South Africa now has a President who, both through his words and his actions, is doing damage to that struggle," stated Democratic Alliance leader Helen Zille (Guyson 2010). President Zuma has failed to lead by example.

When legislators fall from grace, it is not entirely appropriate to question the legitimacy of government *per se*. However; when the Head of State as the symbolic leader of the country falls, the damage can potentially engulf the entire nation. If the failure of a Head of State is not acknowledged and repented, citizens can rightfully begin to question not only the regime, but if not satisfactorily prosecuted, the idea of representative democracy altogether.

In 2006, the Israeli government was rocked by multiple disclosures of crimes allegedly committed by those in high office. President Moshe Katsav was charged with the rape of two female employees and the further sexual abuse and harassment of eight more, all topped off by accusations that he wiretapped his office to spy on employees. If the president is indicted on all the charges, he faces up to 16 years in prison (Mitnick 2006).[1]

Yet, Israeli citizens were not to find solace at any level, as at the same time President Katsav was struggling to save his position, other inquiries were underway investigating charges of bribery related to Prime Minister Ehud Olmert and others from the Kadima Party. Both incidences followed closely on the heels of the indictment of Justice Minister Haim Ramon for sexual harassment, forcing him to take a leave of absence (Mitnick 2006).

Although not all the failings of leadership were related to sexual crimes or impropriety, it was the frequency and depth of accumulated failings that proved to be de-legitimizing. "This accumulation pushes this issue to a strategic danger. I think Israel's enemies are quite satisfied," said Avraham Diskin, a political science professor at Hebrew University, "There is a very deep mistrust among the Israeli public of politics and political leaders" (Mitnick 2006). "There's a convergence of trends that have been building up here over the past year, which has led to the current mood of despair in the moral and leadership capabilities of our politicians," concludes Yossi Klein Halevi, a fellow at the Shalem Center (Mitnick 2006). Asking citizens about the recent spate of government scandals, particularly those of President Katsav, Moshe Katzir, a technology worker protesting outside the Israeli presidential residence said,

> The problem is not only an issue of sexual harassment; it's a problem of democracy.[Mr. Katsav] has lost his honor. . . . We're sick of leaders who are "not guilty." We want leaders who are moral and clean. (Mitnick 2006)

The Trustee-type representative bears a far greater burden than the "delegate," who only has to deliver the goods, say "No" when bribed, and not spend public funds on hookers. The trustee embodies the virtues of the democratic state, the character of a people, the vision of who "we" are when "we are" better than "I am." All share disgrace and ill-repute when the trustee-type shows him or herself to be deeply flawed. Perhaps this explains why constitution writers and citizen reformers focus their greatest attention on prohibiting The Flawed from gaining high political office—the argument to be taken up next.

Keeping the Scoundrels Out! Constitutional Qualifications for Public Office across the World

Given the depth and breadth of real harm caused to the public's interest by The Panderer and The Flawed, the question arises as to how reformers are able to keep out candidates who may succumb to temptation and to encourage representatives to keep their contracts with the electorate. Most countries, such as the United States, have chosen to rely upon the periodic judgment of the electors to kick the bums out of office, so long as the malfeasance during office does not rise to the level of a crime. Other countries have established independent ethics commissions with broad oversight authority. The most extreme, and rare response is the focus of the following discussion; that of writing into a country's constitution a range of qualifications whose aim it is to keep citizens who have a demonstrated potential to become The Panderer or The Flawed out of office.

Constitutions and Qualifications: An Introduction

At the turn of the twentieth century, the comparative study of constitutions was a standard in the field of politics. However, what scholars soon discovered was that the comparative study of institutions and rules could explain large trends but not specific acts or events. What is true about humans is that we are extremely adept at navigating the wild lands just beyond the intent of a rule. To understand the political impact of this extraordinary ability of ours, a shift in scholarship away from formal rules to informal behavior occurred. Until recently, this marked the end of efforts to understand complex rule sets, such as constitutions, in a comparative framework.

After the Second World War concluded, there was an immediate and pragmatic need to once again understand the nature and function of constitutions as the United States set about writing Japan's governing document and newly de-colonized states set out to create authentic national mandates, which only intensified in the 1980s as a new slate of states emerged from Soviet rule. In the early 1990s, scholars and leaders alike declared that liberal democracy had gained global ascendancy; citizens and reformers across the world began to look anew at their constitutions—revisiting enumerated lists of rights, the distribution of power between executive and legislative branches, the power and autonomy of the courts, military responsiveness to elected officials, and the qualifications for public office.

Theories about representative government also underwent significant revision. Behaviorism dominated political science and research on representation focused primarily on the negotiated relationship that occurred between elected officials and their constituency during elections. It was assumed that the legal requirements for candidacy were relatively minimal, thus, the nature of electoral competition could largely be explained through the informal processes of party politics, fundraising, and campaign messaging. Much as scholarship at the turn of twentieth century rightfully claimed that only half the story was understood by studying formal structures, the same is true today when studying only informal ones. The case of Pakistan is instructive.

In 2002, President Pervez Musharraf signed into law the Political Parties Act, which added onto an already very long list of qualifications in Pakistan's Constitution the additional requirement that a candidate for federal or provincial office must have a college degree or its equivalent. This left 97 percent of Pakistan's citizens disqualified from elected office (Botteron 2006, 2007). Interestingly, the justices of the Pakistan Supreme Court who took up a challenge to the order expressed comfort with this qualitative gap between the elector and elected (Botteron 2006, 176). The written opinion of the Court is telling.

Justice Makhdoom Ali Khan argues that, "Being uneducated the members of the legislative chambers did not assert themselves and easily succumbed to allurements and indulged in floor crossing for reasons altogether ulterior" (Botteron 2006, 176). In essence, lack of education resulted in the corruption of the representative.

According to Advocate General of Punjab Maqbook Ellahi Malik, lack of education also leads to loss of virtue or character failure (Botteron 2006, 176–177):

> No doubt wisdom is not related with degrees but this is an exception to the rule. Education certainly broadens the visions, adds to knowledge, brings about maturity and enlightenment, promotes tolerance and peaceful coexistence and eliminates parochialism. We are convinced that the educational qualification prescribed for membership of Assemblies will not only raise their level of competence and change the political culture but will also be an incentive to education. (Quoted in PML(Q) Case pp. 1027–1028 in Botteron 2006, 179)

Given that only 3 percent of Pakistan's citizens could vie for the status of "representative," the representative would not, by definition, "represent" the public as they are, worrying about daily chores, meals, and finances. Rather, the representative would be the "wise, responsible elite," who was "better able to discern the true interests of their country" (Pitkin 2004, 338–339). Living and leading by example, resisting corruption, pursuing what is in the public's interest; the fate of the nation rests firmly on the shoulders of both the Delegate and the Trustee, whose biographies were carefully constructed far in advance of their public début.

Pakistan is not unique. When looking across the constitutions of the world, it is clear that drafters and editors used qualifications for national office to craft the biography and character profile of their preferred representatives. Coming to understand the details of this strategy required a precise yet global analysis of the qualifications for office. It is to the study and findings we now turn.

Qualifications for Public Office: Crime, Character, and Codes of Conduct

The *Constitutional Qualifications for Public Office: A Global Comparative Study* draws from the totality of 186 last-revision constitutions of the world more than 69 different qualifications a candidate must meet in order to compete for one of four national offices (i.e., Head of State, Head of Government, Upper House Member, and Lower House Member). Organizing the 69 qualifications into logically coherent categories, one finds eight general types.

There is a small set of capacity-based requirements; such as, good mental and physical health, and minimum and maximum age limits. A larger set enumerates required skills, such as literacy, ability to speak a named language, and education. There are many more sets of qualifications that define and demand "integrity"; for example, disqualifying those who have been convicted of a felony, banning those with obvious divided loyalties to country and the regime, and prohibiting those with "authoritarian" aspirations. Other qualifications require a candidate to affirm ethnic, national, or religious affiliation or to deny it (Botteron and Greenberg 2010).

There are three specific qualifications that can be used to keep the Panderer and Flawed from gaining elected office if the vetting process is strict and backed by those with the will to enforce it. The first prohibits those previously convicted of "Crimes of Vice and/or Moral Turpitude"; the second requires that a candidate have "Good Character and/or Reputation"; and the last bans those who had been forced from public office for violating the country's Leadership Code of Ethics; each qualification is discussed in more detail below.

Disqualified If Previously Convicted of Crimes of Vice and Moral Turpitude

Should a citizen have previously been convicted of a "crime of vice and/or moral turpitude they are disqualified from running for public office" is the standard language used in approximately 8 percent of the world's constitutions. "Vice" is commonly understood as an *immoral habit or trait* while "moral turpitude" relates to *crimes of a vile nature or those marked by deep depravity*. It is left to the legal codes to define which acts, specifically, constitute vice and/or moral turpitude. The term, "moral turpitude," was used to describe the case of the Malawi Second Deputy Speaker Bester Majoni for having an affair with the wife of a junior colleague. Recall from the earlier discussion, he was impeached for having committed an act of "moral turpitude"(*Malawi Standard* 2003). The United States has seen a recent spate of elected officials with similar failings (i.e., Bill Edwards and Mark Sanford), but in this legal system, similar acts do not rise to the level of vice or moral turpitude, nor are citizens banned from running for public office if they have been convicted of such a crime.

It is to be expected that each country will define these crimes or failings differently. It is also expected that the legal codes themselves will change over time as culture and, thus, ideas about moral behavior evolve. Regardless, until a constitution is amended, what does not change is that the crime categories of "vice" and "moral turpitude" ban from office those who succumb to the ephemeral temptation of illicit, illegal sex. When a constitutional qualification prohibits these types of convicts from seeking public office, a country broadcasts to the world and to its citizens that all means have been taken to keep The Panderer or The Flawed from holding the reins of electoral power.

Who employs this strategy? Out of the 185 countries that have a Head of State, 13 prohibit candidacy and of the 131 countries with a Head of Government, eight do. There are 94 countries with an Upper House; of those, only five disqualify citizens convicted of crimes of vice and/or moral turpitude specifically, whereas, for the 186 countries with a Lower House, 15 prohibit candidacy (See Table 9.1).

These findings are rather unique when compared to the distribution pattern of the entire set of 69 qualifications, which generally indicate a strategic use of qualifications across offices. For example, the requirement that a candidate be born in the country and of native parents is at least three times more likely for the Head of State than for any other office. The requirement that one be literate is at least two times more likely for Lower House members than the Head of State, and prohibitions on elected officials having financial or economic links to the private section are at least four times more likely for the Head of Government than any other office. Here, as Table 9.1 illustrates, the distribution of the prohibition against running for public office by citizens convicted of Crimes of Vice and/or Moral Turpitude are relatively evenly distributed across the offices, the Head of Government having a marginally smaller frequency, but not a statistically significant one.

What can be said about countries using this qualification? Minimally, when these states are concerned about candidates who have been convicted of Crimes of Vice and/or Moral Turpitude, they are concerned about them generally as no single office appears to be of greater focus than any other. One may tentatively conclude that succumbing to this crime-type is viewed as damaging to government in its entirety rather than a more symbolically focused concern as is demonstrated by Good Character and/or Reputation.

There is the question; however, as to the target of this disqualification. Given both content and focus of "vice" and "moral turpitude," one might ask if the primary aim is to keep out of national office the potential Panderer, Flawed, or both?

To answer that question with any certainty, one must look at how the harm to the public's interest is framed. For example, acts of solicitation or marital infidelity, both of which have been used to describe this crime type, can be linked to bribery, extortion, or the misallocation of public funds. All of these harms define the Panderer. On the other hand, harms to the reputation, image, and legitimacy of government that define the Flawed can also result from acts of solicitation or marital infidelity depending upon the full context of the crime as we have seen from previous examples.

It is difficult to determine the precise target of this prohibition because the framing of the harm that defines the representation type is unknown. What is certain; however, is that concern about convicts of a lascivious type is high enough in 8 percent of the countries of the world that they have taken the extraordinary measure of banning them from seeking national public office.

Requirement That One Have "Good Character and/or Reputation"

Unlike crimes of vice and/or moral turpitude, the qualification framed as "Good Character and/or Reputation" usually required fuller elaboration as to the specific acts

Table 9.1 ¹Countries that Prohibit Candidates Convicted of Crimes of Vice and/or Moral Turpitude

Country	Head of State (185 Countries)* (18 Countries)**	Head of Government (131 Countries)* (12 Countries)**	Upper House (94 Countries)* (7 Countries)**	Lower House (186 Countries)* (18 Countries)**
Antigua and Barbuda	No Mention	Yes	Yes	Yes
Bangladesh	Yes	Yes	No Office	Yes
Barbados	No Mention	No Mention	Yes	No Mention
Cyprus	Yes	Yes	No Office	Yes
El Salvador	Yes	No Office	No Office	Yes
Ghana	Yes	No Office	No Office	Yes
Iraq	Yes	Yes	No Mention	No Mention
Malawi	Yes	No Office	Yes	Yes
Maldives	Yes	No Office	No Office	No Mention
Pakistan	Yes	Yes	Yes	Yes
Qatar	No Mention	No Mention	No Office	Yes
Sri Lanka	Yes	No Mention	No Office	No Mention
Sudan	Yes	No Office	No Office	Yes
Tanzania	Yes	Yes	No Office	Yes
Turkey	No Mention	Yes	No Office	Yes
Uganda	Yes	Yes	No Office	Yes

| United Arab Emirates | No Mention | No Mention | No Mention | Yes |
Uruguay	Yes	No Office	Yes	Yes
Total Number of Positive Hits	13	8	5	14
*The Percentage of Countries that Use the Qualification for a Specific Office relative to All Countries.	7.03	6.11	5.32	7.53
**The Percentage of Countries that Use the Qualification for a Specific Office relative to Countries that Use the Qualification.	72	66	71	77

In general, the Head of State is akin to the President of the United States and the Head of Government would typically be a Prime Minister in a parliamentary system. An Upper House is analogous to the U.S. Senate and Lower House would be similar to the House of Representatives. A 'No Mention' means that the country uses the office, but the Crime of Vice and/or Moral Turpitude was not a disqualifier for that office. 'No Office' means that the country does not use that particular office.

or character dispositions prohibited or required of a candidate. Some constitutions framed this qualification in very general terms; for example, "In order to run for office, a candidate must be a person of good character and/or one who is known to have a good reputation." Others were more specific in naming targeted behavior. Take the case of Mexico where one cannot run for public office if a known vagrant or drunk.

There is not a single case in the world where a citizen is banned from running for public office if he or she is a known "whore," "whoremonger," "sexual deviant," or a thousand other sex-specific activities or dispositions. Drawing upon the framing of the case studies presented earlier, the specific demands within the Good Character and/or Reputation qualification that could conceivably be used to keep a salaciously challenged candidate from running for office are: "good morality," "piety," "good standing," "not abusing power," "not being corrupt," and so forth. The countries that framed the Good Character and/or Reputation requirement along these lines are provided in Table 9.2.

The findings here are far more consistent with the distribution of the full qualification set that demonstrates strategic use. As illustrated in Table 9.2, the Head of State receives most of the focus, three-quarters of the state that require a Good Reputation for candidacy use it for this office. Thinking about the duties and symbolic role played by a Head of State, concern over the damage caused by a flawed candidate is understandable.

A Head of State is the embodiment of the spirit of a people, even if it is a mere symbolic position. When the Head of State falters, it is "the people" who defend or deny this individual to the world. During the 2000 presidential election in the United States, George W. Bush stated many times that he would bring dignity and respect back to the White House and to the nation, making a clear appeal to the people that he wanted to become the country's Trustee-in-Chief. The appeal was strategically brilliant, as citizens in the United States had likely heard enough sordid details about stains on dresses, cigars, thongs, and the anatomical peculiarities of President Clinton.

Harm caused by the failings of the Head of State, by definition, cannot be contained at the sub-state level, as his or her constituency is the nation. In this context, should electoral bonds be shredded, the damage runs border to border and it is "government" and "country" that is threatened with disrepute.

President Silvio Berlusconi of Italy serves as an example, although perhaps an extreme one. After the revelation of his "bunga-bunga" party involving 20 nude women dancing around a nude Berlusconi, supporters in Italy are, metaphorically, turning their backs on him. The Catholic Church only recently declared that "personal sobriety and decorous respect of the public office one represents is the minimum" citizens should expect from their Head of State (Barigazzi 2010a). Business interests, too, are backing away, a major trade association saying that it is necessary for Italy's Head of State to regain "a sense of dignity . . . otherwise it is not possible to go ahead" (Barigazzi 2010a). The question in Italy is whether Berlusconi can rise to the demand that he take care of the country's interest rather than his own. As Berlusconi falters, citizens fear Italy stumbles (Barigazzi 2010a)

We are now brought back around to the same question posed earlier, what is the intent of the "Good Character and/or Reputation" qualification. Is it the reformers' aim to save the state from the Panderer, the Flawed, or both?

Recalling earlier illustrations of the harm caused by each representation-type; the "Delegate" Panderer faced accusations of corruption, embezzlement, abuse of power, vote trading, and so forth. The Flawed "Trustee" was charged with causing the office or party to lose dignity, to fall into disrepute, failing to lead or serve as a good example, causing moral outrage, and damaging the image of the state.

Taking specific descriptions as to required dispositions in the constitutions, the "Trustee-type" would be characterized as needing "good morality," "good reputation," "integrity," "respectability," "irreproachable morals," "grand probity," and so forth (see Underlined terms in Table 9.2). Disqualifications speaking directly to the "Delegate-type," such as "abuse of power," "corruption," "dishonesty," "defrauding the state," among others are highlighted (see Highlighted terms on Table 9.2). Terms that could serve either are both underlined and highlighted.

Over the entire table, there are 51 cells containing either highlighted, underlined, or both highlighted and underlined requirements or prohibitions. *Sixty-nine percent have underlined terms*, whereas 41 percent have highlighted terms (35 and 21, respectively, which will not add up to 51 because some cells contain both). If we take this as evidence of intent, a good argument can be made that constitution drafters or reformers used this qualification thinking very much about their elected officials as Trustee-type representatives.

More interestingly, when looking at the distribution of restrictions related to the Trustee-type as opposed to the Delegate-type representative across offices, the Head of State is overwhelmingly conceptualized as the Trustee-type in that out of 20 positive cells, 12 mention Trustee-type restrictions alone, with an additional six containing both. Although the Upper House has few overall cases, it, too, is disproportionately defined by Trustee-type restrictions, with four out of six cells containing only this type and one cell with both. Out of ten positive cells, the Lower House is evenly split, with four cells containing Trustee-type qualifications alone, and an additional four cells with both. Only the Head of Government contains no cells with Trustee-type qualifications alone.

Even when disaggregated across offices and qualification-types, "Good Character and/or Reputation" is generally construed as a Trustee-type consideration that weighs most heavily on the Head of State, perhaps because of the office's profound symbolic meaning to a country and its people. This should serve as fair warning to an aspiring politician that he or she must not succumb to the temptation of the forbidden, as Advocate General of Punjab, Maqbook Ellahi Malik concluded earlier (the quote has strategic editing by this author to make the point):

We are convinced that the educational [Good Character] qualification prescribed for membership of Assemblies will not only raise their level of competence [virtue] and change the political culture but will also be an incentive to education [good behavior]. (Botteron 2006, 179)

Table 9.2 Countries that Require Good Character and/or Reputation

	Good Character			
Country	Head of State (185 Countries)* (29 Countries)**	Head of Government (131 Countries)* (17 Countries)**	Upper House (94 Countries)* (14 Countries)**	Lower House (186 Countries)* (29 Countries)**
Benin	Candidate must have **good morality** and honesty.	No Office	No Office	No Mention
Central African Republic	Candidate must have **good morality**.	No Mention	No Office	No Mention
Chad	Candidate must have **good morals.**	No Mention	No Mention	No Mention
Colombia	Candidate must be in **good standing.**	No Office	Candidate must be in **good standing**	Candidate must be in **good standing**
Comoros	No Mention	No Mention	Candidate must be **honorable.**	No Mention
Congo, Republic	Candidate must have **good morality**.	No Office	No Mention	No Mention
Cote D'ivoire	Candidate must have **good morals and grand probity.**	No Mention	No Office	No Mention
El Salvador	Candidate must have **well known morality.**	No Office	No Office	Candidate must have **well known morality.**
Gambia	If while holding the Presidency, he or she is terminated or dismissed or forced to retire or found guilty of a criminal offense or found liable for **misconduct,** negligence, **corruption, improper behavior,** he or she is disqualified from running for any office.	No Office	No Office	No Relevant Mention[1]
Ghana	Not qualified if found guilty by the Commission of **defrauding state or abusing power.**	No Office	No Office	Not qualified if found guilty by Commission of **defrauding state or abusing power.**
Guatemala	Candidate must be in **good standing.**	No Office	No Office	No Mention
Iceland	No Mention	No Office	No Office	Candidate must have an **unblemished reputation.**

Iran	Candidate for Supreme Leader must be aware of circumstances of age, be courageous, resourceful, with proven administrative ability. Must be an expert in Islamic Law. Must be just and **pious**.	Candidate must have a good past record and convinced belief in the principles of Iran and Madhhab of country.	No Mention	No Mention
Iraq	Candidate must have **integrity, righteousness,** and exhibit fairness.	Candidate must have **integrity, righteousness,** and exhibit fairness.	No Mention	No Mention
Italy	Candidate must not be **deemed morally unworthy.**	No Office	Candidate must not be **deemed morally unworthy.**	Candidate must not be **deemed morally unworthy.**
Nigeria ***	Within less than 10 years, a candidate found guilty of violating the Code of Conduct for Public Officials is not eligible to run.	No Office	Within less than 10 years, a candidate found guilty of violating the Code of Conduct for Public Officials is not eligible to run.	Within less than 10 years, a candidate found guilty of violating the Code of Conduct for Public Officials is not eligible to run.
Pakistan	Candidate must be sagacious, **righteous,** honest, ameen, non-profligate. **Islamic instructions as to good character** apply. A candidate is disqualified if, in previous service, he or she was dismissed or compulsorily retired for **misconduct involving moral turpitude, abuse of power,** or convicted by a court (in general).	Candidate must be sagacious, **righteous,** honest, ameen, non-profligate. **Islamic instructions as to good character apply.** A candidate is disqualified if, in previous service, he or she was dismissed or compulsorily retired for **misconduct involving moral turpitude, abuse of power,** or convicted by a court (in general).	Candidate must be sagacious, **righteous,** honest, ameen, non-profligate. **Islamic instructions as to good character apply.** A candidate is disqualified if, in previous service, he or she was dismissed or compulsorily retired for **misconduct involving moral turpitude, abuse of power,** or convicted by a court (in general).	Candidate must be sagacious, **righteous,** ameen, non-profligate. **Islamic instructions as to good character apply.** A candidate is disqualified if, in previous service, he or she was dismissed or compulsorily retired for **misconduct involving moral turpitude, abuse of power,** or convicted by a court (in general).

Table 9.2 (*Cont.*)

Country	Good Character Head of State (185 Countries)* (29 Countries)**	Head of Government (131 Countries)* (17 Countries)**	Upper House (94 Countries)* (14 Countries)**	Lower House (186 Countries)* (29 Countries)**
Papua New Guinea	No Mention	Candidate must be mature, <u>in good standing, and has the respect of the community.</u> A person dismissed from office for misconduct is ineligible to run or be appointed to federal office or a local body for a period of 3 years after the date of dismissal.	No Office	Candidate must be mature, <u>in good standing, and has the respect of the community.</u> A person dismissed from office for misconduct is ineligible to run or be appointed to federal office or a local body for a period of 3 years after the date of dismissal.
Rwanda	Candidate must have <u>irreproachable morals and probity.</u>	No Mention	Candidate must have <u>irreproachable morals and probity.</u>	No Mention
Samoa	Candidate cannot be known for <u>misbehavior.</u>	No Mention	No Office	No Mention
Sierra Leone	Candidate cannot have been barred from practicing any profession.	No Office	No Office	Candidate cannot have been barred from practicing any profession.
Singapore	Candidate must be a person <u>of integrity with good character and reputation.</u>	No Mention	No Office	No Mention
South Africa	Candidate cannot have been previously removed from office for <u>bad conduct.</u>	No Mention	No Mention	No Mention

Sri Lanka	While President, cannot have been dismissed for corruption or abuse of power.	No Relevant Mention	No Office	No Relevant Mention
Tanzania***	Candidate cannot have Violated the Code of Ethics that prohibits conduct and behavior that tend to portray that a leader is dishonest, lacks integrity, or which tends to promote or encourage corrupt practices in public affairs or jeopardizes public interest or welfare.	Candidate cannot have Violated the Code of Ethics that prohibits conduct and behavior that tend to portray that a leader is dishonest, lacks integrity, or which tends to promote or encourage corrupt practices in public affairs or jeopardizes public interest or welfare.	No Office	Candidate cannot have Violated the Code of Ethics that prohibits conduct and behavior that tend to portray that a leader is dishonest, practices favoritism or lacks integrity, or which tends to promote or encourage corrupt practices in public affairs or jeopardizes public interest or welfare.
Thailand	No Mention	Candidate cannot be addicted to narcotics nor previously dismissed from office on charges of corruption.	Candidate cannot be addicted to narcotics nor previously dismissed from office on charges of corruption.	Candidate cannot be addicted to narcotics nor previously dismissed from office on charges of corruption.
Turkey	No Mention	Candidate may not have been banned from public service.	No Office	Candidate may not have been banned from public service.
Turkmenistan	Candidate must have gained high authority.	No Office	No Mention	Candidate must have gained high authority.
United Arab Emirates	No Mention	No Mention	No Mention	Candidate must be known for **good conduct and respectability.**
Total Number of Positive Hits	22	7	7	14

Table 9.2 (*Cont.*)

Country	Good Character Head of State (185 Countries)* (29 Countries)**	Head of Government (131 Countries)* (17 Countries)**	Upper House (94 Countries)* (14 Countries)**	Lower House (186 Countries)* (29 Countries)**
* The Percentage of Countries that Use the Qualification for the Office relative to All Countries.	12	5	7	7
** The Percentage of countries that use the qualification for the office relative to ALL countries that use the qualification.	76	41	50	48

1 No Relevant Mention' means that character attributes or traits were listed, but could not feasibly be used in this context.

Keeping Out Those Who Had Been Kicked Out: Leadership Codes of Ethics

Leadership Codes of Ethics serve a very different function in the structure of constitutions from other types of requirements. Their intent is to formalize the expected behavior of public officials and the penalties for transgression. Should an official violate the codes, one of two outcomes is possible. The first is that he or she could be dismissed from office and/or brought up on additional criminal charges, depending upon the nature of the violation. The second outcome takes the punishment a step further, banning the individual from holding office in the near to distant future. For our purposes here, only when a country's Leadership Code of Ethics includes the possibility of disqualification from future public office are they listed in Table 9.3.

Out of 186 countries with written constitutions, the fact that only five use this mechanism makes it globally unique, but may in fact be one of the most effective means of containing the behavior of the dissolute. In essence, Leadership Codes broadcast to the political class that after having spent an enormous amount of time, energy, and money vying for public office, if you "exchange" your vote for a carnal indulgence, if you succumb to earthly temptation to the degree you cannot focus on the public's interest, if you rob the public treasury to satiate your fleshly desires, not only will you lose the position you desired, but it will be forbidden to you in the near to distant future.

What is, then, the focus of the Leadership Codes of Ethics? Are states using them to punish the Panderer or the Flawed?

Using the same technique as that employed in the previous section where Trustee-type concepts are underlined and Delegate-type concepts are highlighted, it is very clear that the Panderer is overwhelmingly the focus of concern: bribery, corruption, conflict of interest, and abuse of power dominate the content of these Codes. Papua New Guinea is the only state with any mention of attributes associated with the Trustee-type to any degree.

Although it is clear the target is the Delegate-type representative, one is still left wondering why ban a failed public official from further office rather than impose a sentence, a fine, or an official sanction? If we set aside the obvious deterrence function the Codes likely serve, the only other reason to ban a failed public official from future office is the belief that past practice is indicative of future behavior.

Interestingly, in one of the revisions of representation theory, Jane Mansbridge (2003) added a temporal aspect to the Delegate-type representative; speculating that during campaigns, Delegate-type candidates fall into two camps: "promissory" and "anticipatory." The promissory-type candidate will solicit votes on the *promise* that they will fight for a specified set of policies and programs if elected. The anticipatory-type candidate is the incumbent who asks his or her constituency to look at their past performance and by it, *anticipate future actions* (Mansbridge 2003). It appears the drafters of these Codes of Ethics could not agree more: Once a satyr always a satyr without a forced "pause" for reform!

Table 9.3 Countries with Codes of Ethics Whose Violation Leads to Disqualification

Country	Description of Prohibited Conduct	Penalty
Nigeria	Fifth Schedule: No person shall offer a public office any property, gift or benefit of any kind as an inducement or bribe for the granting of any favor or the discharge in his favor of the public officer's duties. A public officer shall not do or direct to be done, in abuse of his office, any arbitrary act prejudicial to the rights of any other person knowing that such act is unlawful or contrary to any government policy.	Fifth Schedule: Code of Conduct Tribunal may impose the following: Vacation of office, disqualification from membership of a legislative house and from the holding of any public officer for a period not exceeding 10 years, any arbitrary act prejudicial to the rights of any other person knowing that such act is unlawful or contrary and forfeiture to the State of any property acquired in abuse or corruption of office.
Papua New Guinea	Article 26 Responsibilities of Office: A person to whom this Division applies has a duty to conduct himself in such a way, both in his public or official life and his private life, and in his associations with other persons, as not—to place himself in a position in which he has or could have a conflict of interests or might be compromised when discharging his public or official duties; or to demean his office or position; or to allow his public or official integrity, or his personal integrity, to be called into question, or to endanger or diminish respect for and confidence in the integrity of government in Papua New Guinea.	Article 26: A person who has been dismissed from office under this Division for misconduct in office is not eligible--to election to any elective public office; or for appointment as Head of State or as a nominated member of the Parliament; or for appointment to a provincial legislature… for a period of three years after the date of his dismissal.
Swaziland	Chapter 16: Leadership Code of Conduct: The person who holds one of the enumerated offices shall not assume a position where personal interest conflicts or is likely to conflict with the performance of functions of office; and engage in conduct that is likely to compromise the honesty, impartiality and integrity of that officer; likely to lead to corruption in public affairs; or which is detrimental to the public good or welfare or good governance.	Section 242: An officer who contravenes the Code may, after due process of law, be dismissed or removed from office by reasons of such breach or abuse and may be disqualified from holding any public office either generally or for a specified period.
Thailand	Section 270: A person holding one of the enumerated positions who seriously violates or fails to comply with ethical standards, may be removed from office by the Senate.	Section 274: A person who is removed from office shall be deprived of the right to hold any political position or to serve in the government service for five (5) years.
Tanzania	Section 132: Basic rules of ethics for public leaders shall prohibit conduct and behavior which tend to portray that a leader is dishonest, practices favoritism or lacks integrity, or which tends to promote or encourage corrupt practices in public affairs or jeopardizes public interest or welfare.	Article 67: One cannot be a candidate if, within a period of five (5) years had been convicted and sentenced to imprisonment for an offence contravening the law concerning ethics of public leaders.

Keeping Scoundrels Out of Elected Office: A Conclusion

Do the constitutional qualifications discussed, in fact, keep the potential Panderers and Flawed from gaining political office? It is a very difficult question to answer, because to do so, one must prove a negative to be true. In this context, one would have to find cases where an individual was intent upon running for public office but changed their mind or was prohibited from filing candidacy papers for reasons of "sexually scandalous" behavior. Although not numerous, two relatively recent cases illustrate how these prohibitions can keep the lubricious from sliding into elected office if the vetting process has a mind to do so.

Vietnam has very minimal requirements in their constitution for aspiring Deputies of the National Assembly. In the constitution is an oblique reference to a candidate-vetting body called the Commission for Verification of the Credentials of Deputies to the National Assembly. As one might infer from the commission's name, its purpose is to provide the National Assembly with a set of recommendations whether to accept or not accept "the credentials" of candidates. In 1997, a "high-ranking official [had] withdrawn his candidacy for the National Assembly because of his 'failure to meet [the] standards of the candidate'" (*Deutsche Presse-Agentur*1997).

What had the candidate done to merit denial of his application? "43-year-old Nguyen Van Bu from Ho Chi Minh City was forced to withdraw his candidacy because of his involvement in a sex scandal." He stood "accused of having simultaneously extramarital affairs with two women" (*Deutsche Presse-Agentur* 1997). When the vetting body wanted to apply the rule, they did. Whether the rule had been uniformly applied in the past is unclear, as other cases could not be found. The prohibition was, in this case, effective.

Italy provides an interesting contrast. In its constitution is the provision that one may not run for office "in cases of moral unworthiness as laid down by law" (The Constitution of the Italian Republic, 1948 as Amended to 2003, Article 48). As one might anticipate, the definition of what constitutes "moral unworthiness" is sufficiently vague and can either capture or fail to capture candidates at will. In the case of Marrazzo, discussed earlier, he may have had this constitutional provision in mind when he decided not to run for another term as governor. We will not know. We return to the case of President Silvio Berlusconi. In October and November 2010, stories of new sexual escapades appeared in the international press. As a quick overview, Berlusconi has been accused of soliciting a teenage girl for a "bunga-bunga" party (a Muammar Kadaffi creation, by the way), for placing phone calls to the police encouraging them to release one of the "bunga-bunga" party girls from detention on charges of larceny, and for throwing very extravagant sex parties at his villas, where it is alleged he paid approximately $14,000 to a woman for services rendered (Barigazzi 2010b)."

Milan's chief prosecutor says Berlusconi has not broken any laws as the age of consent in Italy is 14 years old and prostitution is not illegal, although making money from it is (Barigazzi 2010b). As rival political parties are scrambling to put together coalitions that could force an early election in 2011, it is clear that Berlusconi is still, officially, "morally worthy" to hold elected office. It appears Berlusconi's political future ultimately rests on the "informal" processes of party and electoral politics.

Being entirely forthright about the data at hand, very few countries employ the strategy of embedding in their constitutions qualifications that could be used to ban character-flawed citizens from vying for public office. Most countries, like the United States, rely on a system whereby citizens judge the worthiness of candidates through regular free elections and, if need be, through impeachment when transgressions pass a critical threshold. Throughout this volume, it has been amply demonstrated that American democracy does not eradicate bad behavior of elected officials. Demonstrated in this chapter, constitutional qualifications for office do not prohibit the character-flawed from successfully gaining elected office if there is no political will to use them.

What do we conclude from this? First, that human beings are incapable of devising a strategy or of writing a rule that will not be creatively dodged, broken, or sidelined by others whose motives are of a lubricious nature. When oversight or implementation of a rule fails, it does not appear to matter whether citizens place restrictive qualifications into constitutions or whether they choose to leave it to the voter to discern who might be corruptible. Universally, we end up with some poorly behaving, if not criminal, elected officials.

Second, that humans are not angels gets to the heart of the conundrum of representative democracy. It is the incontrovertible fact that the corrupt, weak, and fallen find their way into public office and when they do so, it is ultimately up to citizens to determine how the matter is to be handled. Constitutional qualifications are one means among many to weed out those who present the most obvious problematic profile, albeit an imperfect one.

Lastly, what this chapter and volume have demonstrated is that citizens are determined and continue in the struggle to devise effective strategies to reign in and punish elected officials for their ruttish behavior. Rather than view this as a failure of representative democracy, it is more accurate to see these ongoing efforts as a testament to citizen's creativity and to their unyielding belief that representative democracy is the best form of government we have yet to devise because it holds out the promise of carrying forward what is in the common interest.

Works Cited

Barigazzi, Jacopo. "'Bunga-Bunga' Batters Berlusconi." *Newsweek*, November 8, 2010a.
———. "Silvio Gets Taken Down." *Newsweek*, November 15, 2010b.
Botteron, Cynthia. "Validating Educational Qualifications As a Prerequisite to Hold Elective Office: The Supreme Court and the Pakistan Muslim League(Q) Decision," in *Pakistan 2005*, edited by Charles H. Kennedy and Cynthia Botteron. Islamabad: Oxford University Press, 2006: 158–198.

———. "Striking at the Heart of Democracy: Leadership Educational Requirements in Musharraf's Constitutional Order," in *New Perspectives on Pakistan: Visions for the Future*, edited by Saeed Shafqat. Islamabad: Oxford University Press, 2007: 276–308.

Botteron, Cynthia, and Michael Greenberg. "A New Way to Think about Representative Democracy: A Typology Based on Qualifications for Public Office." *68th Annual National Conference of the Midwest Political Science Association.* Chicago: Midwest Political Science Association, 2010: 229.

"The Constitution of the Italian Republic, 1948 as Amended to 2003, Article 48 " *Constitutions of the Countries of the World* Lslf Edition,Oceana Law Online, Oxford University Press.

Dahl, Robert. *On Democracy.* New Haven: Yale University Press, 1998.

Deutsche Presse-Agentur. "Hanoi official withdraws candidacy for parliament in sex scandal." July 2, 1997.

Eggleton, Terry. *Italymag.* November 12, 2009. Accessed October 22, 2010 (www.italymag. co.uk/italy/politics/marrazzo-affair-guide).

Fearon, James. "Electoral Accountability and the Control of Politicians: Selecting Good Types versus Sanctioning Poor Performance," in *Democracy, Accountability, and Representation*, edited by Adam, Przeworski, Susan Stokes, and Bernard Manin. New York: Cambridge University Press, 1999.

Guyson, Nangayi. "Zuma in a New Sex Scandal." *Africa News; SA*, February 2, 2010.

Kershner, Isabel. "Former President of Israel Is Convicted of Rape." *New York Times*, December 30, 2010.

Hyun-kyng, Kang. "Lawmakers Urge Zero-Tolerance for Sex Scandal." *Korea Times*, April 2, 2009.

Korea Times. "Dirty Scandal." April 2, 2009.

Kwai-Yan, No. "Sex Trip Creates Conduct Quandary." *South China Morning Post (Hong Kong)*, March 26, 1999a.

———. "Councillors to Face Sack for Misconduct: Proposal in Wake of Sex Scandal." *South China Morning Post (Hong Kong)*, March 31, 1999b.

Malawi Standard. "Malawi Parliament to Impeach Second Deputy Speaker." *Africa News*, March 22, 2003.

Manin, Bernard. *The Principles of Representative Government: Themes in the Social Sciences.* Cambridge: Cambridge University Press, 1997.

Mansbridge, Jane. "Rethinking Representation." *American Political Science Review*, 2003; 97(4): 515–528.

Mill, John Steward. *Considerations on Representative Government.* New York: Liberal Arts Press, 1861.

Mitnick, Joshua. "Katsav Absent from Parliament; President, Others Reeling from Wave of Scandals." *Washington Times*, October 17, 2006: A15.

Pitkin, Hanna. "Representation and Democracy: Uneasy Alliance." *Scandinavian Political Studies*, 2004; 27(3): 335–342.

Robles, Raissa. "Lawmakers Linked to Prostitution Scandal: Allegations Are Raised That Public Funds Were Used to Pay for Sex with Actresses." *South China Morning Post*, August 16, 2004: 8.

Saroso, Oyos. "Sex Scandal Hits PDI-P Legislators." *Jakarta Post*, April 25, 2002.

South Africa Department of Health. *National HIV and Syphilis Antenatal Prevalence Survey in South Africa: 2002–2007.* Government of South Africa, 2007.

South Africa Human Sciences Research Council. *South African National HIV Prevalence, HIV Incidence, Behaviour and Communication Survey, 2008.* South Africa Human Sciences Research Council, 2008.

Notes

1   30 December 2010, an Israeli court convicted the former President of two counts of forcible rape of one female victim known only as A., one count of sexual abuse and harassment of another female victim, and additional count of harassment of a third female victim. Former President Mosh Katsav will be sentenced sometime in January 2011. Rape verdicts carry a minimum sentence of 4 years and a maximum of 16 (Kershner 2010).

Index

Page numbers in **bold** denote tables.